JUNG THE MYSTIC

ALSO BY GARY LACHMAN

Rudolf Steiner: An Introduction to His Life and Work

Into the Interior: Discovering Swedenborg

The Dedalus Occult Reader: The Garden of Hermetic Dreams

A Dark Muse: A History of the Occult

In Search of P. D. Ouspensky: The Genius in the Shadow of Gurdjieff

A Secret History of Consciousness

*Turn Off Your Mind: The Mystic Sixties and the
Dark Side of the Age of Aquarius*

The Dedalus Book of Literary Suicides: Dead Letters

Politics and the Occult: The Left, the Right, and the Radically Unseen

WRITTEN AS GARY VALENTINE

*New York Rocker: My Life in the Blank Generation
with Blondie, Iggy Pop, and Others, 1974–1981*

JUNG THE MYSTIC

The Esoteric Dimensions
of Carl Jung's Life and Teachings

A NEW BIOGRAPHY

GARY LACHMAN

JEREMY P. TARCHER/PENGUIN
a member of Penguin Group (USA) Inc.
New York

JEREMY P. TARCHER/PENGUIN
Published by the Penguin Group
Penguin Group (USA) Inc., 375 Hudson Street, New York, New York 10014,
USA • Penguin Group (Canada), 90 Eglinton Avenue East, Suite 700, Toronto, Ontario
M4P 2Y3, Canada (a division of Pearson Penguin Canada Inc.) • Penguin Books Ltd,
80 Strand, London WC2R 0RL, England • Penguin Ireland, 25 St Stephen's Green,
Dublin 2, Ireland (a division of Penguin Books Ltd) • Penguin Group (Australia),
250 Camberwell Road, Camberwell, Victoria 3124, Australia (a division of Pearson
Australia Group Pty Ltd) • Penguin Books India Pvt Ltd, 11 Community Centre,
Panchsheel Park, New Delhi–110 017, India • Penguin Group (NZ), 67 Apollo Drive,
Rosedale, North Shore 0632, New Zealand (a division of Pearson
New Zealand Ltd) • Penguin Books (South Africa) (Pty) Ltd, 24 Sturdee Avenue,
Rosebank, Johannesburg 2196, South Africa

Penguin Books Ltd, Registered Offices: 80 Strand, London WC2R 0RL, England

Most Tarcher/Penguin books are available at special quantity discounts for bulk purchase
for sales promotions, premiums, fund-raising, and educational needs. Special books or book
excerpts also can be created to fit specific needs. For details, write Penguin Group (USA)
Inc. Special Markets, 375 Hudson Street, New York, NY 10014.

The Library of Congress has catalogued the hardcover edition as follows:

Lachman, Gary.
Jung the mystic: the esoteric dimensions of Carl Jung's life and teachings:
a new biography / Gary Lachman.
p.   cm.
Includes bibliographical references and index.
ISBN 978-1-58542-792-5
1. Jung, C. G. (Carl Gustav), 1875–1961.   2. Psychologists—Switzerland—
Biography.   3. Esoteric astrology.   I. Title.
BF109.J86L33 2010   2010004330
150.19'54092—dc22
[B]

ISBN 978-0-399-16199-5 (paperback edition)

Printed in the United States of America
1 3 5 7 9 10 8 6 4 2

BOOK DESIGN BY NICOLE LAROCHE

If you bring forth what is within you, what you bring forth will save you. If you do not bring forth what is within you, what you do not bring forth will destroy you.

THE GOSPEL OF THOMAS

For

Marie-Louise von Franz (1915–1998)
Anthony Storr (1920–2001)
Stephan Hoeller

Helpful guides on the night sea journey

CONTENTS

INTRODUCTION: THE UNDISCOVERED JUNG   1

1. MEMORIES, DREAMS, REFRACTIONS   13

2. AN UNHAPPY MEDIUM   35

3. INTRUDERS IN THE MIND   55

4. METAMORPHOSES OF THE LIBIDO   81

5. TRANSCENDENT FUNCTIONS   105

6. THE JUNG CULT   127

7. THE SHADOW KNOWS   151

8. ARCHETYPES FROM OUTER SPACE   181

EPILOGUE: AFTER JUNG   205

POSTSCRIPT: *THE RED BOOK*   213

Acknowledgments   225

Notes   227

Index   251

INTRODUCTION:
THE UNDISCOVERED JUNG

Was Jung a mystic? Jung didn't think so and he thought little of those who did. In a filmed interview in 1957 with Richard I. Evans, professor of psychology at the University of Houston, Jung, then in his eighties, remarked that "Everyone who says that I am a mystic is just an idiot."[1] By that time, this would have included quite a few people, not the least of whom was Sigmund Freud, Jung's erstwhile mentor and friend. It was the "mystical" character of Jung's first major work, *Symbols of Transformation*,[2] that precipitated Jung's break with the founder of psychoanalysis in 1912 and saddled him with a label he spent a lifetime trying to shed. By the time of Evans' interview, Jung had been at it for nearly fifty years, and as the title of this book suggests, he had had little luck. Till the end of his life and throughout a long and often turbulent career, an exasperated Jung argued that he was first and foremost a scientist and empiricist, and *not* a theorist, metaphysician, philosopher, or, most emphatically, a mystic. His complaints, however, fell mostly on deaf ears, and the onus of mysticism hovers around Jung even today, as I discovered during a visit to the Freud Museum, here in London, while researching this book. Talking with the curator about Freud's embrace of nineteenth-century scientific materialism and its tendency to reduce "spiritual" phenomena to material causes, I casually mentioned that Jung's more "constructive" approach to the unconscious seemed to reject this. "Yes," the curator said, "this is true, but that is mysticism, not science." Jung, I suspect, must have turned over in his grave.

Yet Jung himself was not always the best advocate for his defense. In a series of lectures given at London's Tavistock Clinic in 1935—which form one of the best introductions to his ideas— Jung pointed out that "There is nothing mystical about the collective unconscious,"[3] that inner realm of inherited images and symbols that he had discovered and was at pains to define throughout his many writings. The collective unconscious—or as Jung less frequently but perhaps more profitably called it, the "objective psyche"—is a kind of reservoir of symbols and images that we come equipped with at birth, and over which we later add our own store of "repressed" or forgotten material, the "personal unconscious" that Freud focused on. Like "introvert," "extravert," "anima," and "shadow," the "collective unconscious" is a Jungianism that has gained popular if often inaccurate use, and if people know only a little about Jung, it is this. Yet in the same series of lectures, Jung told his audience, mostly made up of fellow doctors and psychologists, that "Mystics are people who have a particularly vivid experience of the processes of the collective unconscious." "Mystical experience," he told his learned listeners, "is experience of the archetypes"[4]—archetypes being the psychic blueprints, as it were, of the individual images that together comprise the collective unconscious. So while there is "nothing mystical about the collective unconscious," there certainly seems something archetypal about mystical experience, at least according to Jung. And as Jung himself had "a particularly vivid experience of the processes of the collective unconscious," he would, by his own definition, be a mystic.

This ambiguity is common to Jung and is one reason why most members of the scientific community are unwilling to grant him acceptance. According to the psychiatrist Edward Glover, "from the point of view of scientific exposition, Jung is at the best of times a confused writer apparently unable to call a spade a spade and to keep on calling it a spade," the effect of this being to create an "immense lather of verbosity."[5] Even writers sympathetic to Jung can't avoid commenting on his obscurity. For the late Anthony Storr, one of Jung's best interpreters and a respected member of the psychotherapeutic community, "one of the major obstacles in reading Jung is his multiplicity of ill-formulated definitions for the same thing."[6] The "collective unconscious" itself is a case in point. At various times Jung spoke of it in biological and genetic language; in terms of brain structure; metaphysically, as similar to Plato's Ideas; and—dare I say it?—mystically, as something along the lines of what the initiates into the ancient Eleusinian mysteries experienced. Jung's followers argue that his style is suited to his unwieldy material—dreams, visions, and those strange "meaningful coincidences" he called "synchronicities"—rather as devotees of the philosopher Martin Heidegger argue that his gnomic and often impenetrable writings parallel the uncommon territories of Being he explores. Yet others, less convinced of Jung's importance, say they are simply vague and that Jung himself was a muddled thinker. Jung was clearly one of the most influential minds of the last century, but he was also, unfortunately, one of the most frustrating.

But prolixity alone can't be all that bars Jung from the hallowed halls of science or drapes him in the unwanted robes of mysticism. Throughout his career, Jung made no secret of being fascinated with areas of experience any scientist worth his salt would turn his nose up at. From the beginning, Jung was enthralled by the supernatural and what we have come to call the paranormal, and although he began his career at a time when some of the most important thinkers in the world thought these worthy of serious pursuit, for the most part science in his day (as in ours) had relegated the idea of any immaterial or spiritual reality to the intellectual dustbin. Yet even here, Jung's ambiguity causes concern. Jung seemed to have two minds about the supernatural: a public one that wanted to understand it "scientifically," and a private one that acknowledged ghosts, visions, and premonitions as part of the essential mystery of life.

Exactly why Jung "shrouded the origins of his discoveries in a mantle of caution that bordered on Hermetic concealment,"[7] as the Gnostic writer Stephan Hoeller put it, is debatable. For some, a prudent career sense explained it; for others it was to protect the mysteries from profane hands. Yet even Jung's frustrating style can be seen as a product of this "doublethink." Although he could write clearly and effectively—his many introductions and commentaries, as well as his published lectures, confirm this—for the most part, Jung's major works are tough going, and tend to drown the reader in a flood of learned references. As Storr remarks, "Jung has a tendency to pile parallel upon parallel from his very extensive knowledge of myth and comparative religion in such a way that the reader may easily forget what it was that was originally being discussed."[8] It's possible Jung overcompensated for criticisms of his lack of "scientific rigor" by producing weighty, erudite tomes. But it's equally possible that Jung aimed at bludgeoning his readers into acceptance by the sheer volume of his work, what I've come to call the Herr Doctor Professor effect. Reading a great deal of Jung, as I did in preparation for this book, it's difficult to avoid feeling that he is compelled to remind his readers repeatedly that he is indeed—and make no mistake about it—a scientist. One can't help suspect at times that he was not as certain about this as he claimed and that one of the people he was trying to convince was himself.

Yet unfounded scientific pretensions and a verbose, torrential style still seem not quite sufficient to warrant the charge of mystic, if charge it is. What seems to pin Jung to the mystical bull's-eye is his claim to special, secret knowledge, knowledge not obtained through the normal methods of cognition, what some Christian sects of the first centuries after Christ called *gnosis*, direct spiritual experience. Jung often lamented that he "knew things and must hint at things which other people do not know, and usually do not even want to know."[9] And in one of his most important papers, dealing with the central theme of his work, the process of "individuation," through which "one becomes who one is," Jung states flatly that he cannot offer any evidence or proof for its reality, as it is something that must be *experienced*. In "The Relations Between the Ego and the Unconscious," Jung writes that "it is . . . exceedingly difficult to give examples [of individuation] because every example has the unfortunate characteristic of being impressive and significant only to the individual concerned."[10] This puts individuation in the same realm as being in love, aesthetic experience, and, also, mystical states, all of which share the characteristic of "being impressive and significant only to the individual concerned"—we've all known people head-over-heels for someone who doesn't do a thing for us, or gaga over a painting that leaves us cold. And like love and aesthetic and mystical experience—*all* experience, for that matter—this clearly takes individuation out of the realm of science, as the fundamental criteria of science are measurability and repeatability. The idea of somehow scientifically "testing" whether people who underwent Jungian analysis had individuated or not—had, that is, "become who they were"—seems as absurd as the idea of "testing" for love or aesthetic or mystical experience. The only measure of reality for something like this is the people themselves, their lives, and their own sense of "self-actualization," to borrow a phrase from the psychologist Abraham Maslow. Jung never tired of repeating that "the real is what works,"[11] and for someone accused of mysticism, this is an awfully pragmatic credo. In a very significant sense then, the whole idea of whether or not Jung's work was "science" is irrelevant to what is important about it.

But it is this need to *experience* the reality of individuation that led Anthony Storr to include Jung in his book *Feet of Clay: A Study of Gurus.* "Jung was a guru," Storr argued, because he "abandoned the scientific tradition" and "knew he was right." Jung came to his knowledge through his own experience of individuation, that difficult and sometimes dangerous process of unifying the conscious and unconscious minds. "No one who has undergone the process of assimilating the unconscious," Jung wrote, "will deny that it gripped his very vitals and changed him."[12] Jung knew this at first hand, and his own "confrontation with the unconscious" shows what a harrowing ordeal it can be. Yet it is Jung's own experience of individuation that many point to as reason to reject it, claiming that his "confrontation" was little more than a psychotic episode. And as Jung claimed that all of his subsequent work came out of his "confrontation," these critics feel justified in dismissing it as simply the product of madness. Indeed, one critic of Jung has argued that the aim of his "analytical psychology" was to establish himself as the leader of a neo-pagan, sun-worshipping cult, geared toward a spiritual rebirth of Europe with Jung as a kind of Christ-figure, evidence, he argues, that Jung suffered from a Messiah complex.[13]

Although much of this argument has been discredited,[14] as will be seen, even supporters of Jung are uncomfortable with his mystical associations. Some recent Jungian scholars argue that Jung's real legacy has been obscured by his link to the New Age movement. While recognizing that "a distinctive feature of Jung's work was its attempt to provide psychological understanding of the processes of personality transformation which he claimed underlay religious, hermetic, Gnostic and alchemical practices," Sonu Shamdasani also knows that Jung's "non-derisive attention to such subjects was enough to brand him as an occultist," a charge that Shamdasani emphasizes Jung "persistently denied," although "many proponents of the Perennial Philosophy . . . were quick to claim Jung as one of their own."[15] Yet others, such as the Gnostic thinker Stephan Hoeller, claim that to reject Jung's connection to the great western underground "counter tradition"—the Hermetic chain of alchemists, mystics, magicians, and esotericists with which Jung himself felt a deep affinity—would be to produce a denuded Jung, a kind of "Jung-lite," acceptable, perhaps, to the intellectual mainstream and professional psychotherapeutic community, but lacking in any significant spiritual substance.

By now however the horse has surely bolted from the stable. That in his later years Jung came to be seen as a kind of prophet— the "sage of Küsnacht" or "Hexenmeister of Zürich"[16]—argues that to try to corral his influence today is futile. As Hoeller argues, Jung was a late flower on "one of the most important branches of what has sometimes been called the Pansophic Tradition, or the wisdom heritage which descended from Gnostic, Hermetic and Neo-Platonic sources," and his work "cannot and must not remain restricted to the field of psychotherapeutic practice and theory."[17] One reason for this is that only a few can avail themselves of Jungian therapy, which, as Jung himself admitted, is costly and time-consuming. Jung's adoption of the role of "universal guru"[18] in his later years can be seen as his own recognition that his ideas needed to be available to more people than could afford analysis. As Hoeller remarks, "Jung's *Weltanschauung*, his model of reality or world conception" and the "wider cultural and spiritual implications of [his] thought need to be explored."[19]

B y the time I first encountered Jung, as a teenager in the early 1970s, this was certainly happening. Jung may not have been accepted by mainstream intellectuals—Freud was their psychologist of choice—but he had certainly been adopted by the counterculture. When I first read *Memories, Dreams, Reflections*—his "so-called autobiography"—Jung was part of a canon of "alternative" thinkers that included Hermann Hesse, Alan Watts, Carlos Castaneda, D. T. Suzuki, R. D. Laing, Aldous Huxley, Jorge Luis Borges, Aleister Crowley, Timothy Leary, Madame Blavatsky, and J. R. R. Tolkien, to name a few. That his face appeared on the cover of the Beatles' famous *Sgt. Pepper's Lonely Hearts Club Band* album, in a crowd of other unorthodox characters, was endorsement enough. It was through Jung that much of the magic that informed the mystical decade of the 1960s reached people like me. Because of him, obscure works such as the *I Ching* and *The Tibetan Book of the Dead* became mainstays of the love generation, and more than anyone else, he was responsible for the spread of the idea that the Age of Aquarius was just around the corner.

Not surprisingly, Jung's success in mass culture hardened his critics against him, but had he been aware of it—he died just on the cusp of the great "occult revival" of the 1960s—I'm sure he wouldn't have cared. Although still demanding respect as a scientist, Jung didn't turn his nose up at the grassroots audience growing around his later, more esoteric work, and that he had been picked up by the "common" people and rejected by the intelligentsia wasn't lost on him. In an interview given in his last years, a decade before the Beatles put their imprimatur on him, the octogenarian Jung remarked, "Do you know who reads my books? It's the ordinary people, often quite poor people."[20] He also told the story of an old Jewish peddler who once knocked on his door and asked to see the man "responsible for all those books."[21] Sour grapes, perhaps, but although Jung did continue to want acceptance by the scientific community, his real readers were people like myself, interested in ideas about the psyche and its place in the cosmos, and less concerned about provable "facts" than in the kind of guidance those ideas might provide. Again, more than anyone else, Jung is responsible for the widespread resurgence of a more inner-oriented spirituality in the modern world, and his contribution is so fundamental that it can be easily overlooked. In essence, Jung taught more than one generation to look within and to embark on the great adventure of discovering themselves. Many today still take their first steps on that voyage with Jung in hand.

In my own case, Jung's insights have often had a profound

impact on my life, and the most immediate and "factual" evidence for "spiritual reality"—or whatever you'd like to call it—I've experienced has been couched in Jungian terms. I disagree with some of his explanations for these phenomena, but I have no doubt of their reality and significance. Synchronicities happen to me so often that I take them as a part of nature. Dreams have shown me that, as Jung argued, some part of the psyche exists *outside* space and time. They have also displayed a wisdom and insight too often lacking in my conscious self. And Jung's notion of individuation, of "becoming who you are"—a theme that goes back to the Greek poet Pindar and was central to the philosopher Friedrich Nietzsche—is a project that, with any luck, I'm still working on.

Jung's life, his own process of becoming who he was, can, I think, be contemplated with much profit. Not, as some have suggested, because it is a life others should emulate. Jung himself argued that imitating another's life, even if it's Christ's, Buddha's, or C. G. Jung's, is a sin against one's own self, and a sure way of avoiding the hard work of individuation. But we should examine Jung's life because, as with the lives of other creative individuals, the difficulties and challenges we all face are, in their experience, often set out in high relief. We should also not avoid the fact that Jung was an exceptional individual. Some "lives of Jung" aim to cut him down to size, an understandable reaction to others that want to project the image of the infallible master. Neither, however, does Jung nor an interested reader much good, and in any attempt to get Jung off a pedestal, we should avoid focusing solely on his feet of clay.

In his long and often stormy life, Jung was many things; the dichotomy between "Jung the scientist" and "Jung the mystic" highlights only two. Jung was a doctor, a husband, a lover, a friend, a parent, a teacher, a student, a genius. He was also, from another perspective and among other things, an opportunist, an adulterer, a crank, an egoist, an absentee father, and a bully. In this brief account, I've tried to look at Jung from a particular angle, to take seriously his "mystical" side and examine it with a sympathetic but critical eye, staying clear, it's hoped, from either ignorant dismissal or credulous devotion. To applaud or berate Jung for his mystical interests is not particularly useful, but to try to understand them, I think, is.

As Jung reminded his patients, students, and readers time and again, the process of individuation is an ongoing journey into the unfamiliar, unknown, and undiscovered parts of our selves. What I hope readers find in this portrait of Jung the mystic is some hint of how they may encounter and explore these uncharted territories. I also hope that along the way, they may, with any luck, come across an undiscovered Jung, too.

1. MEMORIES, DREAMS, REFRACTIONS

The idea of writing an autobiography came late to Jung, and at first he was wholly against it. When the German publisher Kurt Wolff approached him with the notion in 1956, Jung rejected it, and it took the coaxing of his formidable follower and colleague Jolande Jacobi to convince him. Even when he finally came round to it, he wasn't fully behind it. "I am an ungrateful autobiographer,"[1] he told an American correspondent in 1958; at the time he had already been gathering the material that would eventually become *Memories, Dreams, Reflections* with his secretary Aniela Jaffé for over a year.[2] Jaffé and Jung would meet once a week for an afternoon, and he would speak to her about his life, and she would record his remarks and later edit them into a readable narrative. Jung initially hated these sessions so much that Wolff had to bribe him with a case of expensive Burgundy, telling him to drink a bottle as a reward after each interview.[3]

Eventually Jung's resistance lessened and he began to show enthusiasm for the project, but the idea of a standard autobiography was always an issue. Jung's basic complaint about telling the story of his life was that he didn't remember all those dramatic and sensational incidents that make up the usual autobiographical fare, his meetings with important people, his romances, his adventures, those encounters and turning points that give some autobiographies the pace of a good novel. Given Jung's stature, it wouldn't be unreasonable for a reader first coming to him through *Memories, Dreams, Reflections* to expect to gain some insight into the intellectual currents of the first half of the 20th century. After all Jung met important people; some of the figures whose paths crossed his included Winston Churchill, H. G. Wells, and James Joyce.

Such a reader, however, would be disappointed. For one of the most significant figures in modern Western thought, Jung's account of his life tells us little of the world he lived in, and less about the people in it. Of all his "meetings with remarkable men," the only one who gets any attention is Freud. But then, Jung himself would be the first to admit that he wasn't particularly interested in people.

Toward the end of *Memories, Dreams, Reflections,* Jung guiltily remarks that "I had to learn painfully that people continued to exist even when they had nothing more to say to me,"[4] a lesson not a few "inner directed" personalities have to take on. Jung's lack of interest in people even reached his immediate family. His position as father was so distant that once, on a rare family boating holiday—Jung was a passionate sailor—having bought his children some cakes as a treat, his eight-year-old daughter Marianne exclaimed to her mother, Emma, "Look! Franz's father bought me a little cake!" Franz was her brother, and Emma had to explain to Marianne that Jung was her father, too.[5] That Emma Jung herself maintained a peculiarly formal relationship with her children is true, and much of Jung's familial distance can be chalked up to Swiss propriety and decorum, yet the notion that Jung had an unusual detachment from those around him is hard to shake, as is the recognition that he felt a profound detachment from the world as well. A reader of *Memories, Dreams, Reflections* familiar with Jung's life soon begins to wonder why there is little or no mention of the significant people in Jung's story, people whose encounters with Jung triggered those turning points that made him "who he is." Emma Jung herself, his wife for more than fifty years, is mentioned only once, and that is a reference to her death.

What *did* Jung remember? His interest, he said, had only been held by "little but meaningful things," that he "could not speak about anyway," and in any case he was "so consistently not understood," that he lost all desire "to remember 'meaningful conversations' at all."[6] Jung insisted that he was never interested in the surface phenomena of life; all that was merely an "ephemeral apparition," like the plants that last a season, then die. Underneath, though, in the depths below, lay the rhizome, the roots, which live the year round. Jung had little interest in flowers that bloom, fade, and wither, and if readers were looking for them, they wouldn't find them here. The rhizome, though, was another thing.

The "only events in my life worth telling," he informed his readers, "are those when the imperishable world irrupted into this transitory one." The means by which the imperishable rhizome burst through the mundane surface were dreams and visions, Jung's inner experiences. Jung says that his memories of his travels, his milieu, the people he met, have little life compared to the "fiery magma," the psychic lava, that lay below the surface of events, and which provided him with the alchemical *prima materia* ("basic matter") of his life's work. The echoes of his encounters with this remain powerful and clear, but his cupboard of memorable events, he tells us, is sadly bare.

Yet Jung was not entirely inner directed, and whether he admitted it or not, his life, like that of everyone else, was full of "ephemeral apparitions," of flowers that bloom and die, of people, places, things, and events that led in their own peculiar way to the unique individual he was.

Carl Gustav Jung was born on July 26, 1875, in the village of Kesswil, on the shores of Lake Constance in the Swiss canton of Thurgau. He was his parents' second child; two years earlier, their first, Paul, had died soon after his birth, and until the birth of his sister nine years later, Carl was an only child; even then, the age difference between them meant that their relationship was minimal. Like many who develop a mystical, poetic, or, as Jung would later call it, "introverted" personality, Jung spent much of his early years alone, and this insularity became both a strength and a weakness. Years later, when Jung had become famous, in some reminiscences about their youth, his childhood friend Albert Oeri remarked that when he first met Jung he "had never run across such an asocial monster." Jung, Oeri remarked, wouldn't play with him, wouldn't even acknowledge his existence, but continued to play a game of ninepins by himself, as if Oeri wasn't there. Jung was obsessed with his private games as a child and would become enraged if anyone interfered with them, or even observed him playing them, and this absorption in games remained with him in later years. He was "all by himself," Oeri said, and in many ways this isolation, too, stayed with Jung throughout his life.[7]

Jung's father, the Reverend Paul Jung, was a Protestant clergyman riddled with doubts about his religion that he could neither express nor ignore and saddled with a marriage he didn't enjoy. Although in his early years, Paul Jung showed promise as a linguist and Orientalist, the potential of his student days was never fully actualized, and Jung's remarks about his father suggest that he presented to his son a model of how *not* to grow up. Jung's real role model in his early years—although by reputation alone, as he died years before Jung was born—was his paternal grandfather, Carl Gustav Jung Sr.; Jung even later changed the spelling of his first name Karl to match that of his illustrious ancestor. Famous as a doctor in Basel, he was rector of the University and a grand master of Swiss Masons. C. G. Jung Sr. had a romantic, adventurous life and was a friend of many well-known writers, journalists, and artists, among them the composer Franz Liszt. In Heidelberg, where he studied sciences and medicine, he kept a pig as a pet, talking it for walks as one would a dog. In Berlin, he became involved with the radical politics of the time, and in 1819 a friendship with the assassin—a fellow student—of the conservative dramatist and Russian Counsellor August von Kotzebue led to a stay in prison. When released he emigrated to France, where he drank absinthe in Paris and met the naturalist and explorer Alexander von Humboldt.[8] Humboldt recommended him to a position at the University of Basel—where he unsuccessfully tried to found a chair of psychiatry—and this is how the German Jung became Swiss. Later, when Jung began his studies at Basel, he would feel a mixture of pride and resentment when he heard people remark, "Ah, that is the grandson of the old Doctor Jung" as he passed by: pride at the association with his celebrated ancestor, resentment at the fact that, for his fellow Baselers, this is all he'd ever be.

Jung's penchant for identifying with his powerful ancestor prompted him to lend a sometimes tongue-in-cheek credence to the story that Carl Gustav Sr. was an illegitimate son of the great poet Goethe. Throughout his life, depending on his mood, Jung would affirm or deny the biological lineage; psychologically, however, Goethe became a central role model for young Carl, as he would be for his older contemporary Rudolf Steiner.[9] Both saw in Goethe the image of a fully developed, "whole" personality, and on both his most famous work *Faust* made an incalculable impression.

Jung's mother, Emilie (*née* Preiswerk), comes across as a stronger character than his father, and in many ways Jung seems to have acquired several characteristics from her. The daughter of a Hebrew scholar and proto-Zionist, who was also the Antistes or head vicar of his reformed Protestant parish,[10] she is described as kindly, fat, hearty, sociable, and a good cook, but also as haughty, unattractive, authoritarian, and depressed. By the time Jung was three, disaffection between his parents had reached a crisis level, and Emilie suffered a breakdown and had to be hospitalized for several months. Jung was so affected by this that he developed eczema. The separation led him to a life long mistrust of women and the idea of "love." His father was weak but at least Carl could rely on him. His mother was a different story.

Part of the "unreliability" Jung detected in his mother had to do with the fact that she seems to have been a "split personality." For most of the time Emilie expressed the conventional opinions of her class—although coming from fairly well-off families of high social standing, by the time of Jung's birth both the Jungs and Preiswerks had fallen on hard times—and on the surface she was not out of the ordinary. But occasionally Jung heard his mother speaking to herself in a voice he soon came to recognize as not her own, at least not the voice she normally used. Emilie's remarks then were profound, and expressed with an unexpected authority. This "other" voice had inklings of a world far stranger than the one Jung knew. Emilie's father—the Reverend Samuel Preiswerk, the Hebrew scholar (it's said he learned the language because he believed it was spoken in heaven)—accepted the reality of spirits, and to the consternation of his second wife, he kept a chair in his study for the ghost of his deceased first wife, who often came to visit him. Emilie herself was employed by Samuel to shoo away the dead who distracted him while he was working on his sermons, and she herself developed what would later be called "mediumistic powers" in her late teens. At the age of twenty she fell into a coma for thirty-six hours; when her forehead was touched with a red-hot poker—an extreme means of awakening her—she awoke, speaking in tongues and prophesying. Emilie continued to enter curious trance states throughout her life, and during them she would communicate with the spirits of the dead.

Soon after Jung's birth, the family moved to Laufen, near Schaffhausen and the Rhine Falls, the most impressive in Europe. Water was a central symbol for Jung throughout his life. Rivers, falls, and lakes had a mystical enchantment for him, and it's curious to note that the philosopher Jean Gebser, who knew Jung, argued that water was the mythic element par excellence.[11] Once, crossing a bridge over the falls, Carl slipped and nearly fell through the railing; the maid caught him just in time and this, along with several other childhood accidents—a fall downstairs, another against a stove that led to several stitches in his head—led Jung to suspect he had a suicidal urge, or at least a "fatal resistance to life in this world."[12] Water was source of danger, to be sure; Jung recalled the time when a corpse of a boy had been found near the falls and his father allowed the fishermen to put the body in their washhouse. The four-year-old desperately wanted to see the dead boy, but his mother prevented him, although he did manage to observe water and blood flow down a drain out the back door. Yet other early experiences of water had a less dangerous character. Once, on a visit to Lake Constance, Jung was transfixed by the sun glistening on the waves and the way the sand on the lakebed curled into tiny ridges. Then and there he determined that when he grew up he would live near a lake. Mountains, too, impressed the young boy, not surprisingly, as he lived in Switzerland. One of his earliest memories was of being held up by an aunt and shown the Alps aglow at sunset; the next day he was told that he was too young to join a school outing to the Uetliberg, a mountain near Zürich, and the disappointment was crushing. Years later, Jung would receive what he said was the greatest gift his father gave him, when the impecunious reverend could afford only a single ticket on a cogwheel railway to the top of the Rigi, a nearly 6,000-foot peak, and gave it to Carl.

Other memories suggest an early seeding of a love of nature, but for Jung his first years had their darkness, too. In the cemetery he witnessed burials and was told that Lord Jesus had taken some people back to him. But Jesus, at least according to the bedtime prayer his mother said with him, was his protector, a "comforting, benevolent gentleman" who was especially mindful of little children. What did he have to do with the men in black coats and top hats, who lowered coffins into the cold earth? The paradoxes of Christianity that Jung confronted in his late, controversial work *Answer to Job* had their beginnings in this childhood conundrum. Black-coated men led to still another childhood fear, when Jung saw a Jesuit, and the name and dark robes convinced Jung that the man must be especially dangerous.

Even more disturbing was a dream Jung says he had then, the earliest one he remembered. Standing before a dark hole, he peered into it, and seeing a stairway, he descended into a pit. Pushing aside a thick curtain, he entered a chamber and discovered a throne. On it he saw a kind of pillar, which he first thought was a tree trunk, about twelve feet tall, but which he soon realized was made of flesh. Its rounded head was faceless but crowned by a single, unblinking eye. Terrified the huge worm-like creature would approach him, he was petrified, then heard his mother's voice speaking from above. "Yes," she said, "just look at him. That is the man-eater!" Jung mentioned this remarkable dream of a ritual phallus to no one, and for several nights afterward he was frightened to sleep, fearful he would have another such nightmare.[13]

When Jung was four, the family moved to Klein-Hüningen, a small village near Basel. Water proved a dangerous element there, too; a river running through the village burst its dam and fourteen people were drowned. When the waters receded, their bodies were left stuck in the sand. Determined to see them, Jung found one of a man dressed in black, who had just come from church. Death held a curious attraction for him and was not difficult to find; he once upset his mother by watching a pig being slaughtered. His fears of men in black were increased when during a visit to Arlesheim he passed a Catholic church and dared to look inside, but slipped on a step and hit his chin, opening a large gash. For years after, the association of blood, pain, and Jesuits stayed with him, and he could never pass a church without a shudder.

Problems between Paul and Emilie didn't cease with the move, and they slept apart. Jung slept with his father and the atmosphere at night was tense. Jung began to have visions—or hallucinations, depending on your perspective. From his mother's room he saw a ghostly figure whose head would detach and float in front of it. His dreams were oppressive. Small objects would approach until they grew to enormous size and crush him; telegraph wires strung with birds would expand into thick cables, enveloping him. When he was seven, he developed pseudo-croup, and the choking fits added to his worries. During one, Jung had a vision of a glowing blue circle. Within it moved golden angels, and their presence calmed him. Jung fails to make the connection, but this seems like an early experience of a symbol whose meaning he would spend many years exploring, the mandala, or "magic circle" of Tibetan Buddhism, which Jung would later argue is a natural product of the psyche, and which usually appears in "situations of psychic confusion and disorientation."[14] A young boy seeing floating heads, dreaming of huge penises, and choking because of the "bad air" between his parents seems to meet those criteria.

When he started school, Jung made another discovery that would later appear as a central theme of his work. From being a solitary child, Jung suddenly found himself surrounded by others, and the experience was disturbing. He was happy for the company, but his school friends altered his sense of identity; they made him act in ways he never would at home. He felt alienated from himself, and the presence of a world outside his home seemed vaguely hostile. Jung began to feel "split," as if his inner being was threatened. This is an early surfacing of one of Jung's major insights, what he would later characterize as the conflict between the self and the persona. The self is who we truly are, but the persona or mask (the word comes from the Latin for an actor's mask) is the face we turn to the world in order to deal with it. A persona is absolutely necessary, but the problem is that we often become identified with it, to the detriment of our self, a dilemma that the existential philosopher Jean-Paul Sartre recognized in his notion of *mauvaise foi*, or "bad faith," when one becomes associated exclusively with one's social role. At an early age, Jung felt the first inkling of a problem that years later many of his patients would bring to his door.[15]

Jung's response to the sense of threat was to devise rituals and symbols that would strengthen his sense of self. One involved making little fires in tiny "caves" formed by the spaces between blocks of stone in a wall near his parents' house. Although other children helped gather the firewood, Jung alone was the "keeper of the flame." Another involved a large stone. Throughout his life, stone, like water, had a mystical effect on Jung, and one near the "fire wall" became *his* stone. Jung would sit on it and fall into a metaphysical reverie. "I am sitting on this stone," he would think, but immediately the thought would come to him that perhaps the stone is thinking, "I am lying here and this boy is sitting on me." Jung's sense of identity would drift and he would not know if he was himself or the stone, a riddle the Taoist sage Chang Tsu posed when, after dreaming he was a butterfly, he could no longer determine whether he was Chang Tsu dreaming of the butterfly or the butterfly dreaming of Chang Tsu.

Jung remarks that years later, as a grown man, he again sat on *his* stone and felt a powerful pull into his childhood mind, whose essence, he realized, was timelessness. Later Jung would understand that this timeless quality is the basic characteristic of myth, and when he decided to discover what his *own* myth was, he found that the path to it led through a return to childhood.

Jung added to his repertoire of "self" defense when he took his school ruler and carved a strange figure out of the top of it. Oddly, it had a frock coat and top hat, and he colored it black, just like the Jesuits he feared. He cut the figure off the ruler, dressed it in a little woolen coat, and laid in his pencil case, which he had made into a little bed, along with a stone he had taken from the Rhine and had painted two-toned. This, he said, was *his*, the figure's, stone. He then hid the pencil case—which had become a kind of sarcophagus—on rafters in the attic. No one would know it was there, and his secret made Jung feel whole, no longer at odds with himself.

Whenever problems at school, or with his parents, troubled him, Jung would think of the figure in its bed with its stone and he would feel safe. Occasionally he would climb up to the attic, open the case, and look at the homunculus (little man), leaving him messages he would write on scraps of paper in a secret language. Like the phallus dream, the little man was Jung's secret, and the need to have a secret became a fundamental element in Jung's philosophy. "Like the initiate of a secret society that has broken free from the undifferentiated collectivity," Jung wrote, "the individual on his lonely path needs a secret which for various reasons he may not or cannot reveal. Such a secret reinforces him in the isolation of his individual aims."[16] Without this secret, Jung argues, we too easily fall into the herd-mind of the mass and lose our individuality.

Years later, when Jung was researching the book that made his name, *Symbols of Transformation*, he suddenly remembered his little man and his stone, whom he had forgotten about for years. Reading about "soul stones" found at Arlesheim, and the Australian *churingas*, Aboriginal totem stones, Jung realized that the ritual he had performed as a child had a history, that is to say it formed part of a common human tradition. But he had not known about this at the time. Likewise, the little man was, he discovered, similar to the ancient Greek god Telesphoros, a cloaked figure associated with Asclepius, the god of medicine. But he knew nothing of this either when he made the figure. Later Jung realized that both his little man and his stone were manifestations of what he would come to call the "collective unconscious."

When Jung was nine, his sister Gertrude arrived. Jung was unimpressed, as he was with the explanation that the stork had brought her; Jung knew enough about farm life to know no stork could carry a calf in its bill, so the idea that it had brought his sister was clearly another invention designed to keep the truth from him. Emilie spent a great deal of time in bed anyway, so the fact that she had done so during her pregnancy didn't arouse his suspicion. From his mother's remarks, though, he did gather that something unmentionable was involved in the birth. More immediate concerns, however, soon dominated his mind.

In 1886, when he was eleven, Jung was sent to the Gymnasium in Basel. One of the first things he realized there was his poverty. Most of the other students came from well-off families, and Jung was envious of their big houses, nice clothes, pocket money, and holidays to the mountains and the sea. Jung's family was poor and he often sat with wet socks, because his shoes had holes; sometimes he had no socks at all. Although Jung felt more of a connection with his mother than with Paul, he hated the way she would call after him as he made the long trek from Klein-Hüningen into the city, asking if he had washed his hands or if he had a handkerchief. School itself posed its own problems. As with many creative individuals, Jung found it a bore, and mathematics in particular became a dreadful burden. Jung could never quite grasp what numbers *were*, and algebra was completely beyond him. His whole bent was toward "real things"— trees, flowers, animals—and abstract quantities slipped through his mind as if it was a sieve. In this Jung showed an early sign of his phenomenological approach, and it must have been a comfort to him when he discovered that both Goethe and Nietzsche— another major influence—were also useless at math. Oddly, given his later talent in painting and stone carving, Jung did poorly in drawing, too. Yet again, the explanation is clear. He could, he tells us, draw well, but only when his imagination was gripped. Mere mechanical drafting was uninspired and prompted the appropriate response. A third burden was gymnastics. Jung hated to be told what to do with his body, and the timidity he felt because of his "fatal resistance to the world," and the uncertainty rooted in his mother's early absence, led to a fundamental distrust of life, a sense of *angst*. Life was unstable and demanding, and at twelve Jung hit upon a means of avoiding it.

Standing in the square in front of Basel Cathedral, out of the blue Jung was knocked down by one of his classmates. His head hit the curb, and he almost lost consciousness. But as he felt the blow, the thought came to him that, because of this, he wouldn't have to go to school anymore. Jung was dazed, but aware enough to lie on the cobblestones a bit longer than was really necessary; he wanted to scare his attacker, but also to play up to his injury.

Finally someone picked him up and carried him to the house of some aunts who lived nearby.

Jung recovered—for all his ailments he was becoming a big, strapping teenager—but now, whenever he had to return to school, something peculiar happened. He fainted. He fainted when asked to do his homework, too. Jung fainted every time the issue of school came up and finally his parents dropped the matter. For six months he was left to himself. He indulged in an orgy of reading, daydreaming, and solitary walks in the woods or by the water. Jung drew, and again, a peculiarity of his childhood became a key part of his later work. Jung remarks that he drew pages of caricatures and that "similar caricatures sometimes appear to me before falling asleep to this day."[17] The phenomenon of pictures—faces, landscapes, geometrical designs—appearing at the point of sleep is known as hypnagogia, and Jung remained a strong hypnagogist throughout his life.[18] Later, this capacity to see distinct images in a half-dream state would be transformed by Jung into a method of achieving "individuation," what he called "active imagination."

Jung enjoyed his extended vacation until one day he overheard his father talking about him with a friend. The doctors had no idea what was wrong with Carl, the reverend said; he might even have epilepsy. How will he earn a living? He had nothing to give him. How will he fend for himself?

Jung was struck by his father's concern, and the sudden realization that he was acting selfishly. This "collision with reality" forced him to act. He immediately found his Latin grammar and got to work. Ten minutes later, he felt faint. Jung persisted. Another attack came, then another. Jung persevered, and after a few hours he had faced down the attacks and felt better than he had for months. He had, he tells us, learned what a neurosis is, but more important, he learned how to *overcome* one.

Jung had hit on a technique that his older contemporary and friend, the psychologist and philosopher William James, called the "bullying treatment." In "hyperaesthetic conditions," associated with chronic invalidism, life grows into "one tissue of impossibilities," James said, and the slightest effort causes great distress. In "bullying," the doctor forces the patient to make efforts and to ignore the distress. If he is bullied enough, the patient hits a kind of "second wind" and feels "unexpected relief." James recognized that this is true of all of us, not only neurasthenics. "We live," he wrote, "subject to arrest by degrees of fatigue which we have come only from habit to obey."[19] Jung had acquired the "habit" of fainting when faced with a disagreeable reality—a common enough neurosis. His sudden sense of shame forced him to "bully" himself. In this case, doctor and patient were one, and the result was that his fainting neurosis vanished. The historian of psychology Henri Ellenberger wrote that the first step in Jungian therapy is to "bring the patient back to reality,"[20] and this seems to be precisely what Jung did.

Another experience of Jung's seems to be connected to this. Not long after he stopped his fainting fits, Jung had an intense sensation of his own identity. Walking to school, Jung had a sudden powerful feeling that "now I am *myself*!"[21] He had of course existed before, but at that moment, it was as if he had emerged from a fog or mist and had suddenly woken up to the fact that he was himself. For the first time, he felt he had "authority," that *he* willed and acted. The Russian-Greek-Armenian (no one is quite sure of his exact nationality[22]) esoteric teacher G. I. Gurdjieff would say he had a moment of "self-remembering," more than likely brought on by his "bullying."[23] Jung notes that at the time of his "awakening" he had forgotten all about his man in the attic. Most likely this was because Jung no longer needed him. His personality was becoming solid; he was, as he would later say, "individuating."

This new sense of authority had some side effects. Like the character in Woody Allen's film *Zelig*, Jung overcompensated for his earlier, weaker self. After being told off by a friend's father for recklessness on his boat, Jung found himself enraged at the fat boor shouting at him. How dare he insult ME, Jung thought. A part of him knew he was twelve years old, had acted wrongly, and deserved the dressing-down. But another part felt he was a grown man of importance, worthy of respect. The "split" that Jung had seen in his mother appeared in himself, and from then on he knew he was not one person, but two. This was not merely seeing a "side" of himself he was hitherto unaware of. As Jung's mother did on occasion, Jung literally became two people.

The "Other" was a figure out of the 18th century, a masterful, commanding character who wore a white wig and buckled shoes, drove an impressive carriage, and held young Carl in contempt. Jung never says it outright, but it's difficult to escape the impression that in some ways he felt he *was* this character in a past life. Seeing an ancient green carriage led him to believe that it came from *his* time. Likewise, a terra-cotta statuette of a Basel doctor of the last century had a similar effect. As with his mother, Jung's "No. 2," as he called the Other, had great authority and power and seemed to come from a world very different from the one Jung knew, that timeless world he had touched with *his* stone and the little man. Again, from Jung's description, which is all we have to go on, No. 2 was more than the understandable fantasy self-image of an awkward adolescent. It was rather as if a more mature, more individuated personality already existed within his psyche, an idea that would later become central to Jung's psychology.

If his new No. 2 didn't provide preoccupation enough, around this time Jung had his curious vision of the shitting God. Looking at the glorious Basel Cathedral, Jung suddenly had the idea of an almighty turd falling from heaven and destroying the church, and just as suddenly suppressed it. It obsessed him and like many children, Jung believed there must be something wrong with him to have had such a thought. Jung bottled up this intolerable idea for a time, but eventually the pressure was too great and he had to let it emerge. As with his fainting fits, when he did he felt a great relief, a sense, even, of grace, as if committing the very sin he tried desperately to avoid was a kind of blessing. (It was also good psychotherapy, as Freud later learned with the "talking cure.")

But then the idea came to him that in some way God *wanted* him to think it—wanted him, in essence, to sin—and this proved even more troubling. Like the "mild Jesus" who nevertheless took people into the ground, an all-good, all-loving God had compelled Jung to envision a cosmic defecation. Why? Jung told no one of his vision; it, like the little man, the giant penis, and the stone, became another of his secrets. It made him who he remained, a solitary who knows "things and must hint at things which other people do not know, and usually do not even want to know."24

It also colored his relationship with his father. At that point Jung became obsessed with religious questions that his father's unquestioning but shaky faith couldn't answer. Increasingly, Jung came to see that while his father and his uncles, six of whom were

pastors, spoke to him about dogma and *belief*, he was more concerned with *experience*, with what he would later call *gnosis*, discovering the distinction in the ancient Gnostic Christian sects of
the second and third centuries AD. He was convinced his father
had no real experience of a living God, and after his first Com-
munion proved to be an empty affair ("So that's that" is how he
described it), Jung realized that the Church was the last place he
might find the answers to the questions that plagued him. (Perhaps that's why God shat on it.) Theological and philosophical
tomes he devoured didn't help. Yet the idea that God might in
some ways be like himself offered some possibilities. If he had a
No. 1 and a No. 2, perhaps God did as well? Perhaps He was not
all good. Perhaps He was the source of evil, too?

If God *was* the source of evil, then we certainly lived in an
unfair world. Jung received firsthand evidence of this at school.
Although overcoming his fainting spells made him conscien-
tiousness and diligent, Jung was considered "odd." He tended to
befriend boys from poor families; although he was impatient with
their unintelligence, they at least didn't comment on his "unusual-
ness." Jung remained bored with most subjects, but once his German teacher proposed a composition theme that interested him.
Jung worked hard and produced what he felt was an excellent
essay. Unfortunately, it proved to be too excellent. His teacher
refused to believe he wrote it and accused him of copying it; he
even waited until the end of class to mention his paper, after reading all the others. Not to receive high marks, which he had aimed
at, was catastrophic enough, but to be accused of cheating in front
of the class made Jung feel he was marked for life.

Jung's' schoolmates marked him as well, nicknaming him "Father Abraham," an intuitive nod, perhaps, to Jung's No. 2—or simply adolescent vindictiveness toward a peer more mature than oneself. Yet Jung's own relation to No. 2 was changing. As he became more involved in the public, outer world, Jung began to reflect on the world he was leaving behind, what he called "God's world." This had none of the sentimentality this name might suggest. It was a "superhuman" world of "dazzling light, the darkness of the abyss, the cold impassivity of infinite space and time, and the uncanny grotesqueness of the irrational world of chance."[25] Jung felt a strong affinity with nature and believed that behind it lay a "secret meaning" (plants, he felt, were "God's thoughts"). Yet men and even animals had lost the ability to perceive this. His No. 2 could, but increasingly Jung's personal center of gravity moved toward No. 1. As his knowledge increased, Jung began to articulate consciously the questions he had only felt intuitively. Jung scoured philosophy for insights. He was attracted to the pre-Socratics—Pythagoras, Heraclitus, Empedocles—but his real discovery was Arthur Schopenhauer, who made the same impact on Jung that he had earlier made on Nietzsche.

Schopenhauer moved Jung because, unlike most philosophers, Schopenhauer is readable; Hegel's abstract convolutions only left Jung further in the dark.[26] More important, Schopenhauer dealt with "real life," with pain, suffering, evil—everything that occupied Jung's thoughts. Rather than explain away evil as an illusion, as many philosophers did, Schopenhauer openly declared that there was some fundamental flaw in the universe. Schopenhauer argued that behind the visible universe was a blind Will and that its insatiable unconscious striving led to the suffering of the world. Jung approved of Schopenhauer's "warts-and-all" picture of life—he knew enough about nature to know it was not all flowers and sunshine—but not with his solution, a quasi-Buddhist withdrawal from the Will's craving, and his misgivings led to a reading of Schopenhauer's own inspiration, Immanuel Kant.

Kant is one of the most important philosophers in the Western tradition, and his central insight is that we can never know reality "in-itself," but only as it appears to us through our means of cognition, through the senses and what Kant called "categories" of understanding, such as time, space, and causality. We can never "know" whether the way we perceive things is the way they "really" are, because we can never observe them outside of our means of observation, rather as if we only saw things through a particular pair of spectacles, and have no idea what they look like when we have the spectacles off. This may sound abstruse, but it remained a key idea for Jung, who later argued that we cannot observe the unconscious mind directly (for it would then no longer be unconscious) nor its contents, like the archetypes of the collective unconscious, but only their effects, the symbols they produce. For Jung this meant that all we can ever know and experience directly is the psyche. As he remarked years later "This principle recognizes the objectivity of a world outside ourselves, but it holds that of this world we can never perceive anything but the image that is formed in our mind. . . . In that sense, even external reality is in our heads, but only in that sense, and we must avoid speaking too much of the world as subjective image."[27] The world then, is a subjective image of a *something* we can never know directly; given this, we shouldn't think too much about it. Sage advice, I should think.

Schopenhauer and Kant provided Jung with more than epistemological insights. Using his mind purposively strengthened No. 1

and triggered a fundamental change in Jung's attitude. Before Jung had seen No. 1 as an inept, clumsy, shy, inarticulate schoolboy, where No. 2 was as figure of authority and respect. Now, however, No. 1 felt an insatiable curiosity about everything and a determination to pursue what he wanted. His poverty didn't bother him—Jung would later say that he wouldn't have missed being poor for anything, as it taught him a sense of the true value of things—and he began to make more friends. Yet he still met incomprehension and sometimes ridicule when he spoke openly of his ideas, and his teachers continued to think that, although clearly brilliant, he was still careless and lazy. The truth is that Jung was passionately concerned with deep matters that his schoolmates and masters thought were, or should be, beyond him. When accusations of arrogance and conceit grew too painful, No. 2 would appear and Jung would seek comfort in "God's world."

The conflict between the troubled schoolboy who sought acceptance in the world and the secret Other who knew the dark abyss remained, and burdened Jung, but an attempt at a reconciliation began when he left school and entered university.

2. AN UNHAPPY
MEDIUM

The reconciliation of opposites would be a major theme in Jung's later work, but in his late teens it posed a more immediate necessity. The conflict between No. 1 and No. 2 presented Jung with a situation that would become familiar to him in his work as a psychotherapist. Jung discovered that when faced with an irresolvable dilemma, more often that not his patients solved the problem by outgrowing it. Some third possibility, not given in the initial conflict, would present itself, courtesy of a dream or intuition, and the problem would resolve itself by no longer being a problem. The patient had somehow risen above it, had, in fact, developed beyond it. We will look at this faculty, which Jung named "the transcendent function," in more detail later. Now we can see how it helped Jung.

In 1895, at the age of nineteen, Jung had left the lower Gymnasium and, like many young men, was faced with the unavoidable decision of what he wanted to be in life. In Jung's case, however, the need to choose was particularly stressful. Jung felt attracted by two opposite poles. No. 1 had developed an interest in science; Jung, we've seen, liked "real" things, and science, with its pursuit of "facts," fit this bill. But No. 2 had a deep love of history, religion, philosophy, and all the speculative mystery that surrounds them. Although his father had counseled him to avoid theology, his uncles felt differently. Jung could sense the gentle pressure they exerted at weekly dinners, yet he was repelled by a discipline that ignored the real essence of religion, the living God he encountered and who forced him to think evil thoughts. Faced with his uncles' uncritical faith in unquestioned dogma, Jung moved closer to science and began to feel No. 2 as a real obstacle. Yet Kant and Schopenhauer were never far from his mind, and when he slipped back into "God's world," the problem of having to choose a career seemed infinitely trivial. But No. 1 was always there, and once again Jung had to be "brought back to reality" and face the necessity of living in the here and now. One sign that Jung was ready to face "real life" was his abandonment of a fantasy he entertained himself with on his walks to and from school. Jung daydreamed about a castle in which he worked as an alchemist, transforming some strange energy he collected from the air into gold. Jung entered his fantasy with the same seriousness he devoted to his solitary games, building it with elaborate detail, but after a while he tired of it and turned to making a *real* castle, or at least a model of one, out of mud and stones. Instead of remaining in a cozy but ultimately insubstantial fantasy, Jung made it concrete. Again, this is a technique he would employ in his therapeutic work, when he had his patients paint or sculpt or in some other way make "real" their fantasies and dreams. This "hands-on" work helped strengthen No. 1.

But there were other constraints besides Jung's inner conflict. His parents had no money, and Jung's best chance of further education was to attend the University of Basel. In spring of 1895, Jung took the entrance examination and passed with good marks, except, as we might suspect, in mathematics. His father applied for a grant and received it, and Jung enrolled in April of that year. Jung was happy but also ashamed at his need for charity, and the fact that it would come from people who he felt disliked him. Jung remained convinced that the people in "important" positions knew of his reputation as an oddball and disapproved. And it also narrowed his choices. He wanted to study archaeology, but the university had no department in it. Archaeology would have combined his interest in facts with the romantic pursuit of the past, and it's curious that Freud, too, had a deep interest in the discipline. Jung wavered between following No. 1's love of science and No. 2's passion for the humanities, until he overheard his father lament that "the boy is interested in everything imaginable, but he does not know what he wants." Another collision with reality forced a decision, and he abruptly chose science.

Two dreams preceded this apparently sudden decision. In one Jung was in a wood near the Rhine and discovered a burial mound. Digging in it, he found the bones of a prehistoric animal. He woke excited, convinced that he had to understand the world he lived in. In another dream he was again in a wood, and in a circular pond he discovered a strange round animal, a giant radiolarian—an amoeboid protozoa—three feet across, whose shimmering body seemed made of countless little tentacles. Jung woke from this dream with his heart thumping and a painful hunger for knowledge. The pool and the giant radiolarian seem, like Jung's early vision of the blue moon filled with angels, examples of mandalas: faced with the irresolvable conflict between No. 1 and No. 2, Jung's "transcendent function" produced these symbols, which pushed him out of the deadlock and decided him on his career. Strangely, as his No. 2 self belonged to the timeless world of dreams and myths, it seems that *it itself* decided that he should pursue the world of No. 1. In other words, No. 2 decided it was time for Jung to grow up.

Yet choosing science was only half the battle. The area of science to focus on remained to be decided, and Jung knew the decision would affect the rest of his life. Jung's love of animals suggested zoology—he felt a strong kinship with all warm-blooded creatures because of their nearness to man (reptiles, fish, and insects didn't share in this affection)—but Jung knew that the best he could expect from this would be to teach the subject to someone else later on. That didn't seem promising. To pursue other branches seriously would mean attending other universities, which was out of the question. Jung prided himself on not imitating others— again, an early expression of his "individuation"—but in the end he decided on following in the footsteps of his illustrious name- sake, Carl Jung Sr., and to study medicine. Jung really had no vocation for it, and the hands-on necessity of dissection and vivi- section later filled him with disgust, and he avoided it as much as possible. But, he thought, at least medical studies would allow him to pursue science.

Jung's decision brought the conflict between No. 1 and No. 2 to a head, and the resolution again seemed to be symbolized in a dream. Jung identified No. 2 with Goethe's *Faust*, with its famous line "Two souls, alas, dwell within my breast," and the figure of Faust seemed to him to symbolize man's plight more poignantly than Christ. That Goethe could write of a conflict Jung felt in himself made Jung feel that he wasn't a freak, but that he was liv- ing out the same tensions Goethe had turned into great poetry. Jung dreamed that he was alone, at night, in deep fog, walking against a heavy wind. Cupped in his hands was a candle, and Jung knew he had to keep it lit. Behind him reared a huge dark figure. Jung knew he had to keep going against the wind, and it struck him that the figure behind him was his own shadow, made large by the candlelight reflected on the fog. When Jung woke he realized that the candle was his "I," his own understanding. No. 1 was the light, and No. 2 was the shadow. He had to go forward into life—"study, money making, responsibilities, entanglements, confusions, errors, submissions, defeats"[1]—but this didn't mean that he had to abandon No. 2, who followed him; as Jung would later tell his patients, we all have a shadow which we must get to know. After this Jung's "I" became firmly fixed in No. 1, who had to resist the temptation to stop moving into life, let the candle go out, and sink back into the covering darkness. But No. 2 didn't disappear; instead he took on an autonomous life of his own; he was, for example, the intelligence behind Jung's dreams.

Other experiences besides dreams had moved Jung toward a closer identification with No. 1. Yet not all of them, perhaps, were pleasant. When he was fourteen, Jung went on his first solo holiday, a kind of rest cure for his ailing appetite; he had not yet got over the illnesses that plagued him in his childhood. He was sent to Entlebuch, near Lucerne, where he stayed in the house of a Catholic priest. It's possible it was then that he had a homosexual encounter, which traumatized him and which he kept secret for many years; we know of it because he mentioned it briefly in a letter to Freud at the beginning of their relationship. Jung was on his own for the first time in the adult world, and it excited him. One of the other guests at the house was a chemist. Jung "revered" the chemist as the first person he "had ever met in the flesh who was initiated into the secrets of nature." But the chemist, a young man, taught Jung little of his secrets and seemed more interested in teaching him croquet. On another occasion, he and Jung visited a distillery where Jung got drunk for the first time; the experience for Jung was a "premonition of beauty and meaning" although it came to a "woeful end."[2] In his letter to Freud where he mentions his homosexual experience, Jung says "as a boy, I was the victim of a sexual assault by a man I once worshipped."[3] It's possible that Jung's chemist was this man.[4]

On a later holiday Jung had an early experience of his anima, the feminine element in man—or, less technically, a teenage crush. Visiting his father in Sachseln—where he took his frequent holidays away from home, a practice Jung himself would adopt in later life—Jung hiked to the nearby hermitage of Flüeli, which housed the relics of the fifteenth century-mystic Nicholas of Cusa. On the way back he met a pretty young girl. Jung had little experience of girls, and he felt, as most teenaged boys would, awkward and shy. Jung was immediately attracted to her and believed she felt similarly, and his imagination ran wild, wondering if fate had thrown them together; Jung had a strong penchant for "love at first sight." Yet his reflections soon convinced him it could not be, and he felt unable to speak with her about all the deep thoughts that obsessed him, which was probably just as well, as *Faust*, Schopenhauer, God, and the Devil might have scared her off. So he settled for the weather. They soon parted, but her memory stayed with him for the rest of his life. Other early experiences of women suggest Jung had a strong predisposition for the opposite sex, regardless of the uncertainty his mother bred in him. A maid who cared for him as a child was linked in some way "with other mysterious things I could not understand," and a young woman who walked with him in the autumn sun remained a powerful memory; she, though, would return in Jung's later life.[5]

Around the same time that Jung entered the University of Basel, his father's health took a bad turn. He had for some time been increasingly depressed and irritable, and had developed hypochondria, complaining of stomach pains, for which the doctors could find no cause. The arguments he and Carl had over religious matters didn't help; in fact, all they accomplished was to make it clear to Paul Jung that his faith was founded on nothing. Jung had a piercing insight into his father's spiritual state when Paul accompanied Carl on a student outing with the Zofingia fraternity Carl had joined. Paul himself had belonged to it in his student years, and at a wine-growing village, his old student self revived briefly. He sang the student songs, enjoyed the wine, gave an entertaining speech, and Jung realized that for all practical purposes his father's life had ended when he graduated. Jung recalled how his father would often brood on his unhappy marriage, smoking his old student's pipe, remembering his early days, and now he saw that although his father once showed great promise and potential—his dissertation on the Arabic version of the Song of Songs was considered excellent—all that ended early on. It may seem cruel that Jung considered his father a failure, and some have questioned his account of his life, but it makes Jung's later emphasis on the psychology of the second half of life, as opposed to Freud's fixation on childhood, understandable. Jung couldn't understand why his father's inner life ended when he was still a young man, and his later concern with "individuation," the unending work of "becoming who one is," can be linked to his recognition of his father's sadness.

Paul Jung's physical life ended less than a year after this incident. His condition worsened, and in January 1896, he died; from what is still unknown, although he does seem a victim of what the playwright Bernard Shaw called "discouragement," and what Colin Wilson has labeled "life failure." He was only fifty-three. Jung's curiosity about death hadn't left him, and he sat by his father's side, fascinated, as he passed away. A few days later, Emilie spoke to Carl in her No. 2 voice. "He died in time for you,"[6] she said. Jung was struck by this, but it soon became clear what she meant. It was Carl's time now. He moved into his father's room and became the head of the household. Jung's mother was useless with money, and Carl had to dole out the finances. Soon after this, he had two dreams of his father, both so vivid that he seriously began to consider the possibility of life after death. It was a thought that would occupy him for the rest of his life.

Not long after Paul's death, the family had to abandon the parsonage for their father's successor. They moved to an old house near Binningen, named Bottminger Mill, on the outskirts of Basel, where Emilie's sister and her husband lived. The house was said to be haunted, and Jung, Emilie, and Jung's sister, Gertrude, occupied the second floor. Paul had left them little and Jung had to borrow money from an uncle, and he showed considerable entrepreneurial flair by helping his aunt sell an antique collection. Jung haggled for the best price and received a commission on every sale. Even so, he was always strapped for cash, and he was so frugal that a box of cigars he received as a gift lasted a year.

Jung's entry into university seemed to effect a change in his personality. From being an outcast and oddball, a typical introvert, he became something of a celebrity; he earned his nickname, "the

Barrel," because of his large intake of beer, although he seldom got drunk. And although he never cared for dancing, he discovered he was actually good at it and, during one waltz, fell in love with a French-speaking girl. Sadly, the twenty centimes he had to purchase two wedding rings the next day were not enough, and handing them back to the jeweler, he forgot his sudden marriage plans and, apparently, the girl. Jung was a regular at the "Breo," an old tavern, and got a reputation for telling spooky stories on the way home through the Nightingale Woods, which were considered haunted. Jung carried a revolver, and along the way would point out where a murder was supposed to have happened, or a suicide, and offer the pistol to a friend who, having walked Jung to his door, now had to carry on alone.

The commanding character of No. 2 seemed to have melded with his student self, and Jung became a dominant voice at the Zofingia lectures and debates. By his early twenties, he had become the tall, handsome, vital, muscular, and often domineering character who was determined to make his mark on the world. Jung enjoyed captivating his fellows with his controversial talks "On the Limits of Exact Science" and "The Value of Speculative Research." Like some others at the time Jung rejected the reign of scientific materialism and argued that philosophy and metaphysics must again take central place in Western thought. More daring, though, was Jung's uninhibited interest in spiritualism, which by this time had become a controversial topic on both sides of the Atlantic, ever since 1848, when the Fox sisters of Hydesville, New York, discovered they could communicate with the spirit of a dead man. Soon after this, mediums, table turning, floating tambourines, ectoplasmic limbs, and a variety of other otherworldly phenomena became the focus of an international craze; the flood of disincarnate appearances led one investigator to speak of an "invasion of the spirit people."[7] Colorful characters like the Russian medium and mystic Helena Petrovna Blavatsky were involved, but also scientists and philosophers like William James, Oliver Lodge, William Crookes, and Frederick Myers. It is difficult for us today to realize that at the time, many of the most famous men and women in the world were involved in spiritualism, to one degree or another. Thomas Edison, for example, who joined Blavatsky's Theosophical Society, hoped to be able to record spirits on his "Spirit Phone." Yet, for all this, the reductionist thought that dominates the academic world today was already securely in place, and Jung was risking his future career by openly advocating the unbiased study of the paranormal.

Jung came across a book about spiritualism in the library of a friend's father, and reading it led to a serious study of the literature. Books by Professor Johann Zöllner (an astrophysicist fascinated with the spirit world), the aforementioned William Crookes (the chemist famous for inventing the Crookes tube), and Carl du Prel, the philosopher who wrote on dreams, trance states, and hypnotism; Justinus Kerner's classic *The Seeress of Prevorst*, about the psychic Frederika Hauffe; seven volumes of the Swedish scientist and visionary Emanuel Swedenborg, who anticipated many modern discoveries in astronomy and neuroscience, as well as Immanuel Kant's study of Swedenborg, *Dreams of a Spirit Seer*— these and other similar works occupied Jung as much as did his studies of anatomy, physiology and internal medicine.

Jung realized that much of what he read in these books was familiar to him from the stories he had heard when he was growing up. He of course knew of the supernatural background of his mother's family, and the stories of his grandfather talking to his dead first wife. His own recent dreams of his father, in which he had "come back" and seemed more alive than ever, added to this. Jung was not, as many of his critics believe, gullible, or if he was, he was in some highly esteemed company. (Goethe before him had a deep interest in the occult and "spirit world.") As many do today, he recognized that science had created unnecessary boundaries to its explorations and that the phenomena described in these books and in the tales he heard as a child weren't illusions or lies but pointed to dimensions of reality that had only recently, in the last two centuries, become "off limits." Jung led a group of students who performed various occult experiments; yet when he spoke to his fellows about these ideas, or lectured to them about the need to take them seriously, he met with resistance and rejection, and the tone he took in some of his talks suggests that once again, he had found himself in the position of the outsider. Apparently he had greater luck with his dachshund, whose name has not come down to us, who he felt understood him better and could feel supernatural presences himself.[8]

University, however, wasn't the only place Jung could confront the spirits. There was a much more active access to them at home. Along with his readings in spiritualist literature, and his discovery of Nietzsche's *Thus Spake Zarathustra*, a work that would obsess Jung for many years, around this time Jung soon experienced some firsthand encounters with the paranormal. The house in Binningen was the site of two very well reported incidents of psychic phenomena in Jung's life. Sitting in his room studying, Jung suddenly heard a loud bang, like a pistol shot. He rushed into the dining room, from where the sound came, and found his mother startled. He looked at the round, walnut table that had come, he tells us, from his father's mother and saw that it had cracked from the edge past the center. The split didn't follow any joint, but had passed through solid wood. Drying wood couldn't account for it; the table was seventy years old and it was a humid day. Jung thought, "There certainly are curious accidents," and as if she was reading his mind Emilie replied in her No. 2 voice, "Yes, yes, that means something."[9]

Two weeks later a second incident occurred. Jung returned home in the early evening and found the household in a state of distress. About an hour earlier another loud crack had been heard, this time coming from a large sideboard. Jung's mother and sister could find no crack in it and had no idea what had produced the sound. Jung inspected the sideboard himself, then thought to look inside. In a cupboard where they kept the bread, Jung found a loaf and the bread knife. The knife had shattered into several pieces, all neatly arranged in the bread basket. Jung's mother had used the knife for four o'clock tea, but no one had touched it nor opened the cupboard since. When Jung took the knife to a cutler, he said that there was no fault in the steel and that someone must have broken it on purpose; it was the only way he could account for it. Jung kept the shattered knife for the rest of his life, and years later he sent a photograph of it to the psychical researcher J. B. Rhine.

There's some controversy about the chronology of these events. In a letter to Rhine about the knife, Jung says that he was in the garden when it shattered, and that it happened before the table splitting.[10] In his letter, however, he mentions something that later became even more controversial: his relationship with his cousin, Helene Preiswerk. Jung refers to her as a "young woman with marked mediumistic faculties" that he had just met around the time of the incident, and that he felt she could have been responsible for the explosions. In fact, Jung had known Helly—as she was called—for some time, and everything we know about her suggests she was in love with him.

In *Memories, Dreams, Reflections,* Jung says that he became involved in a series of séances with his relatives after the incidents with the table and knife. Yet at the time these occurred, he had already been participating in the sessions for months. His study of spiritualism led him to want firsthand experience, and with the encouragement of his mother—or at least her No. 2—he organized a group at the parsonage. Although Paul was still alive, he was confined to his bed and was apparently unaware of what went on. Attending were Jung, Emilie, Jung's cousin, Luise—known as Luggy—Luggy's sister, Helly, and her best friend, Emmy Zinnstag. Jung had a crush on Luggy, who was attractive, intelligent, and lively. Her younger sister, apparently, was not. In the doctoral thesis that emerged from these proceedings, *On the Psychology and Pathology of So-called Occult Phenomena*, Jung describes Helly as "exhibiting slightly rachitic skull formation," "somewhat pale facial color," and dark, piercing eyes. She was absent-minded and reserved, but could sometimes become boisterous; wasn't particularly intelligent or talented; didn't like reading, wasn't well educated and had rather limited interests. Not a particularly flattering account. The dissertation dates the séances from 1899 to 1900, but they had started years before. Gerhard Wehr politely suggests that "the doctoral candidate was obviously at pains to conceal his own role, and especially his close kinship relationship, thus forestalling from the start any further critical inquiry that might have thrown the scientific validity of the entire work into question."[11] Which in plain English means that Jung the scientist thought it a good career move to obscure Jung the mystic's personal involvement in the business. Jung may have wanted to save the idea of the scientific study of the paranormal from the ridicule it would nevertheless receive, but that distancing himself from the séances, as if he was only a curious, scientific researcher, would look better than admitting his own passionate involvement in them, must have been on his mind. And if his personal advancement coincided with helping to keep the door open on studying these phenomena, then so much the better.

Sitting around the same table that would later crack—and which, contrary to Jung's account, came from the Preiswerk side of the family[12]—the participants touched fingers lightly. Then Helly went into a trance, making clear that she had inherited a good portion of the mystical Preiswerk blood. She fell to the floor, breathed deeply, and began to speak in the voice of old Samuel Preiswerk. She sounded, Jung noted, more serious and mature, and had somehow duplicated the old Hebrew scholar's voice, speaking in High German rather than her usual Swiss dialect, although she had never heard him speak. She began to tell the others that they should pray for her elder sister Bertha, who, she—or Samuel Preiswerk—said, had just given birth to a black child. Bertha, who was living in Brazil, had already had one child with her half-caste husband, and gave birth to another on the same day as the séance, as later corroboration confirmed.[13] Further séances proved equally startling. The table moved, taps sounded, and at one point Samuel Preiswerk and Carl Jung Sr., who in life disliked each other, reached a new accord. A warning came for another sister, who was also expecting a child. She would lose it, the medium said, although her grandfather tried to help her. In August the baby was born premature and dead.[14]

There were other séances, but at each Helly reached more feverish states and Luggy worried for her health. It was agreed that they should be postponed until after her confirmation. Another reason for stopping may have been Luggy's suspicion that Helly was using them as a means of getting Jung's attention. At one point she had even conveyed a message from Samuel that Carl should not read so much Nietzsche.[15] And when Helly began to utter messages that were surprisingly similar to those in Kerner's *The Seeress of Prevorst*, which Jung had given her as a birthday gift, her reliability became shaky.

When the séances started again—prompted by the splitting table, which Emilie believed was a sign from Samuel—Helly produced an array of voices. Among others, dead relatives, a girl who spoke in a strange mixture of Italian and French, and some unknown character named Ulrich von Gerberstein, turned up. But the most interesting was a spirit named Ivenes, who called herself the *real* Helene Preiswerk. Ivenes made spectacular claims, such as that she had once been a clergyman's wife whom Goethe had seduced or Frederika Hauffe or a noble woman burned for witchcraft or a Christian martyr. But what Jung found most remarkable was that Ivenes was so much more mature, confident, and intelligent than Helly. What was the source of this more mature personality?

Although in this context this question referred to Helly's disembodied guests, it would become central to Jung's ideas about "individuation." As with Helly, other mediums, schizophrenics, and the related phenomenon of multiple personalities, amidst the chatter and often spurious metaphysical pronouncements, a more serious, developed, adult personality will appear, one that seems to prefigure who the person could become, if guided in the right direction.[16] Jung came to understand that in this regard, we are all fragmented, and that the work of individuation is to fuse our disparate parts into a new, more competent whole; as he remarked years later "so-called normal people are very fragmentary . . . they are not complete egos."[17] Jung's method to accomplish this, active imagination, has its roots in the questions he put to Helly's different "spirit guides," which in the dissertation he argued were really splinters of her own personality. In his first official pronouncement on the occult, Jung argued that the phenomena were produced by the unconscious mind, a position he held for most of his career, although, as we will see, he changed his mind on occasion. That he may have encouraged her to "dissociate," i.e., to produce the voices in order to keep his interest, has led some critics to question the value of Jung's early work.[18]

Eventually, Helly's performance flagged, and the séances became dominated by rather trivial spirits. And when Jung discovered Helly cheating—in order to maintain his interest—he knew it was time to stop. She admitted to this, but not before she communicated a complicated metaphysical system that pictured the universe as a series of seven circles; years later, when working out his ideas about mandalas, Jung recognized one in Helly's "system." Helly dropped her mediumship, as well as her attempts to catch Jung, and sometime later left Switzerland to become a successful dressmaker in Montpellier, France. She died at thirty from tuberculosis. Jung later suggested that her unconscious, somehow aware that she would die young, had created Ivenes in order for her to experience to some degree the kind of mature, middle-aged woman she wouldn't have the chance to become. They met for the last time in Paris. By this time Jung's thesis had been published. He had tried to obscure her identity—referring to her in it as "S. W."—and that of her family, but the ruse didn't work, and his account of Helly and his suggestions that insanity ran in her side of the family created a scandal in Basel; some suggest Helly was unable to find a husband because of it.[19] Neither Helly nor Jung mentioned any of this during their last meeting. Helly's interest in Jung had long faded, yet Jung, who by that time was engaged, found himself attracted to her. In many ways she had become who she really was.

During the time of the séances, Jung had taken a course in psychiatry, but it hadn't stirred any deep interest in him. Jung was again undecided about his future. No. 1 knew he had to master his medical studies, so he would be ready for a career as a physician, but No. 2 wanted to transcend what he saw as the artificial limits of science and to tackle the big mysteries: life, death, the soul, time, space, eternity. Psychiatry then was considered a kind of dead end; it meant a career caring for hopelessly incurable lunatics in dreary asylums. Jung's experiences with Helly brought him a deeper understanding of the psyche, of how No. 2 personalities form, and how they become integrated into the Self. Yet a second course in psychiatry again failed to arouse Jung, and when it came time to take the state examination in order to graduate, he waited until the end to tackle the psychiatric textbook. This was a classic work by the psychiatrist and sexologist Richard von Krafft-Ebing, responsible for coining the terms "sadist" and "masochist." Jung was already familiar with it, but now it was as if he was encountering it for the first time. Jung was struck by Krafft-Ebing's remark that psychoses were "diseases of the personality." When he read it, his heart pounded and he had to take a breath. Jung realized that he had finally found a discipline that could combine No. 1 and No. 2. Here his two passions, for empirical facts and metaphysical speculation, could meet. But what also thrilled him was Krafft-Ebing's comment that the psychiatrist's *own* personality was brought into his practice; he confronted the "sick" personality of his patient, not with cold, "scientific" detachment, but with his whole being, which would, presumably, be affected by the encounter. Yet it should also be clear that for someone like Jung, who felt it was his destiny to plumb the secret meaning of nature, psychiatry offered an open field, a fresh, new pursuit in which he could make his name. This as much as anything else must surely have helped him to decide on pursuing it.

It was not absolutely foreign to him, though. His father had for a time been the official pastor of the Friedmatt asylum in Basel, and as we've seen, his namesake, Carl Jung Sr., had tried unsuccessfully to establish a chair of psychiatry at the University of Basel. Some have even suggested that Jung's real reason for entering psychiatry was fear for his own sanity, prompted by his recognition that there was a hereditary strain of mental illness in his family. Samuel Preiswerk's ghosts, his mother's No. 2, and his own sense of inner duality may have suggested that confronting insanity head-on, might be the best way of dealing with it in himself.[20]

Jung's friends certainly thought he was crazy when he told them of his decision. His professor in internal medicine, Friedrich von Müller, was equally amazed; Müller had been offered an important position in Munich, and had asked Jung to join him as his assistant. It was the kind of chance someone like Jung should have jumped at; it meant an excellent start in what could have been a prestigious, if conventional, career. Why, his colleagues asked, had Jung thrown it away? Again, the old feeling of being an outsider returned, yet the sense that in psychiatry he would find his destiny overruled everything.

Jung passed his exams brilliantly, and as a reward he went to the opera, the first time in his life. Although in later life Jung hated attending concerts—he told his wife, Emma, who loved concerts, that after listening to people all day the last thing he wanted to do was to sit and listen to something else—on this occasion Bizet's *Carmen* intoxicated him. He had saved enough money from his antique deals to afford a holiday in Munich and Stuttgart, where he enjoyed the museums, a pleasure, like concert going, he later lost. But now he relished it.

It was just as well that Jung enjoyed himself. He had applied and been accepted for a position at the famous Burghölzli Asylum in Zürich. Entering there, he said, was like joining a monastery. But in leaving Basel, he was giving up more than cultural delights. For the first time he was striking out on his own. His mother and sister were unhappy with his decision, but Jung was beginning to feel that Basel was cramping him. The business with Helly hovered over him, and he would never shake off the fact that he was old Carl Sr.'s grandson. Basel, he felt, was weighed down by tradition and heritage; Zürich, on the other hand, was little more than a commercial village. In Basel, Jung knew people who had seen great figures like the historian Jacob Burckhardt, the mythologist Johann Bachofen, and even Nietzsche walk the streets; it had centuries of culture behind it. Zürich lacked this and for most

Baselers it was a city of philistines and merchants. But what Jung needed now was a blank slate, and Zürich provided it. After serving his first period of mandatory military service—something required of all Swiss males, and an obligation Jung thoroughly enjoyed—he headed southeast to meet his destiny.

3. INTRUDERS IN THE MIND

J ung started work as an assistant at the Burghölzli Mental Hospital in Zürich in December 1900. He was twenty-five. Being accepted at the Burghölzli was, in its way, as prestigious a coup as working with his teacher Friedrich von Müller would have been. At the time, it was the most famous mental clinic in Europe, having achieved this distinction under its previous director Auguste Forel, a diverse thinker of many achievements, whose study of brain structure led to the cofounding of neuron theory. When Jung arrived, Forel had handed over his directorship to Eugen Bleuler, a renowned psychiatrist who was responsible for coining the term *schizophrenia*, to replace the older *dementia praecox*. Bleuler championed an approach to mental illness that Jung himself adopted and which the psychiatrist R. D. Laing would make famous in the 1960s. Instead of regarding a patient's delusions as merely unintelligible symptoms, of no value in treatment, and which doctors could rightfully ignore, he tried to understand what his patients were saying, and saw their seemingly nonsensical remarks as a relevant, if unproductive, response to their problems. He spent time with them, gave them simple tasks, showed sympathy and interest, and in general treated them as human beings, rather than as simply broken machines, as the reigning orthodoxy, which regarded all mental illness as organic in origin, did. Sadly, with its emphasis on the chemical basis of mental illness, to a great extent mainstream psychiatry still takes this approach today.

As a boy Jung had vowed to one day live near a lake; entering the Burghölzli, he did exactly that. Assistants were required to live in-house, and the clinic, an austere, domineering building, was perched on a hilltop, overlooking Lake Zürich. Neither the doctors nor the patients, however, had a good view of the water. In the patients' case, this was to avoid encouraging thoughts of suicide. Given the living conditions and workload of the doctors, a similar concern may have applied to them, too. A colleague of Jung's, Alphonse Maeder, called the Burghölzli a "kind of factory, where one worked hard and was paid badly."[1] Bleuler was fanatically hard-working, dedicated, and serious, and he expected his assistants to be the same. Their day started at 6:30; they had to make their rounds before 8:30, when a general meeting was held. There was often another meeting at 10:00, and an evening one at 5:00 that lasted until 7:00. Jung and his colleagues spent the rest of their evenings typing out their notes, and an average working day ended at 10:00 pm, when the doors to the clinic were locked for the night. Only senior doctors had keys, and assistants had to borrow one if they intended to come home late. Every doctor was required to have a working knowledge of all the case histories of all the patients. When Jung arrived, there were 340 patients to four doctors.

Bleuler was teetotal, and all of his assistants were required to give up alcohol; for the Barrel this was quite a sacrifice. Jung, however, had little opportunity for socializing. He knew practically no one in Zürich, and in any case, having only one pair of trousers and two shirts put a damper on his night life. Jung's talent for solitude helped, and for the first six months he dedicated himself to reading through fifty volumes of the *Allgemeine Zeitschrift für Psychiatrie* (*Journal of Psychiatry*). Jung's seriousness matched Bleuler's—indeed, his monkish lifestyle raised questions about his "psychological abnormality" among his colleagues[2]— and it's unfortunate that his remarks about Bleuler and the Burghölzli in *Memories, Dreams, Reflections* are less than flattering. In his account of the Burghölzli, Bleuler isn't mentioned, and Jung sums up the professional atmosphere there by saying that "From the clinical point of view which then prevailed, the human personality of the patient, his individuality, did not matter at all," and that in the doctors' diagnoses, "the psychology of the mental patient played no role whatsoever."[3] Both remarks are untrue, and Colin Wilson suggests that the reason Jung made them is that he "regarded Bleuler with the unconscious jealousy of a man who feels that someone else has anticipated his own discovery."[4] The inference is that Jung unintentionally wanted to get credit for developing the "patient-friendly" approach to mental illness that has become such a mainstay of humanistic psychology. True or not, this won't be the only occasion in which Jung will be accused of taking credit for the work of others. Jung did, however, speak well of Bleuler in other contexts; when identified by a correspondent as a Freudian, Jung corrected this and pointed out that as a "student of Bleuler's" he had already acquired "a scientific reputation when I began supporting Freud." And in a letter to Bleuler's son, he said that the "impressions and suggestions I received from your father are all the more vivid in my memory, for which I shall always be thankful to him."[5] Yet in his central public statement about his life, these acknowledgments are missing.

If Jung had been excited by the prospect of understanding how "the human mind reacted to the sight of its own destruction,"[6] at the Burghölzli he had ample opportunity. Patients ate their own excrement, drank their urine, and masturbated continually; one smeared herself with her feces and asked Jung if he found her attractive. They would switch from polite conversation to violent abuse and wails of despair to catatonic silence within a matter of moments. Most of Jung's colleagues refrained from Bleuler's example and avoided interacting with their patients; however, Jung, who soon got a reputation for being as fixated on work as Bleuler—which the others read as ambition—would sit patiently and listen to the incessant word salad. Remarks like "Naples and I must look after the world with noodles," "I am the triple owner of the world," and "I am double polytechnic irreplaceable," strangely prefigured the kind of "automatic writing" the Surrealists in Paris would produce in the 1920s, in works like André Breton and Philippe Soupault's *The Magnetic Fields*. One patient in particular, an old woman named Babette, who had been in the asylum for twenty years, fascinated Jung. She had been born in poverty; her father had been a drunkard and her sister a prostitute. She had spent most of her life in squalor, and the rest in madhouses. Jung listened to her "crazy" remarks, such as "I am Socrates' deputy," and "I am plum cake on a cornmeal bottom," and realized that they weren't meaningless, but attempts to increase her sense of self-worth by claiming a kind of importance. She was, Jung saw, compensating for the low self-esteem that had led to her retreat from reality.

Jung gained his insight into the meaning of Babette's gibberish through his work on word-association tests, to which he had been assigned by Bleuler. These tests were originally developed by Sir

Francis Galton—Charles Darwin's cousin—to test physiological reaction time to stimuli, but Jung saw that there were psychological applications as well, an approach the psychologist Wilhelm Wundt had already developed. Jung would read out a list of "trigger" words, and the test subject was required to respond with the first word that came to mind. The reaction time and the response were noted, and if the subject hesitated, or produced an unusual response, Jung suggested this indicated a "block" of some kind. Noting similarities between words, reaction times, and responses, Jung argued that the problematic words were associated in the subject's mind with certain emotions, which clustered to produce what Jung called a "complex." Often the subject was unaware that he or she had hesitated, and Jung concluded that the complexes operated in the subject's unconscious. Jung also worked on measuring skin and sweat gland responses with a galvanometer, and his early studies led to the development of the lie detector. Jung even employed the word-association test in order to help solve crimes. In one case, a boy thought to have stolen money from his employer was given a string of trigger words; after hesitating on words such as "thief" and "police," Jung cut to the chase and accused him of the theft. He denied it, then broke down in tears and confessed; his "repression" of unpleasant thoughts—his guilt—betrayed him. Jung's work on word association is clear evidence that he was aware of and investigating approaches to the unconscious well before he had encountered Freud. Indeed, he had read Freud's *The Interpretation of Dreams* before coming to the Burghölzli, but hadn't been impressed, and it was only on reading it a second time, in order to make a report on it for Bleuler, that he grasped its importance. Clearly, the work he did on word association and his insights into complexes, which gave Jung his own evidence for an unconscious mind, led to his recognizing the significance of Freud's work. But by the time he did, Jung had already achieved recognition in psychiatric circles for the work he was doing at the Burghölzli.

While a student at the University of Basel, Jung visited an old family friend in Schaffhausen; she was Berta Rauschenbach, the "young woman who walked him in the autumn sun" as a child, mentioned in the previous chapter. Now she was a middle-aged woman with a family of her own. On that occasion, while paying his respects, he saw another young girl, a pigtailed teenager of fourteen, standing on the stairway. Out of the blue Jung turned to the friend he was with and said, "That girl is my wife!" Years later, recounting the incident, Jung told Aniela Jaffé that he was deeply shaken by this; he had only seen her for an instant, but knew with utter certainty that he would marry her. Jung was right. Emma Rauschenbach—Berta's daughter—was well educated, attractive, and charming, and she came from a wealthy family; at one point she would be considered one of the richest women in Switzerland. Her father was an extremely successful industrialist, and at the time he first saw her, Jung's chances of marrying her were pretty slim. Understandably, his friend laughed at his outburst; Jung had yet to speak with the girl, and in any case, his own prospects as a poor student were strictly limited. Yet Jung's sudden intuition proved correct. Jung saw Emma again six years later at a fete in Winterthur, just north of Zürich, to which he had been invited by a family acquaintance. Jung's social life was practically nonexistent and the opportunity must have been welcome. A few months later, Berta Rauschenbach invited Jung to a ball at their summer home in Olberg. The impecunious Jung must have been impressed by the setting: several acres, footmen in livery, carriages, horses, spacious rooms, costly furnishings: rather a different environment from the Burghölzli or Jung's family life. Jung danced with Emma, but he made a bad first impression; he was clumsy and decidedly underdressed. Yet Berta must have got wind of Jung's premonition, because she asked him to visit again. When Jung finally proposed to Emma, she turned him down. Neither Jung nor Berta was satisfied with this. Eventually they convinced Emma to reconsider, and soon Emma and Jung were engaged.

It has to be said that marrying Emma—which Jung did in February 1903—was probably the luckiest thing that ever happened to him. Although Jung eventually drew extremely well-heeled patients from both sides of the Atlantic, it was Emma's wealth that allowed him to pursue his research without worrying about making a living; because of it he could eventually leave the Burghölzli and set himself up in private practice.

Before this, though, Jung spent the winter of 1902 to 1903 in Paris, attending lectures by the renowned Pierre Janet, the psychiatrist and philosopher who coined the terms "dissociation" and "subconscious," and whose belief that early traumas were responsible for a patient's present condition predated Freud's similar belief by some years. Freud himself had studied under the great Jean-Martin Charcot, Janet's instructor at the Salpêtrière Hospital in Paris, as had Bleuler, and Janet later believed that his own work was confirmed in that of Freud's; indeed, that "confirmation" for Janet often drifted into plagiarism. Although Freud is most often cited as the greatest influence on Jung, Janet and another French psychologist, Alfred Binet, are serious challengers. Janet argued that there are two basic neuroses, hysteria and psychasthenia, and Binet likewise developed the typology of "introspection" and "externospection." Both Janet's and Binet's ideas were influential on Jung's studies on "introversion" and "extraversion," which form the basis of his most influential book, *Psychological Types*.

Janet's central concept was what he called the "reality function." Like Bleuler, he believed that mental illness was a result of a "loosening" of consciousness, a slackness in our grasp of reality, as if the mind was a hand too feeble to hold anything properly. We even tell someone who seems on the verge of hysteria to "get a grip." Mental health, Janet believed, was determined by our ability to focus, to concentrate our attention (again, we often say "pull yourself together" to someone who is in danger of "losing it"). Janet called this act of concentration "psychological tension," and he believed it was something people could develop intentionally. The patients in the Burghölzli had lost contact with reality because their consciousness had become dangerously slack, and Bleuler recognized this by giving them various "tasks" to perform. Jung himself had experienced the truth of Janet's insight when he "cured" himself of his fainting fits and later of his indecision about his career: in both cases a "collision with reality" threw Jung into purposeful action (and we recall that Henri Ellenberger remarked that the first step in Jung's therapy was to "bring the patient back to reality").

Janet had also developed the idea that when someone's psychological tension becomes extremely slack—what he called "the lowering of the mental level," through either sleep, hypnosis, or illness—the personality separates into autonomous fragments that seem to have a "mind" of their own, which is very close to what Jung was discovering about complexes, and what he felt he had experienced during the séances with Helly. So historians of psychology like Sonu Shamdasani, who argue that Jung has an equal if not more of a link with French schools of psychology than with Viennese, are correct, yet Jung himself didn't seem to have appreciated Janet's influence at the time. This may be because Janet's optimistic and common sense approach struck Jung as smacking too much of French Enlightenment thinking; it was too rational. Freud's ideas were more in line with Jung's early reading of Schopenhauer and Nietzsche, and his mysterious realm of the unconscious mind appealed too strongly to the romantic in Jung.

Besides, Jung was on something of a holiday in Paris, and he had more on his mind than Janet's ideas. He attended lectures only once a week; the rest of the time was his own, and he spent it enjoying the city, its art galleries, concerts, and cafes, taking classes in English at a Berlitz school, and anticipating his coming marriage. It was during this trip that he saw Helly Preiswerk again and found himself strangely attracted to her. He also seems also to have developed a fascination with a Jewish girl; Jewish women, in fact, exerted a strong pull on the Teutonic Jung. At 27, Jung was a handsome man and he was beginning to understand that women found him attractive. It was an insight his fiancée, Emma, would have to come to terms with.

After his return, the couple were married and they honeymooned in Madeira and the Canary Islands. Emma quickly discovered what being married to a psychiatrist would mean, and the reality of living in the Burghölzli was at first something of a shock. The newlyweds took a flat above Bleuler's in the clinic; this time they did have a view of the lake. Emma was used to quality, and she ensured that her new home was well furnished. Jung's impecunious days were over. He began to live in style, eating and dressing well, and entertaining friends. It was a way of life he quickly came to appreciate, and although he never outgrew the effects of the poverty he had known for most of his life, Jung took to being well-off with panache.

In 1904 Jung was made a senior doctor and clinical director; other advancements soon followed, and before long he was Bleuler's "second in command," although later promotions evaded him, a slight by Bleuler that Jung felt keenly. His hard work and enormous vitality were difficult to ignore, and at the beginning he and Bleuler were on friendly terms; soon, however, their relationship became rocky, mostly because of Jung's irrepressible drive and self-confidence. It also didn't help that at bottom, Jung considered Bleuler a cross "between a peasant and a schoolteacher."7 One stimulant to Jung's emerging genius was the arrival at the Burghölzli of a female patient who developed a relationship with him that others would also have: that of Jung's muse. Eventually the position would be occupied on a near permanent basis by Toni Wolff, another patient who in 1913 became Jung's mistress, a distinction she would enjoy until the mid-1940s, and which the saintly Emma endured gracefully but not without suffering. Before Toni there were others. At his lectures at the university, Jung was ogled by a clutch of well-heeled groupies, locally known as the *Zürichberg Pelzmäntel*, the "fur-coated ladies," and by the time he emerged as the founder of a new school of psychology (or self-transformation), he was rarely without a flock of admiring females, a blessing (or curse) he shared with other "teachers" such as Rudolf Steiner and Gurdjieff. That Jung had sexual relationships with some of his patients has, not surprisingly, lent much ammunition to his detractors.

Sabina Spielrein arrived at the Burghölzli in August 1904. She was an eighteen-year-old Russian Jew (her grandfather was a rabbi) who wore pigtails and dressed like a child. Previous time in a private clinic proved unhelpful. She was highly sensitive, deeply emotional, intelligent, well-spoken, and suicidal. She cried, laughed or screamed uncontrollably, avoided eye contact and stuck her tongue out at anyone who touched her. Hysteria ran in her family, and Jung was surprised when Bleuler suggested he psychoanalyze her. Although Freud had introduced the idea almost a decade earlier, he hadn't provided a manual, and Jung, in a sense, had to wing it. He met with Sabina for an hour or two every other day. Combining word association with the "talking cure," he got her to tell her story. A beating by her father on her bare bottom when she was three aroused her (and seemed confirmation of Freud's ideas about childhood sexuality, about which Jung maintained strong reservations), as did the sight of her father beating her older brother. Afterward she believed she had defecated on her father's hand; this led to obsessive thoughts about excreta. When she reached her teens, Sabina couldn't eat or see anyone else eating without thinking of feces, and the sight of her father's hands excited her sexually. Anger at the sight of punishment turned into sexual fantasy, which gave way to open masturbation, depression, and rage.

Talking about her problem helped, but Jung took a lead from Bleuler and asked her to help him in his work. Sabina wanted to become a medical student and Jung had her research material for his *Habilitationsschrift*, the paper that would qualify him as a lecturer at the University of Zürich; she also assisted him in the word-association tests. She proved an excellent assistant, and with Sabina, for the first time Jung made "full use of his ability to give a patient a more flattering image of herself than she would have formed without his help."[8] Although at the time women had more obstacles in the path of their individuation than did men, the need for a strong, positive self-image transcends gender, and throughout his life, Jung had an enviable knack for making people think better of themselves; in his later work, this would move beyond merely achieving a "normal" level of competence, into more creative possibilities. In Sabina's case, providing an opportunity to use her talents was as much of a "cure" as psychoanalyzing her, an insight the psychologist Abraham Maslow, who shares much with Jung, also discovered.[9] Sabina proved so good a helper that Jung encouraged her to become a psychiatrist. His intuition was correct; she later became one of the first female psychoanalysts, and there's evidence that her ideas influenced both Jung and Freud.

Yet with Sabina, Jung learned the truth of Krafft-Ebing's belief that in psychiatry, the whole personality of the doctor is involved, and that in responding subjectively to a patient, one's own problems emerge, a phenomenon later dubbed "counter transference." During his talks with Sabina, Jung spoke of Emma, and his conventional views about women surfaced. Like most Swiss he believed that as his wife, Emma should be interested only in keeping a home and making a family (something she proved exceptionally good at, producing five children) and in sharing his interests, a prejudice that, for all his celebration of the feminine, remained with Jung throughout his life. Years later he told an interviewer, "A man's foremost interest should be his work. But a woman—man *is* her work and her business."¹⁰ Sabina, he said, was exceptional. He would find other female patients exceptional, too.

Although Jung has been criticized for taking advantage of his patient, Sabina was really the seducer, and as Bruno Bettelheim grudgingly admits, her affair with Jung is probably what cured her.¹¹ After only eight months of treatment, Sabina was released from the clinic and she started classes at the university. Jung realized that her growing emotional involvement with him gave her support, and withdrawing it could cause a relapse. But he also discovered his own growing dependence on her; as with the Jewish girl he met in Paris, Sabina's dark "otherness" attracted him. Although Emma took an active interest in his work, and wanted to be the kind of intellectual partner he desired, she never was (although not through any fault of her own), and with Sabina, Jung started a pattern of relationships with women that combined the pursuit of ideas with that of the erotic. In Sabina's case this led to a fantasy of having Jung's child, which they named Siegfried, in honor of Wagner's character from the *Ring of the Nibelungen*.

Jung talked to her about his ideas, and about his determination to capture "the intruders in the mind,"¹² that he had already encountered with his cousin Helly and was meeting daily with patients like Babette. They didn't become intimate until 1908. Jung held her off, but eventually he succumbed. But a few months later Jung tired of the affair and of Sabina's possessiveness (at one point during the breakup, she pulled a knife on him); he was, after all, a rather conventional Swiss and when he heard that Sabina had introduced herself to one of his colleagues as his mistress, alarm bells went off. He also loved Emma and his growing family (four of his children were born during the time he knew Sabina), and was concerned she would be hurt.

Jung realized he had to extricate himself from the business and he did it rather clumsily, in a letter to Sabina's mother, which was in response to an anonymous letter—most likely written by Emma—telling her that her daughter was involved with her doctor, who was a married man. (By this time though, Sabina had been discharged from the clinic, and as Jung was no longer receiving a fee for his services, technically he was no longer her physician, a point he made in his letter.) Jung took the role of the injured party, claiming that her daughter had spread stories about him, simply because he had denied himself the pleasure of making her pregnant. The business shows Jung in a rather unattractive light, and he knew this himself; however, it is true that at the time, analyst/analysand ethics were not yet as fixed as they are today, and as critics such as Bruno Bettelheim admit, Sabina benefited by the affair, although the same could not be said for Emma.

One positive thing to come of the Sabina Spielrein affair was that it strengthened Jung's developing relationship with Sigmund Freud. Increasingly, Jung saw that the work he was doing with word association confirmed many of the findings of this still obscure doctor in Vienna. And Jung's own deep interests in dreams made Freud's insights seem like revelations. In early 1906 Jung sent Freud a fan letter, the opening gesture in what would become a voluminous correspondence, and a copy of his book *Diagnostic Association Studies*. He had, though, reservations about Freud's emphasis on sex as the sole origin of neuroses, and communicated them to Freud from the start, but in the light of the new realms of the psyche Freud was exploring, these differences seemed minor. Jung must have been thrilled when Freud wrote back almost immediately saying he had already purchased a copy of Jung's book, and more or less invited Jung to join him in his work; with Müller and Bleuler, Freud quickly joined the ranks of those who recognized Jung's worth early on. Yet Jung must have felt some hesitation, as he waited several months before replying, thus beginning a pattern that would continue throughout their friendship, with Freud often eagerly awaiting a reply from the tardy Jung. When the correspondence did begin, one of the first things Jung discussed was Sabina. Although at first he didn't mention her by name, he did say that her case had taught him about his own polygamous tendencies. In another, later letter he also confessed that the formula for a successful marriage was a tolerance of infidelity.[13]

Freud quickly became a father figure for Jung, and Jung soon confided his personal problems to him. The age difference helped; Freud was twenty years older and Jung had lost whatever emotional connection he may have had with Bleuler, which was minimal at best. From Freud's viewpoint, Jung was a catch. Bleuler was already sympathetic to his ideas, and to have his second-in-command on his team, too, was attractive. As mentioned, Jung had already made a name for himself, and not only in Switzerland. Freud would tell his Viennese circle—who were mostly Jewish—that psychoanalysis needed Jung, a Protestant, so that it couldn't be characterized as a strictly "Jewish science." Sadly this is precisely how the Nazis would characterize it thirty years later.

What followed was in many ways a kind of love affair, with

wooing letters, words of praise, and mutual admiration. That there was an element of courting in the burgeoning friendship has been suggested more than once, and Jung's admission to Freud that he had been abused by a man he once looked up to was a signal to Freud that Jung needed to maintain some distance. Intimacy in general, he told Freud, was difficult for him, a nod to the distrust he developed during the months his mother spent in a mental hospital when he was a boy.

Freud saw Jung as his "crown prince," the non-Jew who would carry the banner of psychoanalysis into the wider world. Jung saw Freud as the "first man of real importance" he had encountered. He was "altogether remarkable,"[14] yet it shouldn't surprise us that Jung would surely think that helping Freud's cause could advance his own. It's true that championing Freud in the early days of psychoanalysis was dangerous; as he did in his Zofingia lectures on metaphysics, Jung was aligning himself with a recherché cause. But Jung had a sense that the psychological future would be Freudian, at least for a time, and Jung enjoyed debate and, in William Blake's phrase, "mental fight." Jung had superabundant energy and throwing himself into the psychoanalytical battle would put it to good use. Inarguably, psychoanalysis wouldn't have gained the reputation it did nor reach so wide a field without Jung's tireless promotion.

The two first met in 1907, when Jung and Emma visited Freud and his family in Vienna. Freud in middle age had yet to achieve the recognition he desired, and he was happy to welcome his new champion. Most of his circle were mediocre camp followers (characteristics the dictatorial Freud usually preferred), and the brilliant, energetic Jung must have seemed like a godsend. The two spoke for thirteen hours straight. Freud let Jung unburden himself of a torrent of ideas and observations; then, when the flood receded, he calmly began to clarify things. Most accounts of the visit emphasize that Jung showed little interest in Freud's family; he was, if we're to go by them, rude and boorish, focused solely on his conversation with the master. Although he had a rich wife and a growing reputation, Jung was not always socially adept and his lack of interpersonal skills could be explained by simple shyness; later, when he met Freud's circle, Jung felt out of place amidst the café intellectuals. Yet his earthy vitality and relentless drive must have seemed like a hurricane of fresh air in the decadent atmosphere of fin-de-siècle Vienna, a recognition Freud acknowledged when in 1910 he appointed Jung president of the International Psychoanalytical Association, over the heads of people such as Alfred Adler, Wilhelm Stekel, and Sándor Ferenczi, who had been faithful members of his Psychological Society for years. Freud quelled dissent about this coup by explaining that psychoanalysis needed a non-Jewish representative; he also knew that if his work was to survive his death, a genius like Jung would be a great help.

For his part, Jung eagerly took up the Freudian cudgel and struck out at his new mentor's critics. Even before he met Freud, he defended his ideas from the attacks of the psychiatrist Gustav Aschaffenburg at a conference in Baden-Baden, although some of Freud's followers, and Freud himself, felt he didn't defend the master quite aggressively enough. Soon after they met, Jung spoke in favor of Freud at a conference in Amsterdam, where he delivered a paper on hysteria. Jung certainly had more than enough on his own plate: by this time he was lecturing at the university as well as dealing with his patients, and had his family life and his own research to contend with, not to mention the complications around Sabina Spielrein. But typically he saddled himself with organizing the first congress of the International Psychoanalytical Association in Salzburg, in April 1908, and took on Freud's suggestion that he edit a new psychoanalytical yearbook.

Although Jung threw off concerns about overwork, the strain led to a flu. One suspects that as in his early reluctance to go to school, Jung's unconscious was at work, and while on the surface he was the psychoanalytical man of the hour, the recognition that his own independent work would suffer by his becoming Freud's bulldog must have played a part. Other illnesses, sudden holidays, and delays in correspondence throughout their relationship suggest a resistance built up in him, even from the start.

The congress, however, was a success, and one of the speakers was an eccentric character who would have as great an influence on Jung as the dark Sabina did. Otto Gross was the son of the judge and criminologist Hans Gross, whose lectures the writer Franz Kafka attended; Hans Gross' ideas about degenerate "criminal types"—those who had not yet committed a crime but were bound to, a theme updated in Philip K. Dick's "The Minority Report"—can be felt in Kafka's disturbing novel *The Trial*, about a man who is arrested but never discovers why. (Hans Gross also had a link to Jung, when Jung accused two of his students of stealing credit for the use of the word-association test in determining guilt.) Otto Gross became disgusted with his father's authoritarian views and threw himself into a variety of "liberationist" ideas, most excessively "free love"; he fathered several illegitimate children, and was also a morphine and cocaine addict. He was also severely disturbed: he refused to bathe, wore several layers of clothing in the hottest weather, talked rapidly in a torrent of grandiose ideas, encouraged narcotic use in others, and was even said to have supplied poison to a suicidal woman.

Gross was a habitué of the decadent bohemian café society of Munich's Schwabing district—a kind of early-twentieth-century Haight-Ashbury—and embraced the radical social ideas prevalent in Monte Verità, the "Mountain of Truth," an early alternative community established in Ascona, Switzerland, in 1900, where as the historian Martin Green argued, "the counterculture began."[15] Notables such as Hermann Hesse, Rudolf Steiner, Isadora Duncan, and many more made the trek to Monte Verità to take the nature cure, practice nudity (not Steiner), meditate, grow their own vegetables, enjoy "free love," and in general cast off the ills of an increasingly mechanized society. Gross was initially drawn to psychoanalysis because, with its emphasis on the dangers of sexual repression, it seemed a potent weapon against authoritarianism. He soon discovered, however, that Freud was more repressive than he thought. At the conference Gross argued that Freud's ideas could be used as the basis of a cultural revolution, claiming that a sexually liberated society would be neurosis-free, in many ways anticipating the Freudian-Marxist mélange made popular in the 1960s by Herbert Marcuse. As R. D. Laing did, Gross argued that sickness was an appropriate response to a repressive society, and at the conference he made no attempt to hide his own eccentricities. The bourgeois Freud was shocked, much as he would be years later at the ideas of another sexual-liberationist, Wilhelm Reich, who taught his patients how to masturbate; for someone who believed sex was at the bottom of everything, Freud was oddly repelled by anyone who took this belief seriously. Rejecting any link with social change, Freud claimed that he and his followers were only doctors, and should remain so. Gross disagreed.

It was as a doctor, however, that Jung met Gross, when Freud sent the young rebel to the Burghölzli, after his father asked him to cure Gross of his addictions. Jung was at first put off by Gross' ideas about sexual liberation, believing that sexual repression was necessary for civilization. Yet Gross' charisma soon overcame Jung's antipathy, and the proper Swiss came to feel that the anarchic Gross was like a twin brother. He spent hours with him, taking time away from his other patients, and the two fell to analyzing each other. On one occasion, as with his first conversation with Freud, Jung and Gross talked for twelve hours straight. Gross introduced Jung to the ideas he absorbed in Schwabing's cafés[16] and amidst the sun worshippers on Monte Verità, among them paganism and the notion of an ancient matriarchal society, that had been advocated by Johann Bachofen, like Jung a Baseler. The rather straight-laced Jung found himself questioning his whole attitude to life, society, marriage, and the family; Gross, for his part, cut down on his drug intake and tried to conduct himself with a bit more stability.

Jung felt that his analysis had been successful and that Gross was on the mend, but soon he realized that Gross was a classic example of what Jung would later call a *puer*, a kind of eternal youth, a Peter Pan personality, unable to accept the responsibilities of being an adult. Gross proved him right when, unable to resist the craving for drugs, he climbed a wall and escaped the asylum. Jung never saw him again, and Gross died alone and homeless in a Berlin suburb in 1920, by then having been forcibly interred for a time in another psychiatric institution by his father. Jung was crushed at what he felt was Gross' betrayal. It was his first defeat. Yet Gross unquestionably changed Jung. For one thing, it was after their encounter that Jung jettisoned his scruples and, by all accounts, became Sabina's lover. His polygamous tendencies had broken through, prompted by Gross' urgings, and the respectable

Jung found himself an advocate of rebellion; his affair with a Jew can be seen as a product of his new contempt for social norms, if they inhibited one's true identity. In many ways, Jung's determination to "become who he is," and to aid others in doing so, can be linked to his brief but intense encounter with Otto Gross.[17]

Jung, however, was never as visible a rebel as Gross. He wasn't an exhibitionist, and his own anti-authoritarianism produced a new version of his old No. 1 and No. 2. No. 1 loved his wife, his children, and the new home in Küsnacht, on the shore of Lake Zürich, which they would soon move to, and where Jung would live for the rest of his life. No. 2 wanted to explore the possibilities of life that Gross had unexpectedly revealed to him. No. 1 was the capable, tireless propagandist for psychoanalysis; No. 2 was becoming increasingly dissatisfied with what he saw as the narrowness of Freud's ideas. No. 1 was the highly respected senior physician at a world famous clinic and a popular lecturer at a prestigious university; No. 2 wanted to dig deep into his own ideas, to push aside all the demands on his time and focus on his own work. Not an unfamiliar dilemma, and it goes to show that the reconciliation of opposites, the central motor of Jung's ideas about self-transformation, isn't limited to the alchemist's laboratory or the mystical products of a dream. It's a challenge most of us face most of the time.

One product of the inner tensions Jung was beginning to feel was the episode of the poltergeist in Freud's bookcase. Visiting Freud again in Vienna in 1909, Jung asked Freud about his attitude toward parapsychology. Freud was a total skeptic and dismissed the whole subject as nonsense.[18] Indeed, during a later meeting, Freud practically begged Jung to never abandon his sexual theory, because for him it had to be secured as an "unshakable bulwark" against the "black tide of mud of occultism."[19] Jung couldn't accept this; although he often obscured his true feelings about the paranormal, Jung had enough experience of it to know it was real. Now, sitting across from the master, Jung held back from rebuking Freud, but he began to feel his diaphragm glow, as if it was becoming red-hot. Suddenly they heard a loud bang coming from a bookcase, and both jumped up, afraid it would come crashing down. Jung said to Freud, "There, that is an example of a so-called catalytic exteriorisation phenomena!" Jung's rather long-winded circumlocution for a poltergeist, or "noisy spirit." Freud said, "Bosh!" Jung disagreed and predicted that another bang would immediately happen. It did. Jung said that from that moment on, Freud grew mistrustful of him, and that his look made he feel he had done something against him.[20]

Pro-Freudians have always argued that, as in the case of the oak table, it was nothing more than drying wood or some other "perfectly normal" explanation, a belief Freud himself was at pains to maintain in a letter he wrote to Jung about the incident. What is interesting is that the event occurred, as Freud writes, "on the same evening that formally I adopted you [Jung] as my eldest son, anointing you as my successor and crown prince . . ." Knowing the tensions Jung felt at the time, this anointing was bound to have an effect on him, to which Freud's shallow dismissal of something Jung held dear—the world of No. 2—could only add. Jung felt certain that in some way *he* had caused the bang, and it is curious to wonder if he, too, was responsible for the crack in the oak table and the shattered bread knife, and not, as he suggested to J. B. Rhine, Helly Preiswerk. The fact that *Memories, Dreams, Reflections* is full of similar and related phenomena suggests that either Jung had remarkable luck in being on hand for a number of psychic experiences or that he himself had a part in them. For example, Jung tells the story of how he experienced the suicide of a patient, who had manifested a strong "transference," while in bed in a hotel room after giving a lecture. The patient, who relapsed into depression, shot himself in the head. Jung awoke in his hotel, thinking that someone had come into the room, and feeling an odd pain in his forehead. The next day Jung discovered that his patient had shot himself precisely where Jung felt the pain, at the same time Jung woke up.[21] More to the point, a visitor to Küsnacht once remarked about Jung's "exteriorised libido," how "when there was an important idea that was not yet quite conscious, the furniture and woodwork all over the house creaked and snapped."[22]

Freud himself felt that Jung had some curious effect on him. At the time of the incident of the bookcase, Freud admitted to being moved by the experience, but in his letter he changed his mind. "The phenomenon was soon deprived of all significance for me," he wrote, and his "readiness to believe vanished along with *the spell of your personal presence* [my italics]."[23] In other words, while Jung was there, the skeptical, hard-nosed Freud was somehow moved enough to accept that Jung could have been right. But in his absence, he reverted to type, and set about explaining it in purely rational terms. Freud's emotional investment in Jung may be enough to account for this, but I wonder if the mistrust Freud began to feel toward Jung was at least in part a recognition that Jung somehow had the kinds of "powers" Freud had so easily dismissed? Without Jung's presence, the "mana" Jung had exhibited faded, and Freud, unwilling to accept that anything paranormal could actually happen, basically talked himself out of it.[24]

I n a letter to Freud a few days after the event, Jung spoke apologetically of his "spookery," yet he goes on to speak of what he calls a "psychosynthesis," which he opposes to psychoanalysis.[25] He calls it a "quite special complex" associated with the "prospective tendencies in man," "which creates future events," something in his thesis on Helly's séances he called the "attempts of the future personality to break through" and which seems to prefigure his later idea of individuation. Jung arrived at this conclusion through his observation of a patient who produced "first-rate spiritualistic phenomena." He speaks also of "the objective effect of the prospective tendency," which seems to mean its ability to arrange events in the external world. This seems like a remarkably early presage of what Jung would later call synchronicity. If nothing else, it's at least an admission that Jung recognizes a part of the psyche that somehow *reaches out* from inside the mind and affects the world *outside*.

In the same letter Jung informed Freud that one effect of the poltergeist was that it freed him "from the oppressive sense of your parental authority."[26] In reply Freud tried to deny this, and in dismissing the poltergeist as nothing but everyday sounds, he had to "fall back into the role of father" toward Jung. In denying the poltergeist, he was denying Jung's maturity, and he chastised his errant offspring for the delight with which he expressed his "coming of age." Like a good Jewish mother (or father), Freud tried to make Jung feel guilty about it. Jung had separated his commitment to psychoanalysis from his emotional dependence on Freud. "Your cause must and will prosper," he told him. He still had the yearbook ahead of him, but he was no longer in thrall to the master. With someone as sensitive to how others perceived him as Freud, this was, whether he acknowledged it or not, something of a challenge. Anyone familiar with the history of Freud's circle knows that more than one follower who expressed independent thought met with a bad end. Victor Tausk, and later, Herbert Silberer—whose writing on alchemy and psychology predated Jung's by decades—both committed suicide after being excommunicated by Freud for expressing reservations about the master's theories. Wilhelm Reich had a breakdown after being rejected by Freud, and Jung, too, would go through a crisis once the psychoanalytical umbilical cord was cut.[27]

It was still a few years ahead, but in hindsight it seems inevitable. Jung's own "prospective tendency" was at work, and the "attempts of his future personality to break through" had already started. Freud's belief that the son invariably wants to kill his father and possess his mother may seem far-fetched and a bit obsessive. But he certainly had good reason to be wary of what his crown prince had in store.

4. METAMORPHOSES
OF THE LIBIDO

Jung left the Burghölzli as a full-time staff member in March 1909, although he remained affiliated to it for a time as a voluntary doctor, which allowed him to supervise doctoral candidates and gave him access to patients. His position there took too much time away from his own research, he said. Given that he could depend on Emma's support, he could make a stab at setting up in private practice, and Emma herself pressured Jung to leave the clinic.[1] While all this was true, other factors may also have been involved. His commitment to psychoanalysis demanded more and more of his time and energy. Bleuler clearly felt there was a conflict of interest and this had soured their already bad relationship. Jung's breezy tendency to act as if he was in charge, and eagerness to get through his workload as quickly as possible, couldn't have helped. His colleagues complained that Jung was only interested in his patients' dreams and that he was more focused on his own work than on his administrative obligations. There's also suspicion that Jung's real reason for leaving was the Sabina Spielrein affair. Some have suggested that because of it Bleuler asked for his resignation. Jung had, in fact, resigned earlier, when Bleuler, for unclear reasons, refused his request to study with Janet in Paris, but he was soon reinstated. Whatever may have precipitated it, Jung was happy to leave. The nine years he spent there were crucial to his development, but it was time to move on. For one thing, the Barrel could drink again. And in any case, the fates seemed to approve of his decision. On the same day that he resigned, Jung was handed an important patient, practically on a silver, if not golden, platter.

Joseph Medill McCormick, heir to a Chicago newspaper empire and later a US senator, was rich, powerful, alcoholic, and in the middle of a breakdown. He arrived at the Burghölzli from Berlin demanding to see Dr. Jung and no one else. After two weeks as Jung's private patient (an arrangement Bleuler disliked but had to accept) Jung "cured" McCormick, at least temporarily, by breaking his debilitating dependency on his domineering mother, who owned the *Chicago Tribune*, where Medill (as he was known) worked. Jung used what he called a "kill or cure" method. Jung wrote to the paper, explaining that Medill was incapable of performing his duties and must be relieved of his responsibilities; the newspaper men, aware of his uselessness, agreed and were happy to see him go. His mother was less so. She had lost her hold on him, and Medill was free, for a time at least. (He committed suicide in 1925.) It was Jung's first independent success, and he had hit the jackpot. Not only did the McCormick family own the *Chicago Tribune*, Medill's cousin Fowler was married to the daughter of John D. Rockefeller, one of the richest men in the world. Medill's great-uncle was Cyrus McCormick, inventor of the McCormick Reaper, later to play a large part in International Harvester. That Medill returned to Chicago cured, if only temporarily, gave Jung an enviable cachet among rich, neurotic Americans, and a flow of them soon headed for his door.

This was, however, no longer at the Burghölzli. Six years

earlier Jung had purchased land in Küsnacht, a small suburb on the shores of Lake Zürich. The typically Swiss house he had built there, described as "comfortable" and "full of Biedermeyer furniture and family pictures"[2] was closed off and extremely private and became his home for the rest of his life. It remains an attraction for pilgrims, and in later years, Jung remarked that to achieve psychic wholeness, a strong connection to the land was necessary, and aid to individuation some must forgo. Jung, Emma, and their children moved there in June. Jung's mother and sister moved to a nearby house earlier in the year; both would become fixtures in the new house, Trudi (Jung's sister) working as his secretary, and Emilie helping with the children. At Küsnacht Jung had room to work and to see his patients and to retreat into the solitude that was as much a necessity for him as eating or breathing (and with a by now large family, there seems no mystery in this). It was on the lakeshore and allowed Jung to indulge in sailing, which became a passion. Jung was always an outdoors type; he loved hiking, cycling, and camping and enjoyed the stint of military duty he had to perform each year. Jung was an extremely physical man, who found relaxation in hard, physical work, supplemented by the occasional detective story. Jung had little use for most modern literature but apparently was a fan of Agatha Christie and Georges Simenon.

Other doctors might have thought that leaving a world-famous clinic was a bad career move, but almost immediately Jung received a boost to his already boundless self-confidence when he was invited to lecture on his word-association tests at Clark University in Worcester, Massachusetts. Freud, too, was invited, and although Jung suggests that his invitation was totally independent of Freud's, the fact that he was Freud's most well-known supporter certainly had a hand in it; there's even suggestion that Jung was invited as a second-best, when a first choice was unable to attend.³ When Freud learned that Jung was lecturing as well, he was delighted. Jung's feelings, however, were perhaps not so straight-forward, and for that matter, perhaps neither were Freud's. Jung had come to see that Freud was in the grip of his ideas, obsessed by them in fact. Even on that momentous first meeting, Jung had powerful reservations which, in deference to Freud's greater experience, he kept to himself. What troubled Jung most was Freud's tendency to *reduce* any expression of spirituality—in a cultural or philosophical sense—to something *smaller*. Freud sniffed out sex everywhere; it was the central motive behind everything, and if it was not immediately visible, this was because it was camouflaged. Remarking that if he was right, then all culture becomes merely a facade, masking repressed or sublimated sexual desire, Jung was aghast when Freud replied, "Yes, so it is, and that is just a curse of fate against which we are powerless to contend." With Marx and Nietzsche, Freud is one of the great practitioners of what the philosopher Paul Ricoeur called the "hermeneutics of suspicion," the idea that the *real* meaning of a text or cultural work is not what it presents on the surface, but what is hidden below, and which is usually much less idealistic or high-minded. For Marx it was the class war, for Nietzsche the "will to power," and for Freud it was sex. This is behind Freud's notorious reduction of works of art to various manifestations of sublimation, "displacement activity" or wish fulfillment.⁴ Jung, a romantic, couldn't accept this assessment, but at that stage of their relationship, he didn't feel confident enough to question the master. Soon he did.

Another of Freud's followers, the Hungarian Sándor Ferenczi, was invited to lecture as well, and the three arranged to meet in

Bremen, Germany, and spend a day before sailing. There occurred one of the two famous fainting fits that Freud had in the presence of Jung. During lunch, talk moved to some prehistoric corpses that had been discovered in North Germany. Ronald Hayman makes the point that after his near-decade long abstinence, Jung wasn't used to the wine he drank, became drunk, and mixed up the prehistoric corpses with the peat-bog mummies recently unearthed in Belgium.[5] Drunk or not—and as the Barrel was a large man used to copious portions, he would have had to imbibe quite a bit to get intoxicated—Jung's talk of corpses had a peculiar effect on Freud: it made him faint. Freud claimed the wine and exhaustion had caused it, but another reason suggests itself: that Freud felt Jung harbored a death wish against him, something he had detected in a dream of Jung's as well. Three years later, at a conference in Munich, Freud fainted again, when Jung argued against the idea that the pharaoh Amenophis IV held a death wish against his father, Amenhotep. Jung remarks that when he picked Freud up on that occasion and carried him to a sofa—his followers standing around helplessly—Freud looked at him "as if I were his father."[6] (Ernest Jones, Freud's biographer, remarks that Freud himself said, "How sweet it must be to die," as the powerful Jung carried him away.) Whether Jung had a death wish against Freud or not, Freud seems to have believed he did strongly enough to produce a neurotic reaction in him whenever the combination Freud-Jung-death popped up. On the other hand, with his increasing unvoiced reluctance to play the role of crown prince, while at the same time devoting a considerable amount of energy to it, the reflection that life would be easier without Freud must have crossed Jung's mind.

Crossing the Atlantic then was quite an adventure, and to pass the days, Jung and Freud decided to analyze each other's dreams. This proved disastrous. Trying to analyze one of Freud's dreams— Jung doesn't give the details, and in fact remained silent about them for the rest of his life, but it involved Freud's wife and sister-in-law, with whom Freud is thought to have had an affair—Jung remarked that he could do a better job if Freud provided him with more insight into his private life. Freud again looked at Jung as if he suspected him of something, then refused. His reason was that doing so would risk his authority. This had the opposite effect. By putting his personal authority above the truth, for Jung he lost it entirely. At that point the relationship ended, at least for Jung; what remained was the painful process of admitting it.

Freud himself struck out when it came to Jung's dreams. One in particular was very important for Jung; in it, he said, he glimpsed for the first time what he came to call the collective unconscious. He dreamt that he was in a house he didn't know, although it was "his." It had two stories. The upper was furnished in rococo style. The lower one seemed much older, and suggested the fifteenth or sixteenth century, even the Middle Ages. He then followed a stone stairway into a cellar. Here everything was even more ancient and seemed of Roman origin. He saw a ring on one of the stone slabs of the floor and, pulling it, discovered yet another stairway. Descending, Jung entered a low cave; dust covered the floor, and on it Jung saw broken pottery, bones and two ancient human skulls.

What strikes a reader is the similarity to Jung's earliest dream, of the huge ritual phallus; in both he goes *down*, below, into the underground. What struck Freud, however, were the skulls, understandably, given that he felt the man he was sailing with wanted him dead. Jung tells us that Freud kept returning to the skulls and asking Jung if he could detect any wish associated with them. Jung, realizing Freud's obsession, and inwardly acknowledging that he wouldn't be able to explain his own interpretation (and most likely wanting to avoid an argument that could last the rest of the trip), decided to lie to Freud and admitted that the skulls may have been those of Emma and her sister. Freud was pleased, curiously happy that his crown prince wanted his wife dead. Jung felt guilty because of the lie, but saw that it was unavoidable, and privately took his own counsel. The house in the dream, he felt, represented the psyche. The upper story was his consciousness. The ground floor, which was in an older style, was the top layer of the unconscious. The cellar and cave below represented older, much deeper levels, the crumbling bones and skulls the earliest appearance of man. Jung surmised that if he had gone even lower, he would have encountered animal remains. Jung's dream—perhaps stimulated by the fact that he had recently moved into a new, still strange house that was nevertheless "his"—was showing him that his modern consciousness, the upper level of his psyche, was part of a much larger and much *older* structure, whose foundations reached into the earth itself. It argued that something of an altogether *impersonal* character lay beneath the personal unconscious, which, Jung recognized, was where Freud's explorations ended. Freud's obsession with death wishes prevented him from seeing this *objective* nature of the deep unconscious, and the obstinacy with which Freud maintained his theories more than likely produced a death wish in Jung, too. (It should also be noted that as Jung was increasingly grappling with his polygamous tendencies, some part of him may have wanted Emma dead after all.)

In spite of this, the trip to America was a great success, and although Freud disliked the new world and stoically endured his time there, Jung enjoyed himself immensely.[7] Letters to Emma tell of his adventures in New York's Chinatown, a visit to a pale-ontology museum, the train to Boston; although his books are often tough going, readers can discover a different Jung here, one full of vivid observations and charm. The lectures went well and Freud noted that Jung had toned down the sexual element in his. Both men were awarded honorary doctorates, and Jung met many important people, but the one he felt most taken with was William James, who shared Jung's interest in parapsychology and concern with religion. James was equally taken with Jung and wrote to their mutual friend the psychologist Theodore Flournoy about the meeting. Yet while Jung made a very pleasant impression on James, Freud struck him as a man obsessed with fixed ideas, something, we know, Jung had already come to accept.

On his return to Zürich, Jung undertook a deep study of mythology, something that would occupy him for the rest of his life. His dream had *shown* him something, and Jung was determined to discover what it was. He had already come to the conclusion that Freud was wrong to think that dreams try to *hide* something from us, that their "manifest" content camouflaged "latent" material. Dreams, Jung saw, were natural products of the psyche, and were not, as Freud believed, something the unconscious cooked up in order to disguise our primitive urges from our "super ego." Dreams did not *conceal* truths, Jung recognized. Rather they *revealed* knowledge unknown to the conscious ego, in a symbolic language that was not the sexual semiotics Freud insisted upon. Jung is said to have once quipped that "the penis is merely a phallic symbol," meaning that it, too, was an expression of an archetype that informed various manifestations of male creative energy.

One effect of this dream was to rekindle Jung's early love for archaeology, the primitive remains in the dream cave reminding him of the finds being discovered at that time by people such as Arthur Evans at Knossos. Heinrich Schliemann's sensational discoveries at Troy, too, were not too far in the past, and Howard Carter's excavation of Tutankhamun was only a decade away. Growing up in Basel had imbued Jung with a strong historical sense, something that Freud seemed to lack. Now it was coming back to Jung, and telling him that the psyche, too, had to be understood historically, as a product of a process going back in time.

As he had with spiritualism, Jung began to read feverishly, and after years of the clinical grindstone, his plunge into the romance and mystery of myth was delightful. One book struck him powerfully, Friedrich Creuzer's *Symbolik und Mythologie der alten Volker* (*The Symbology and Mythology of Ancient Peoples*), but others were equally absorbing: Richard Payne Knight's *Two Essays on the Worship of Priapus*, Thomas Inman's *Ancient Pagan and Modern Christian Symbolism*, Erwin Rohde's *Psyche*, as well as Jacob Burckhardt's *History of Greek Civilization*, and the work of Herodotus, the "father" of history himself. Jung began to see a connection between the strange narratives of myth and the products of the "intruders of the mind" he encountered in his patients, as if in their delusions his patients were somehow using mythological material. Most of Jung's patients were uneducated, uncultured people such as Babette, which meant that it was unlikely they could have absorbed this material through reading or some other conscious method. It began to dawn on Jung that it was coming straight from the unconscious itself, and that the psyche of his patients—and of everyone else, presumably—had somehow *inherited* it from past generations.

Although it has subsequently been rejected, Jung was deeply influenced by the work of the then immensely popular evolutionary thinker Ernst Haeckel, who argued that, in its own development, each individual organism goes through the previous evolutionary stages of the species. Haeckel expressed this in the neat formula "ontogeny recapitulates phylogeny," which means that from conception to birth, while in the womb, each of us repeats the entire evolutionary process.

Now if, as Haeckel argued, the present physical organism goes through the past evolutionary stages of its species, then, thought Jung, perhaps this is true of the psyche, too? Nietzsche had come to a similar conclusion as well when he remarked that "in sleep and dreams we repeat once again the curriculum of earlier mankind."[8] Mythologies were the earliest dreams of mankind, and in the psychotic delusions of his patients, Jung believed he was encountering those dreams again. Freud, too, believed that the psyche retained archaic vestiges, remnants of our earlier mental world. But for Freud these were a burden we were forced to repress. Jung instead would see them as a reservoir of vital energy, a source of meaning and power from which, through the overdevelopment of our rational minds, modern mankind has become divorced.

Jung was an insatiable reader, but there was so much to assimilate, and he had so many other things to attend to—a wife, a family, his patients, his lectures at the university, his work for the psychoanalytical movement—that he needed helpers. One was Sabina Spielrein; another was Johann Jakob Honegger. Like

Sabina Spielrein and Otto Gross, Honegger was another brilliant but unstable individual who came into Jung's orbit. Honegger's father—also named Johann Jakob—had been a doctor at the Burghölzli and for a time its acting director; unfortunately a deterioration of his brain led to insanity, and he became a patient himself, dying there at the age of forty-five. Honegger himself developed a severe dependence on his mother and exhibited obsessive and hysterical traits. Eventually Honegger, too, would succumb to madness; in 1911 he committed suicide by a lethal injection of morphine.

As with Sabina Spielrein and Otto Gross, Jung's first contact with Honegger was as his physician; Honegger consulted Jung after a delusional episode during which he ominously identified with his father and was determined to become a psychiatrist, too. Jung recognized that Honegger was probably incurable, but suggested analysis as a means of staving off the inevitable. Honegger's interest in mythology, history, and symbolism suggested that, as with Sabina Spielrein, putting him to work would be the best treatment. While Jung was in America, Honegger was assigned to familiarize himself with current mythological studies and to observe a patient Jung had been fascinated with since 1901, Emile Schwyzer, "the Solar Phallus Man." Honegger's assignment was to gather enough material on Schwyzer to form a dissertation.

Schwyzer was admitted to the clinic in 1901 when he was forty; he had been in other institutions for twenty years before this. He suffered from delusions of persecution and megalomania and had attempted suicide. In many ways Schwyzer was a typical case, but one delusion in particular gripped Jung. Schwyzer maintained that he was able to control the weather, and when Jung asked how, he explained that the sun had an enormous penis, and when he looked at it through half-closed eyes and moved his head from side to side, the penis moved, too. This made the wind, and through this, the weather. Schwyzer used a strange archaic language when he spoke of this; it had no connection to anything in his past, and Jung was mystified as to where he could get this idea.

Although Schwyzer was able to learn English and had even traveled to London—where his delusions began—he came from a poor, uneducated background. Although incapable of logical thought, Schwyzer had an interest in current events and some knowledge of geography; some of his delusions involved royalty such as Queen Victoria. There was nothing in his past to suggest that Schwyzer would have any knowledge of or interest in mythology, yet his fantasies about the sun's penis suggested an origin in myth or folklore. Even if he had come across a book on mythology—which seemed unlikely, as none of the previous clinics he had been in had a patients' library, and his family in Zürich had no interest in books at all—his inability to concentrate would have made it difficult for him to retain anything he had read. But if he didn't get it from books, where did the idea come from?

Jung himself had come across a reference to a solar phallus in Albrecht Dieterich's *Eine Mithrasliturgie* (*A Mithras Liturgy*) and *A Mithraic Ritual* by the Theosophical scholar G. R. S. Mead; he had also come upon the idea in a painting by an unknown early German artist, in which a tube descends from heaven, and shoots up the skirts of the Virgin Mary; the Holy Ghost in the form of a dove flies down this, impregnating her. (It was also around this time that Jung came across the references to the "soul stones" mentioned previously and recognized his homunculus as the Greek god Telesphoros.) Jung had instructed Honegger to record all of Schwyzer's ramblings and to collect any drawings he made and to work this material into a paper that could be presented at the Second International Psychoanalytical Congress, scheduled to be held at Nuremberg in March 1910. Jung urged Honegger to work quickly. He had already written to Freud about his interest in mythology, and Freud had expressed his own interest in studying it, predictably, in order to show that myths, too, had their origin in sex. As Jung's student, Honegger would establish Jung's leadership in the psychoanalytical study of myth, something Freud himself was encroaching upon, and his paper would indicate the direction Jung's thought was taking. In other words, it would be the first step in establishing the idea of the collective unconscious (although Jung didn't yet use this term); understandably Jung wanted to get there first.

Yet although brilliant and subject to flashes of genius, Honegger, like Gross, was unreliable and Jung complained that his wayward student wasn't meeting the rigorous standards he had set for him. And when Honegger finally presented his findings at the conference, his performance was disturbing. Echoing Otto Gross, Honegger made no attempt to hide his eccentricities; his paper was "a morass of confusion and distress, at times an incoherent melding of the author's voice with the subject's visions," and his conclusion was expressed in a "garbled, lofty, omnipotent, and paranoid prose."[9] Honegger ended by saying he would present conclusive evidence for his claims with a more detailed paper, but none was forthcoming. He unexpectedly fled Zürich soon after the conference—another of Jung's patients to fly the coop—and Honegger's subsequent behavior, a series of erratic decisions and grandiose plans, suggests no paper was ever written or, if it was, wouldn't have clarified much. But the disappointed Jung determined to complete the work left undone by his manic assistant.[10]

The ambiguity around the affair—some accounts have Honeg-ger fantasizing the solar phallus, some have Schwyzer telling *him* about it, some have Schwyzer telling Jung—led to accusations that Jung "stole" Honegger's work and that the idea of the collective unconscious originated with him, and not Jung.

If Jung had his hands full with the mess Honegger left behind, his life was complicated even more with the arrival of yet another brilliant but unstable individual. Before the dark and trou-bled Toni Wolff entered Jung's life, he had already had encounters if not affairs with two women, Mary Moltzer and Martha Bod-dighaus. The two became rivals for his attention, a development Emma couldn't fail to notice. Moltzer, a nurse at the Burghölzli, came from a rich family like Emma; she was heiress to the Bols liquor empire but kept this information secret and led a modest existence. Whether they became lovers or not, Jung was strongly attracted to her and later admitted she was the inspiration for his idea of the anima, the feminine component in the male psyche; this credential will become important later. There's no ambigu-ity however about Jung's relations with Toni Wolff. When she arrived at the clinic at the age of twenty-two she was dangerously depressed over the death of her father and close to madness. She came from a cultured family and had led a sheltered life, some-thing that would continue for years to come; until her fifties she lived with her mother. As with Sabina, Jung recognized her intelligence—like him she had a strong interest in mythology—and that what she needed was some purposeful activity to occupy her considerable energies. Once again, his support, interest, and encouragement brought a potential wreck back from the edge.

And as with Sabina, Jung "cured" Toni by involving her in his work, giving her research assignments; she became, as one biographer put it, "the first in a long line of women who gravitated to Jung because he allowed them to use their intellectual interests and abilities in the service of analytical psychology."[11]

At first Emma saw in Toni only another of Jung's successes. Her recovery was so complete that, like Emma, she had become a vital member of the Zürich psychoanalytic community and both attended the third International Psychoanalytical Association conference in Weimar in 1911; a photograph from the conference shows them both seated prominently in the front row. Yet it soon became clear that she was something more. As Sabina did, Toni talked with Jung about his work and ideas (which he rarely did with Emma) and she seems to be the one responsible for his renewed interest in the occult. She suggested he read works on Theosophy and astrology, a development that troubled Freud. The "transference" between Jung and Wolff was strong but hadn't yet crossed the line into an affair; when the treatment was complete both were unhappy but knew they had to end their close relations. Two years later, however, they were back together, in the clearest expression yet of Jung's polygamous tendencies.

Emma had the patience of a saint but felt so troubled by her marital problems that she started writing in secret to Freud about them. On three different occasions she threatened to divorce Jung; each time he became so ill that she couldn't leave him, a return, it seems, to the neurosis he adopted as a boy in order to avoid school.[12] Her letters to Freud were also concerned with the obvious distance growing between the two men. The main reason for this was Freud's lack of response to the first part of Jung's work *Wandlungen und Symbole der Libido* (originally published in English as *The Psychology of the Unconscious* and later changed to *Symbols of Transformation*), which had appeared in the yearbook in August 1911; both parts were published in book form in 1912. Throughout the first half, Jung more or less continues to toe the Freudian line, but he makes one major change: he no longer accepts Freud's definition of libido as purely sexual energy and instead sees it as simply vital or psychic energy, which can be directed to sex, but to other pursuits as well. After all, hunger and self-preservation are clearly urges as primal as sex; more primal in fact, as it is difficult to think about sex if you're starving or about to be killed. Sex had no monopoly on our energies, and Jung was interested in showing how our life energy, or libido, transforms itself when one avenue of its expression is blocked.

Yet Jung's main theme, developed in the second half, is that, rather than forms of sublimated sexual energy, our spiritual strivings are as much a part of our nature as our sexual instincts, an idea that Freud vehemently rejected. The sexual content in myths, Jung suggested, was really a symbolic use of sexual themes in order to convey a spiritual or religious meaning. One sexual theme favored by Freud, incest, is not, Jung argues, meant to be taken literally, but symbolically; the idea of entering the mother shouldn't be seen as a form of forbidden sexual gratification, but as a symbol for spiritual rebirth; in other words, as a symbol of individuation. This argument is set out in exhaustive and at times confusing detail in the second part of the book. Knowing that this stance would cost him his friendship with Freud, Jung put off finishing the book and spent months unable to pick up his pen. Tellingly, the most offending chapter is entitled "The Sacrifice."

Symbols of Transformation set Jung on his own path and is an important work in the history of analytical psychology; it's here that Jung begins his exploration of the "archetypes of the collective unconscious," although, again, he was yet to use these terms. But more than any other it confirms the psychologist Anthony Storr's remark that Jung was "severely hampered . . . by his own difficulty in expressing his thoughts with clarity." "I know of no creative person," Storr writes, "who was more hamstrung by his inability to write."[13] Anyone who has tried to read *Symbols of Transformation* will, I think, agree, and, like myself, will no doubt be thankful that Jung has commentators such as Storr, Marie-Louise von Franz, and others who are more able to convey his ideas with brevity and precision. (Jung is one writer who is well served by books such as *The Portable Jung* or *The Essential Jung*.) In many of his writings, Jung gives the impression that he is trying to cudgel the reader into acceptance by the sheer volume of references—the Herr Doctor Professor effect—but none achieves this with greater force than this early work. Jung himself was never happy with it, and in later life he rewrote it, without, however, achieving much in greater clarity. It overflows with quotations from dozens of sources—often in Latin or Greek—and gives the impression that Jung is trying to jam everything he's read in the last few years between its covers. Its main focus is a series of hypnagogic visions by a young woman writer who used the pseudonym Frank Miller; the case was originally presented by Jung's friend and mentor Theodore Flournoy, another father figure whose importance to Jung is overshadowed by the presence of Freud. The central point is that Ms. Miller's fantasies suggested to Jung that through them she had somehow tapped into the archaic residue he had encountered in Emile Schwyzer's solar phallus.

The flood of references, allusions, and associations—which later became Jung's method of "amplifying" unconscious material—was aimed at showing that Ms. Miller's visions had parallels in the world's religions and literature. It was in many ways a tour de force, but the main effect it had was to make clear that Jung was no longer Freud's crown prince.

It wasn't the only thing that did this. Petty slights had a hand, too. Jung took offense when Freud visited the psychologist Ludwig Binswanger, a student of Jung's who later went on to develop existential psychology, without inviting him along. Binswanger was the director of a sanatorium in Kreuzlingen, which was not far from Zürich, and the incident became known as "the Kreuzlingen gesture." It was all a misunderstanding, or so they both later agreed. Yet neither really wanted to meet but were both loath to admit this, and foisted the blame for the missed opportunity on the other. Although ostensibly still open to reconciliation, both men were looking for a way to make a clean break. When Freud heard that on a recent successful lecture trip to America—this time without Freud, a fillip to Jung's ego—Jung had been critical of Freud's insistence on the centrality of sex and had promoted his own revised version of psychoanalysis, he wrote a critical letter headed "Dear Dr. Jung," rather than the usual "Dear Friend." Freud admonished him not to enter his success in a "credit column," because "the farther you remove yourself from what is new in psychoanalysis, the more certain you will be of applause,"[14] meaning that Jung's self-promotion, through watering down Freud's ideas, was more important to him than the "cause."

It's understandable Freud was concerned. He had already dealt with Alfred Adler's defection (he went on to develop his own school of "Individual Psychology") and was having trouble with

Wilhelm Stekel; he was worried, too, that the "Zürich school," which included Bleuler and Jung's colleague Alphonse Maeder, would turn on him. Like a king in fear of his throne, Freud demanded absolute obedience and saw treachery in those around him. On Emma's prompting, he had finally given Jung faint praise for the first part of *Symbols of Transformation*, saying it was a fine work but that its author would produce something even better; i.e., closer to Freud's own view. The apprehension that Jung was diving into forbidden waters was clear.

Jung himself faced another conflict between his No. 1 and No. 2, and as had happened before, a dream brought this home to him. Although Jung clearly wanted to blaze his own trail, he continued to see Freud as a father figure, worthy of respect, and told himself that he still had much to learn from him; to do this he needed to keep his own ideas in check. But Jung's unconscious thought otherwise. In a dream Jung found himself in the mountains on the Swiss-Austrian border, a clear symbol of the demarcation between himself and Freud. There he found an elderly customs official, decked out in an ostentatious Imperial Austrian uniform. He looked anxious and troubled, as if he was concerned about contraband crossing the border. He ignored Jung and someone in the dream explained that he was the ghost of an old customs inspector, and that he belonged to those who "couldn't die properly." Consciously Jung maintained an image of Freud he had outgrown, but his unconscious was telling him that he was really an anxious old customs inspector who was a "ghost of his former self" and should really be dead. Here Jung's unconscious *compensated* for an exaggerated and unrealistic conscious attitude, a process that Jung would later refer to as the "self-regulating" character of the psyche, its means of achieving wholeness.

In another dream Jung was in a modern Italian city, and at the stroke of noon, amidst the crowds he discovered a knight from the Crusades, dressed in armor and wearing a white tunic emblazoned with a red cross. Jung associated the knight with his own long fascination with the story of the Holy Grail, which would later return in his studies of alchemy. Contrasting the knight with the peevish custom official, Jung concluded that while Freud was obsessed with discovering what people had hidden in their baggage, Jung's deepest interest was in something sacred, with the Grail quest. His whole being, he said, "was seeking for something still unknown which might confer meaning upon the banality of life."[15] Growing up in the country among peasants and farmers, Jung had early on learned all about sex, and the kinds of perversions Freud was uncovering were no revelations to him. That life could be ugly wasn't news, and Jung found that the neurotics who were supposed to be cured by making their neurosis clear to them, more often than not wallowed in it. What they needed was the realization that there was something *more* than the sort of thing Freud was revealing to them; to tell them that they should now find a "normal" place in society after being shown how "abnormal" we all are seemed pointless. Jung's knight seemed to symbolize that "something *more*."

Yet as in many dysfunctional relationships, making a clean break was difficult, and after years of friendship and collaboration, the old affection was still strong. During a meeting in Munich, Freud and Jung took a walk and apparently patched things up; till the end, Jung wanted to remain with the psychoanalytic fold he had done so much to promote. Although he didn't accept Freud's version of it unreservedly, he was still in full support of the cause. Freud accepted this, at least for the moment. Soon after, however, occurred Freud's second fainting fit, and the old charge of the crown prince wishing the aged king dead re-emerged. That followers such as Ernest Jones and Lou Andreas-Salomé—lover of Rilke and one-time confidante of Nietzsche—urged Freud not to trust Jung couldn't have helped. When Freud wrote to Jung about the incident, he said a migraine was behind it, but admitted that "a bit of neurosis" he hadn't looked into was at least partially to blame.[16] Jung replied that he knew that bit of neurosis well, as he had suffered from it already more than once. And Freud's offhand remark that in his explorations of mythology Jung had unintentionally "solved the riddle of all mysticism" by "showing it to be based on the symbolic utilization of complexes that have outlived their function" could only anger him as it showed how Freud continued to underestimate his work by misunderstanding it.

The exasperated Jung explained to Freud that he had the "purely human desire to be understood *intellectually* and not be measured by the yardstick of neurosis;" that is, he wanted his criticisms of Freud's ideas to be taken as valid, *objective* insights, and not as symptoms of his "father complex," "anal anxiety," or any other handy psychoanalytic term that Freud could use to avoid dealing with them honestly. Jung headed his reply with the warning that "This letter is a brazen attempt to accustom you to my style. So look out!" This makes clear that the gloves were off, but also begs the question, after nearly seven years of correspondence: wouldn't Freud have been familiar with his "style" already? Not if, as seems to be the case, Jung had been holding back his true feelings for some time.[17]

Yet the trigger for the final act came, appropriately enough, through a Freudian slip. Jung had expressed his intention of writing a critical review of Adler's *Über den nervösen Charakter* (*The

Neurotic Character), and in a letter Freud approved, saying it would make clear that he wasn't taking Adler's side. Jung wrote back that "even Adler's cronies do not regard me as one of yours" when he meant to say "theirs."[18] Freud couldn't let this slip go past and pointed it out to Jung, asking if he could recognize it without anger.

Apparently not. Jung had had enough, and in his reply he made clear his disgust with Freud's infuriating practice of treating criticism of his ideas as mere psychological resistance to his infallibility. Jung had already complained that "the majority of psychoanalysts misuse psychoanalysis to devalue other people and their progress by insinuations about complexes,"[19] and now he dotted the i's and crossed the t's. Treating his followers like patients, he told Freud, was a "blunder" that produced "either slavish sons or impudent puppies." "I am objective enough to see through your little trick," he told the master. "You go around sniffing out all the symptomatic actions in your vicinity, thus reducing everyone to the level of your sons and daughters who blushingly admit the existence of their faults. Meanwhile you remain on top as a father, sitting pretty. For sheer obsequiousness nobody dares to pluck the prophet by the beard and inquire for once what you would say to a patient with a tendency to analyse the analyst instead of himself." "You see, my dear Professor, so long as you hand out this stuff I don't give a damn for my symptomatic actions; they shrink to nothing compared with the formidable beam in my brother Freud's eye."[20]

Jung was no longer criticizing a narrow view of psychoanalysis; he was criticizing Freud, saying he was as neurotic as anyone else and that he had better look into it. Although he would continue to stand by Freud publicly, privately he would "start telling you in my letters what I really think of you." Jung's temper was piqued as much by Freud's superior tone as by his own prior timidity: he was angry with Freud and with himself for not telling Freud sooner. Freud's reaction was predictable. Jung, he told Ernest Jones, was behaving like a fool; he was crazy and needed treatment. He told Ferenczi the same thing. Jung's letters, Freud explained, exhibited disturbing mood swings, veering unpredictably from tenderness to brutality. If Jung didn't submit to analysis, there was little hope of his recovery.[21] In his last personal letter to Jung—they continued a "business" correspondence for a brief time—Freud wrote that "none of us need feel ashamed of his own bit of neurosis." "But," he continued, "one who while behaving abnormally keeps shouting that he is normal gives grounds for the suspicion that he lacks insight into his illness."[22] Because of this, Freud requested that they abandon their personal relationship entirely. Jung reluctantly agreed. After Freud didn't respond to a letter in which he reminded him that "the understanding of psychoanalytical truths is in direct proportion to the progress one has made in oneself,"[23] Jung wrote another three days later. "I never force my friendship on anyone," he said, acceding to Freud's wish that they cut off their relations.[24] He was crown prince no more, something closer to the disinherited son. Symbolically at least, it was time for Jung to leave home again.

5. TRANSCENDENT FUNCTIONS

Jung broke off personal relations with Freud in January 1913, but his involvement in the psychoanalytical movement continued for more than a year. It was clear though, to him and to others, that his presence really wasn't wanted, and after internal squabbles he finally resigned as president of the International Psychoanalytical Association in April 1914, having left the editorship of the yearbook the previous fall. Around the same time he also gave up his post as lecturer at the university. By now his status as crown prince had shifted to something less admirable; he had become, according to Freud, the "brutal and sanctimonious Jung," a self-seeking bully who used his association with Freud for his own ends, an assessment shared by those who closed ranks around the master. Jung had known what it meant to be an outsider, and now, blackballed by his former colleagues, it all came back. Ernest Jones' paper on "The God Complex: The Belief that One is God and the Resulting Character Traits," encapsulated everything Freud's followers felt about the turncoat. Jones didn't mention Jung, but it was clear he had the ex-crown prince in mind. Such a complex, he said, leads to the sense that one possesses a "key that is available only to the elect" and to a "great interest in the various forms of thought-reading, chiromancy, divination, and even astrology, as

well as in occultism and mysticism in all their branches."¹ Anyone
who knew Jung knew who Jones was talking about.

But if his psychoanalytic standing was low, Jung's pull with
patients hadn't suffered. Soon after the break with Freud, Jung
traveled to America to treat one of the richest women in the world.
Jung had met Edith Rockefeller McCormick—daughter of John
D. Rockefeller (Standard Oil) and wife of Harold McCormick
(International Harvester)—through her cousin, Medill McCormick, whom Jung had treated at the Burghölzli and later in
Chicago. Medill had asked Jung to evaluate Edith, a depressed
introvert suffering from the death of two children and a bout of
tuberculosis. Jung saw she was on the edge and diagnosed latent
schizophrenia. Edith was so impressed by Jung that she offered
to move him and his family to Chicago in order to treat her, an
expression of her extravagance and deep-seated agoraphobia.
Jung was tempted by the idea—unlike Freud, he loved his time
in the States—but Emma refused, so he traveled to New York
and escorted Edith back to Zürich. Her son, Fowler McCormick,
became one of Jung's closest friends and Edith eventually became
a practicing analyst herself, seeing her patients in her suite at the
luxurious Hotel Baur au Lac. She herself rarely left her rooms, her
only regular journey into the outside world being her excursions
to Küsnacht for her sessions with Jung.

But something more than the bad reputation he was getting
from Jones and others troubled Jung. In October 1913, just before
he resigned from the yearbook, Jung had, depending on your perspective, a vision or hallucination. On the train to Schaffhausen,
he suddenly saw a flood covering Europe, between the North Sea
and the Alps. When it reached Switzerland, the mountains rose to
protect the country, but in the waves Jung saw floating debris and

bodies. Then the water turned to blood. The vision lasted an hour and seems to have been a kind of waking dream or, rather, a dream that had *invaded* Jung's waking consciousness. Having spent a decade treating mental patients who suffered from precisely this, Jung had reason to be concerned. The break with Freud had disoriented him, as if he had been abandoned by a partner. Jung felt a constant inner pressure, as if something *inside* was straining to get out. The effect was not all bad. Because of his uncertainty, Jung developed a new approach to his patients. He no longer tried to impress his ideas on them. Instead he let their experience speak for itself, through their dreams, which he no longer tried to interpret; rather he asked his patients what they thought about them. Previously, Jung could be accused of seeing his patients as simply material for his theories. Now he felt more humble. But one question troubled him. After making a monumental study of myths, he had to admit he had no idea what his *own* myth was. It wasn't the Christian one—that was clear. But what?

His own dreams seemed to be telling him something again, reinforcing his sense that they were not eruptions of repressed material but hints pointing him in the right direction. In one he was sitting on a golden chair in a beautiful Renaissance style loggia. A white dove landed on an emerald table, then transformed into a young girl who ran off to play with Jung's children. The girl returned and embraced Jung, then turned back into the dove, who told him that she can turn into a girl only when the male dove is busy with the "twelve dead." Jung couldn't see the connection between a dove and a dozen dead people, but he did know the legend of the "emerald tablet" of Hermes Trismegistus, the mythical founder of alchemy, and wondered if there was some link. He wracked his brains about the mythological significance of twelve—the twelve apostles, the twelve signs of the Zodiac—but nothing clicked, although the dream did have a more immediate effect on Jung's life: it was after it, apparently, that he decided to enter his nearly forty-year affair with Toni Wolff.[2] The idea of the twelve dead persisted, and he found himself fantasizing about dead people returning to life. Another dream took up this theme. Walking through an avenue of ancient tombs in France, Jung kept seeing the dead reawaken; oddly, this happened only when *he* looked at them. Was the dream telling Jung that the dead were still alive in his psyche, but in order for them to come to life, he had to pay attention to them? Again, it was another dream about something old and buried yet still vital, another clue, perhaps, to the collective unconscious?

Jung made a thorough review of his life, especially his childhood; he was afraid of madness and enough of a Freudian to wonder if some childhood trauma was at work. He found nothing. Having exhausted what his rational mind could suggest, he decided to do whatever came to him—whatever, that is, his unconscious wanted. He remembered that as a boy he loved playing with building blocks. He followed the impulse, and the thirty-eight-year-old Jung found himself making castles of stone and mud by the lakeshore. Boaters on the lake may have wondered what the eminent doctor was up to, or if he was as crazy as his patients. In the middle of this he found a stone resembling a pyramid, and as he picked it up he remembered the dream of the underground phallus. Jung would build in the morning before his patients arrived and later after they left. He kept asking himself what he was doing, and the idea that he was participating in some rite came to him. In later years, at the outset of some new work, Jung found himself drawn to chiseling stone as a preliminary step to writing; he seemed to need some hands-on work to release his creative flow. As he wrote in an important paper we will return to shortly, "Often the hands know how to solve a riddle with which the intellect has wrestled in vain."[3]

But the tension didn't dissolve and yet another vision came. Again Jung saw blood and devastation. He had no sense that these visions were a portent of some external catastrophe, a revolution perhaps, and he feared they were the signs of an incipient psychosis. His own dreams seem to confirm his diagnoses; in them he saw Europe covered with ice, as if a new ice age had descended. Only in the third dream of this kind was some kind of salvation suggested. In it Jung saw a tree whose leaves had been transformed into ripe grapes; he plucked the grapes and gave them to the people who crowded around him. In July 1914 he had to lecture in Aberdeen on "The Importance of the Unconscious in Psychopathology," an apt subject, he thought. Then the guns of August fired and ironically Jung was relieved. World War I had broken out and Jung felt that his visions were not solely related to his own psychic turmoil, but were involved in the collective eruption that would devastate Europe for the next four years.

Although Jung's distaste for modern art would preclude it, he would have been relieved to know that his wasn't the only sensitive consciousness at the time plagued with visions of destruction. In 1912 the German Expressionist painter Ludwig Meidner produced a series of "Apocalyptic Landscapes." Meidner depicted cities laid to waste: comets rocket through the sky, the sun blackens, men run screaming through the streets, buildings collapse. Meidner painted his landscapes in a manic rush of inspiration, and his later work lacks this intensity: one is tempted to say that rather than Meidner having a flash of genius, some flash of genius briefly had *him*, the same one, perhaps, that invaded Jung's own mind. Had Jung known of Meidner's work, he would have surely seen it as confirmation of his belief that some individuals are mediums through whom future events are foreshadowed. As he remarked more than a decade later, arguing against the idea that his visions were simple evidence of his madness: "it can be assumed from such fantasies that some profound social disturbance is actually in progress, and at such times there is always more than one person whose unconscious registers the upset conditions."[4] Hindsight helped Jung here, but knowing Meidner's work at the time would have been some assurance that he wasn't simply going insane.

World War I however didn't stop his visions nor end the sense of oppression, and Jung continued to undergo what Henri Ellenberger called a "creative illness," a "deep reaching interior metamorphosis."[5] It was, we could say, the mother of all midlife crises, and it's not surprising that Jung, like Dante, came to see the middle of life—from thirty-five to forty—as the turning point in one's development, and that his later psychotherapy focused on this, rather than childhood. Waves of fantasies washed over him; the tension was so great he had to resort to yoga exercises to calm himself.[6] Yet, while any sane person would have wanted the visions to stop, having calmed down, Jung allowed the fantasies to rise up again. He knew others had been shattered by similar encounters—Nietzsche, the poets Friedrich Hölderlin and Gérard de Nerval—but Jung was driven by the need to *understand* what was happening to him. It was this unshakeable need to *know* that saved him. The only similar encounter I can think of is when the playwright August Strindberg *wrote* himself back to sanity during a psychotic episode in Paris.[7] Jung was also helped by a kind of mantra. In order to anchor himself in the real world, Jung repeated to himself that he had a diploma from the University of Basel, that he was married with a family, that he was a physician and lived in Küsnacht, that people depended on him: a mundane ballast that Nietzsche and the others had lacked.

Yet after months of fighting the feeling that he was cracking up—Jung remarked that he felt as if tremendous boulders were constantly tumbling on to him—he decided to *let go*. It wasn't an easy decision; it meant *allowing* himself to go mad, and Jung, who was still seeing patients, gathered courage from the fact that by doing this he would be able to understand their fantasies better. He was, in fact, becoming the proverbial "wounded healer," and Jung's own bout of madness puts him in a different category from most other therapists, who lack his firsthand encounter with the malaise they treat. In a seminar Jung gave in 1925, he talked about this experience—which was not made public until *Memories, Dreams, Reflections* was published after his death—and commented on how difficult it was to allow the fantasies free reign. "Fantasizing," Jung said, "was a mental process that was directly repellent to me"; it was "altogether impure" and "thoroughly immoral from an intellectual point of view."[8] Perhaps because Jung felt this way and perhaps because of his criticism of what he called "fantasy thinking" in *Symbols of Transformation*, Jung's unconscious felt his ego needed some adjustment.[9] If so, he got it.

Sitting at his desk, frantic with the thought that he was going insane, Jung let himself "drop." (Again there is the motif of a descent.) He felt as if the ground had given way and he was falling. He landed on a soft mass; although he was in complete darkness, he felt relieved, as he did when he finally expressed the thought of the shitting God. Gradually his sight adjusted and he could see the entrance to a cave. There he saw a dwarf with leathery skin.

Entering the cave Jung waded through icy water. He came upon a huge glowing red crystal; lifting it he saw a corpse of a blonde youth, then a gigantic black scarab, then a brilliant sun floating below in a stream. The light blinded him, and trying to replace the crystal, he saw a sudden geyser of blood, like the blood he saw on the train to Schaffhausen. The sight of it sickened him, and then the fantasy stopped. Jung felt that it must be some kind of solar-hero myth of rebirth, like the kind he had explored in *Symbols of Transformation*; the blood, however, seem to suggest the cycle wasn't complete. A week later he dreamt that he and a brown-skinned man, a "savage," were in the mountains at dawn. In the distance he could hear a horn; it was Siegfried, from Wagner's opera. He and the savage were there to kill him, and as Siegfried's chariot—made of the bones of the dead—turned a corner, they shot him down. Jung was disgusted at the crime, but then a sudden downpour washed away the evidence. None would know he was a murderer, but Jung himself felt a terrific guilt.

When Jung woke, he felt that he had to understand the dream immediately; an inner voice commanded that if he didn't, he must shoot himself. Jung kept a loaded pistol by his bed, a habit that caused his family alarm. (Years later his son Franz asked an interviewer, "Can you imagine living with a man who slept with a gun by his bed [and] said that when he could bear it no longer he would shoot himself . . ."[10]) Siegfried, of course, was the name of the child Sabina Spielrein wanted by Jung, and he may have only been feeling unconscious guilt for how he handled that situation. Jung, however, believed that the dream was saying that he had to abandon the heroic model, symbolized by Siegfried, who in Wagner's opera is a kind of superman, and his grief was over jettisoning an old identity. Freud and the others had seen Jung as an engine of efficiency and purpose, but now he saw that he had to curb his will, his ego, and let his unconscious take the wheel. (The fact that the typical solar-hero motif was spoiled by the sickening geyser of blood seems to support this interpretation.)

Soon after Jung again imagined "going down"; he used the fantasy of entering a hole or cave as a trigger for his visions. On one excursion he passed into what sounds like an extraordinarily vivid waking dream. Jung was doing this consciously, but anyone experiencing it spontaneously would have felt they were hallucinating. Reaching an eerie lunar landscape, Jung encountered a white-bearded old man and beautiful girl. He approached them as if they were real people and Jung found that they *spoke* to him, and said things he didn't know. The old man was Elijah, the girl Salome—two well-known biblical characters—and she was blind. Jung also saw a huge black snake, which seemed particularly interested in him. Jung was suspicious of Salome, a caution toward his inner feminine figure that would return. He had never heard of any connection among Elijah, Salome, and a snake, but says that he later understood why the three were together.

Other inner figures appeared in Jung's fantasies, like Ka, a kind of earth spirit. But the most important was Philemon, who became an "inner guru" for Jung. In paintings Jung did at the time, which he collected in what he called *The Red Book*, Philemon is depicted as a bald, white-bearded old man with bull's horns and the wings of a kingfisher.[11] In one of the many synchronicities that accompanied Jung's inner journey, while working on the painting, he came upon a dead kingfisher; the birds were rare in Zürich and Jung had never before found a dead one. One also recalls the Fisher King, a character in the Grail legends that were important to Jung.

Philemon was important to Jung because he showed him that "there are things in the psyche which I do not produce, but which produce themselves and have their own life."[12] If anyone wants a one-line summing up of Jung's significance, this is it. Whatever you might think of the whole edifice of Jungian psychology, this discovery, and the method and process that accompanied it, ranks Jung among the most important inner explorers. It's an example of what Jung means by the "objective psyche," a term I find more profitable than the "collective unconscious," which, like the archetypes, Jung himself defined in a number of different and sometimes conflicting ways.

Jung's 1925 seminar frequently refers to the idea that the figures Jung encountered had a strange life of their own, that in entering the depths of his mind Jung was discovering a strange, new world, that somehow existed *independently* of him, in the same way that the world outside my door exists independently of me. Jung discovered that he seemed to be sharing his mind with *others*. "As soon as one begins to watch one's mind," Jung told his students, "one begins to observe the autonomous phenomena in which one exists as a spectator . . ."[13] The process of achieving this wasn't easy. "It took me a long time," Jung said, "to admit to something in myself that was not myself."[14] Jung spoke of "writing letters to a part of myself with a different viewpoint from my own,"[15] and said that to understand the unconscious "we must see our thoughts as events, as phenomena."[16] Philemon had told Jung that he believed *he* created his thoughts, but that they were really like animals in a forest or people in a room, neither of which depended on him to exist.[17]

The importance of Jung's discovery bears considering. Since the seventeenth century, we've been taught that what is "in our heads" is only "subjective," that we are all island universes, separate worlds, and that everything in those worlds has been furnished with material taken from *outside*, from the senses, as if our minds began as empty rooms, waiting for the mental equivalent of a trip to Ikea. Yet anyone, like myself, who has had precognitive dreams or experienced synchronicities or telepathy or other "paranormal" phenomena knows this isn't quite true. Jung knew this and is saying that there are things in our heads that *have nothing to do with us or our senses.* In his book *Heaven and Hell* Aldous Huxley made the same point. "Like the earth of a hundred years ago," Huxley wrote, "our mind still has its darkest Africas, its unmapped Borneos and Amazonian basins." And while the creatures that inhabit these "far continents" of the mind seem "improbable," they are nevertheless "facts of observation," which argues for their "complete autonomy" and "self-sufficiency."[18] Huxley borrowed the title of his book from another extraordinary inner explorer, the Swedish sage Emanuel Swedenborg, who was a powerful influence on Jung, and who, like Jung, was a practiced hypnagogist and developed a method of entering similar inner worlds.

There was a method to Jung's madness, and I've already mentioned it: active imagination. It, like the transcendent function, which I've also mentioned, are the two most important discoveries Jung made at this time. I would even argue that they were the most important discoveries of Jung's career, and that everything that came later had its roots in these two fundamental insights. This being so, they warrant a bit of attention.

Strangely, Jung seems to have done everything he could to *hide* these discoveries from all but his closest colleagues. The paper which discusses both in any detail, "The Transcendent Function," was written in 1916, while Jung was in the middle of his "deep reaching interior metamorphosis." (He was serving a stint of military duty, stationed near the Gotthard Pass at the time.) Yet it wasn't published until 1957, and only then when Jung was asked to contribute to a student publication, not something many of his readers would see. For forty years it remained in Jung's files, off-limits to the general public. Jung discussed the ideas in seminars and lectures, but usually only with his closest students, rather like an initiate sharing the most profound mysteries with only his most devoted pupils. Although subsequent Jungian analysts have recognized their importance, neither idea plays a prominent role in any of Jung's major works. For example, in *Mysterium Coniunctionis*, Jung's alchemical magnum opus, active imagination warrants only a brief mention, again not by name, and the transcendent function is mentioned only twice. As is often the case with Jung's ideas, we need to go to his followers for anything like a clear definition.[19]

Some suggest Jung kept quiet about active imagination because he considered it possibly dangerous. In a note, he cautioned that through it "subliminal contents . . . may overpower the conscious mind and take possession of the personality."[20] That Jung came upon it precisely when his own subliminal contents were mutinying against his ego makes this a reasonable concern. Yet there may have been other reasons. Weak egos might fragment practicing active imagination, but what would his peers think of a psychologist who talked to people in his head? As with his public and private opinions about spirits and the occult, Jung seems to have kept quiet about things that could threaten his persona as a scientist.

What, then, *is* active imagination? In practice it's exactly what Jung did in his visions and conversations with inner figures such as Philemon, Ka, and Salome mentioned above: entering a fantasy and talking with one's "self"—at least a part of oneself "normally" left unconscious—asking questions and receiving knowledge that one—"you"—did not know. In many ways, it's something we engage in often already, but in a shallow, fleeting way, when we "ask ourselves" what we think or will do about a situation.

More abstractly, it's a method of consciously entering into a dialogue with the unconscious, which triggers the transcendent function, a vital *shift* in consciousness, brought about through the union of the conscious and unconscious minds. Unexpected insights and self-renewal are some of the results of the transcendent function. It achieves what I call that elusive "Goldilocks" condition, the "just right" of having the conscious and unconscious minds work together, rather than being at odds. In the process it produces a third state more vivid and "real" than either; in it we recognize what consciousness *should* be like and see our "normal" state as at best a muddling through. We've already seen how the transcendent function helped Jung when faced with the dilemma of having to choose between science and the humanities. Then it operated through a dream, producing the mandala-like symbol of the giant radiolarian. In the simplest sense, the transcendent function is our built-in means of growth, psychological and spiritual—it's "transcendent" only in the sense that it "transcends" the frequent deadlock between the conscious and unconscious minds—and is a development of what Jung earlier recognized as the "prospective tendencies in man."

As the name implies, active imagination is a means of stimulating this, rather than waiting passively for the unconscious to do it on its own. It's a way of consciously "having it out with it" with the unconscious—the German is *Auseinandersetzung*—that is, not passively accepting it, as we normally do in a dream or reverie, but confronting it, engaging with it, asking it what it wants. It isn't easy. As Marie-Louise von Franz, one of Jung's best interpreters and an acute psychological thinker in her own right, remarks, "if done rightly one is exhausted after ten minutes for it is a real effort and not a 'letting go'."[21]

Although Jung describes several means of "doing" active imagination—painting, sculpting, even dance—the basic method is to allow a fantasy to appear, as Jung did. But rather than drift into "free association"—which only allows complexes to take over—one grabs hold of an element in the fantasy and sticks to it. With practice one can follow the material as it develops and can actually speak with it, as Jung did, which means, of course, that it can speak to you. As Jung explained to a correspondent: "The point is that you start with any image . . . Contemplate it and carefully observe how the picture begins to unfold or to change. Don't try to make it into something, just do nothing but observe what its spontaneous changes are. Any mental picture you contemplate in this way will sooner or later change through a spontaneous association that causes a slight alteration of the picture. You must carefully avoid impatient jumping from one subject to another. Hold fast to the one image you have chosen and wait until it changes by itself. Note all these changes and eventually step into the picture yourself, and if it is a speaking figure at all then say what you have to say to that figure and listen to what he or she has to say."[22]

In a lecture he gave to the Tavistock Clinic in London in 1935, Jung spoke of a patient who couldn't grasp what active imagination was, until one day he found himself looking at a travel poster at a railway station. It showed the Alps, with a waterfall, a meadow, and cows on a hilltop. Jung's patient wondered what he would find if he walked over the hill. In a reverie he did, and found himself in a small chapel, looking at picture of the Virgin. Then a creature with pointed ears popped behind the altar and disappeared. At first Jung's patient thought this was nonsense, but he continued. The creature appeared again, although *he hadn't imagined it there at all*. It seemed to have a "life of its own." After that, he understood what Jung meant.

Again, it sounds easy but it isn't. The critical ego wants to reject the fantasy for a number of reasons—it's silly, obscene, absurd—but it must be disciplined to withhold judgment and allow the material expression. Anyone who does creative work is familiar with this problem, and in many ways active imagination is similar to writing, painting, and so on; all creative work entails a give-and-take between inspiration (unconscious) and execution (conscious). (As I am writing this, for example, I have to allow my intuitions expression before I can start editing them.) The difference for Jung is that the aesthetic quality of the end product isn't important; understanding it is. Nevertheless, one of the best introductions to active imagination are the letters *On the Aesthetic Education of Man* by the poet Friedrich Schiller, a contemporary of Goethe, which discuss in detail the dialogue between the creative (unconscious) and critical (conscious) drives and their union in art, both creating and experiencing it.

I n many ways, active imagination is similar to hypnagogia, and as we know, Jung was a good hypnagogist. His ideas on active imagination and the transcendent function may have been influenced by Herbert Silberer. In 1909 Silberer's paper[23] on hypnagogia was published in the psychoanalytical yearbook, and as editor Jung read it. Silberer discovered that hypnagogic imagery was auto-symbolic: it gave a pictorial or auditory assessment of one's current state, a characteristic Swedenborg had noticed almost two centuries earlier. For example, Silberer was resting and thinking of how to improve an awkward passage in an essay, and as he slipped into a reverie he saw himself smoothing out a piece of wood. Later, again resting, he contemplated the mysteries of human existence and saw himself on a jetty reaching out into a dark sea. Unable to keep an argument of Kant's and of Schopenhauer's in mind simultaneously, Silberer saw himself asking a secretary for information. Silberer concluded that the opposition of two "antagonistic elements"—the effort of thinking while dozing—produced the auto-symbolic effect. This seems very much like the effort to maintain conscious and unconscious processes simultaneously—a wakeful reverie—which is the essence of active imagination, and the symbols produced seem very similar to the work of the transcendent function. Years later Jung paid tribute to Silberer, saying he "has the merit of being the first to discover the secret threads that lead from alchemy to the psychology of the unconscious."[24]

Although one can practice active imagination "cold," most people do because, like Jung, they are faced with psychological distress. Paradoxically, the distress provides the best opportunity to practice active imagination, rather like an ailment containing its own cure. Jung suggests taking a bad mood, and focusing on it, making it as conscious as possible. This crystallizes it into a symbol, fantasy image, or some other representation, achieving an "enrichment and clarification of the affect [emotion]."[25] The unconscious seeks consciousness and Jung discovered that "as soon as the image was there, the unrest or sense of oppression vanished." "The whole energy of these emotions," Jung says, "was transformed into *interest in and curiosity about the image* [my italics]."[26] With no exaggeration, focusing on his dark moods and transforming them into inner images saved Jung from madness.

Yet Jung didn't agree with everything his unconscious said. As he painted his images and recorded his fantasies, Jung asked what exactly it was he was doing. A woman's voice—his "anima"—answered, "art." Jung recognized the voice. It was, he said, that of a "talented psychopath" with a "strong transference" to him."[27] Some suggest the "talented psychopath" was Sabina Spielrein but it seems Jung was referring to Mary Moltzer, mentioned earlier as the Burghölzli doctor Jung may have had an affair with. His resistance to accepting his anima's remarks about art may have been influenced by one of his colleagues at the Burghölzli, Franz Riklin Sr., who worked with Jung on the word-association tests and was also a supporter of Freud. Riklin considered himself an artist and had some small success; for a time he was associated with Hans Arp and Paul Klee. Riklin vacillated between being an artist and a scientist, and in the process often neglected his duties.[28] Later, he and Moltzer teamed up in reaction to what they saw as Jung's dominance.[29] Jung's remarks about artists are usually directed at the "misunderstood genius" type, who talk a good painting but produce little, and he may have had Riklin in mind when he rejected the idea that what he was doing was art. What is curious is that in Jung's first encounter with his anima—an inner figure that will play an enormous role in his system—she is "cunning" (unreliable, like his mother?), and he is wary that she could seduce him into thinking he was a "misunderstood artist" which would have meant he could "neglect reality,"[30] something Jung was determined not to do. Yet anyone who sees Jung's paintings in *The Red Book*, or his stone carvings, or reads the strange work produced during this period, his enigmatic *Seven Sermons to the Dead* (which we will discuss shortly), will recognize that art had as much, if not more, of a claim on him than science—at least after his "confrontation." Even Jung himself saw that what he was doing while speaking with his inner figures wasn't "science," at least not in the sense in which most scientists accept it.[31]

One result of active imagination, according to some reports, is an increase in synchronistic and paranormal phenomena.[32] This was certainly true of Jung. In 1916, Jung again felt that something *within* wanted to get out. An eerie restlessness seemed to permeate his home. Jung, I have to say, was lucky to have his house in Küsnacht, where he retired to a room, his "intellectual cave," decorated in colored glass, to commune with his interior voices; he demanded and got absolute silence, and neither his children nor Emma—nor even the maid—were allowed to enter.[33] As his maternal grandfather did, Jung felt the presence of the dead. His children seemed to feel it, too. One daughter saw a strange white figure; another had her blankets snatched from her at night. His son drew a picture of a fisherman he had seen in a dream: a flaming chimney rose from the fisherman's head, and a devil flew through the air, cursing the fisherman for stealing his fish. An angel warned the devil that he couldn't hurt the fisherman because he only caught bad fish. Jung had yet to mention

Philemon the Kingfisher to his family. Then, on a Sunday after-noon, the doorbell rang loudly when it was clear no one was there. The pressure increased and Jung finally demanded "What in the world is this?" Then he heard the voices. "We have come back from Jerusalem," they said, "where we found not what we sought," the beginning of one of the strangest works of "auto-matic writing," Jung's *Seven Sermons to the Dead*, which he attrib-uted to "Basilides in Alexandria, the City where the East toucheth the West."

Depending on your tastes, the *Seven Sermons* is either a work of Gnostic-Hermetic revelation, the "fount and origin" of Jung's work or, as Jung sometimes referred to it, a youthful indiscre-tion.[34] Whatever it was, like much else, Jung wanted to keep quiet about it, and after distributing a few privately printed copies to close friends, he suppressed it; it only appeared years later as an appendix to a US edition of *Memories, Dreams, Reflections*.[35] One recipient of the *Sermons* was advised by Jung to "find the little book a discreet resting place in your writing desk," which would keep it from profane hands, as well as off a bookshelf.[36] Jung wrote it in three days, locked away in his multi-colored room. In an inflated, quasi-biblical language, which Jung explains is how the archetypes express themselves, Jung spells out his ideas on indi-viduation in a series of prophetic revelations passed on to the dead by Basilides, a Gnostic teacher of second-century AD Alexandria. (Curiously, another influential work of spiritual dictation, writ-ten a decade earlier, Aleister Crowley's *The Book of the Law*, is couched in a similarly highfalutin style.) Jung was influenced by the research of the Theosophical scholar G. R. S. Mead, whose work on the Gnostics, *Fragments of a Faith Forgotten*, is a classic. The *Seven Sermons*, Jung tells us, is what Philemon *would* have written, but by this time, Jung had assimilated this personification of his unconscious, and now Jung had to say it himself. It's a curious work, sometimes reaching poetic power, sometimes reading like pastiche. Its central message is the need to differentiate from the mass, to achieve one's own individuality. "The natural striving of the creature goeth towards distinctiveness, fighteth against primeval, perilous sameness." "Ye all become equal and thus is your nature maimed."[37] (William Blake: "One law for lion and ox is oppression.") Prominent place is given to the Gnostic god Abraxas, who unites the opposites, and who plays a central role in Hermann Hesse's novel *Demian*, which Hesse wrote after undergoing Jungian analysis. Jung met Hesse when Josef Lang, his analyst and one of Jung's pupils, brought him to the Psychological Club in 1916. It's possible Lang was one of the recipients of the *Sermons*, and that he passed on the revelations to Hesse; anyone familiar with both works will see the link immediately. Jung may have sent Hesse himself a copy after reading the novel.[38] This brief sketch does no justice to the rich possibilities in Jung's inspired work, and for an in-depth study of the *Seven Sermons* in light of Gnosticism and the mystery tradition, the reader can do no better than refer to Stephan Hoeller's illuminating *The Gnostic Jung and the Seven Sermons to the Dead*. Whoever the Dead were—and we remember Jung's dream of the dove and the twelve dead people at the start of his crisis—they must have found what they were seeking, as they seem never to have importuned on him again.

Jung's "confrontation" culminated in the last years of WWI, when he was 43 and serving as Commandant de la Région Anglaise de Internés de Guerre in Château d'Oex, overseeing

English soldiers interned in Switzerland. (Although neutral, during the conflict Switzerland's considerable militia was mobilized and combatants who crossed the border—the country was surrounded by warring nations—were interned. Jung always enjoyed his military duty and was happy to put his fluent English to use.) Two things marked the end of the crisis. One was that he broke off relations with Mary Moltzer. She had sent him a letter arguing once again that the images arising from his unconscious should be considered art, and this got on Jung's nerves, because he recognized that some of her arguments made sense, which suggests that he himself was in doubt about it.[39] This led to the second thing: the significance of the mandala. Each morning while in camp, Jung sketched a circular drawing, a mandala, which seemed to somehow represent his psychic state. Jung's first mandala, which he drew in 1916, is an elaborate work he called *Systema Mundi Totius* (*The System of All Worlds*) and presented in pictorial form the cosmology of his *Seven Sermons*; it resembles nothing so much as the kind of Hermetic representations of the universe Jung would pour over a decade later when he plunged into his study of alchemy.[40] The morning after he received Moltzer's letter, he saw that his mandala that day reacted to his irritation. It was off-balanced, inharmonious, its symmetry ruined. From this Jung concluded that the mandala and his inner state, his self, were somehow attuned, and that the aim of the individuation process was a kind of inner mandala. He called this the Self, differentiating it from the ego. He, his ego, was only a part of a larger, more encompassing psychic totality, the Self, which embraced both the conscious and the unconscious mind. It was a mystical insight, to be sure; at first glance the idea of the Self as a kind of inner circle (esoteric puns aside) sounds poetic enough, but doesn't *quite* make sense, at least not immediately. Yet it did to Jung. The goal was to achieve inwardly the kind of harmony and integrity the mandala possessed, and Jung recognized that when moving toward that goal, mandalas appear in dreams or fantasies. It was as if individuation was a kind of spiral or labyrinth in which one moved ceaselessly around a center point. That center was the Self, and after much suffering, pain, and darkness, Jung had found his.

6. THE JUNG CULT

According to Henri Ellenberger, "Jung emerged from his creative illness with an increased propensity to intuitions, psychical experiences, and meaningful dreams." But this wasn't all. Individuals who "have lived through such a spiritual adventure," Ellenberger argues, characteristically "attribute universal value to their own personal experience." Jung was no exception. The anima, the Self, the archetypes, the collective unconscious, all the flora and fauna of Jung's inner voyage became for him "psychological realities that existed as certainly as did the material world around him."[1] Jung was convinced that what he experienced was real, in a literal sense, and not only for his psyche, but everyone's. This is why Anthony Storr included Jung in *Feet of Clay*, his "rogues' gallery" of "gurus." "Gurus," Storr writes, "claim the possession of special spiritual insight based on personal revelation." From this they "promise new ways of self-development, new paths to salvation."[2] From a "spiritual insight which has transformed his own life," the guru generalizes and creates a teaching that he believes is applicable to everyone. Depending on your perspective, what emerges is either of universal benefit or a gigantic delusion.

Whether or not he was a guru, after his crisis, Jung moved

from healing the sick to exploring ways for the healthy to achieve higher levels of maturity, to in fact individuate, based on his own experiences. If, Jung thought, one can survive a psychosis and achieve "normality" by reaching a better balance between the conscious and unconscious minds, why then couldn't one go further, and reach a level beyond the norm, which is really, as Hermann Hesse remarked in his Jungian novel *Steppenwolf*, nothing more than a "bourgeois compromise"?[3] That "much, if not all, of [Jung's] scientific [read psychological] work may be based on visionary revelations,"[4] is for some an endorsement. For others it's reason enough to reject it. Yet it has to be admitted that the critics who argue that Jung's creative illness was nothing more than a psychotic episode can't have it both ways. Even if all he experienced was a colossal breakdown, Jung *did* find a means of coming through it in one piece. In fact he emerged stronger, and he was able to help others through their own difficulties, too. This argues that, "true" or not in some literal sense, Jung's belief in the reality of the objective psyche, and his means of communicating with it, *worked*. And this was enough. As he argued in different ways and at different times, for Jung, what is real in any vital, meaningful sense is what works. Jung had crossed the abyss and come back reborn, and that was proof enough for him.

He hadn't crossed it alone though. Although his wife and children were unsure what was happening to him and were kept at a distance, Jung allowed one person to share his "night sea journey," the hero's voyage into the belly of the beast. Whether or not he would have made it safely to shore without her is debatable. It's unclear exactly when Toni Wolff crossed the line from analysand to mistress and *soror mystica*; the general consensus is that their personal relationship was renewed around the time that Emma became pregnant with their last child, Emma Helene, who was born in March 1914, and that Toni might have taken the lead. Two weeks after "Lil," as the girl was called, arrived, Jung and Toni had a holiday in Ravenna. It's difficult not to feel that Jung, for all his insight into his and others' troubled psyches, had a peculiar blind spot for Emma. While she remained at home cared for by her mother, Jung and Toni became lovers. Years later Toni Wolff would tell Marie-Louise von Franz that sex was never the real bond between them and that Jung himself was not that interested in it.[5] He was, apparently, not a great lover anyway: according to his biographer Vincent Brome, "his sexuality was very straightforward, and all the mythopoeic talk vanished in a cloud of uncomplicated passion."[6]

That his wife would surely feel abandoned, especially following a pregnancy, would occur to most men, yet when confronted with the affair, Jung vacillated between rationalizing about his anima and using it as an excuse.[7] Toni filled the position left empty or only fitfully filled since the contretemps with Sabina Spielrein. Aside from his young son Franz, Toni was the only person Jung allowed to sit by him as he built his castles near the lake. She would sit with him in his library at Küsnacht, listening to him talk about his visions, dreams, and fantasies as he paced around the room, smoking his ever-present pipe. Then she would tell him what she thought, what she felt the visions meant, what she saw happening in his psyche, in a way going through an analysis with him. She read pages from his *Black Book*, where he recorded his experiences (these were later transferred to his famous *Red Book*) and looked at his paintings, the only person to do so. Curiously, Wolff never practiced active imagination herself; presumably she was already too close to the unconscious to need it.[8] Toni soon became indispensable to Jung; she even helped him name some

of his inner figures, and she had a deep, if not sufficiently cred-
ited influence on his work. And although Emma and the children
resented her—the children often made fun of "Aunt Antonia"—
Jung had his way and Toni became a part of the family. After
refusing her demand that he divorce Emma and marry her, this
seemed the only solution. A détente was eventually agreed and
Emma and Toni even analyzed each other. Nevertheless the addi-
tion raised the level of stress in an already tense atmosphere, and
it's difficult not to think of Jung as being a bit spoiled.

Wolff wrote little and was an idiosyncratic analyst, but she
became a central figure in the Psychological Club, started in
Zürich by Edith McCormick in 1916. It was a meeting place for
people who had been analyzed by Jung or one of his students.
Jung knew how his patients behaved when seeing him, but how
would they act in a group? Two years earlier an Association for
Analytical Psychology had started among some of Jung's patients
and students, but now there was an opportunity for a more formal
organization, and in a more lavish setting than the restaurant the
Association had used as a meeting place. An entire building on
Löwenstrasse in the center of Zürich was provided, with living
quarters, a lecture hall, rooms for seminars, a library, a restaurant,
even a billiard table, all through the courtesy of Edith's millions (in
1919 it moved to Gemeindestrasse, where it resides today). Jung,
of course, was the key player, but he refused to accept the presidency or to have anything to do with the administration; Emma
was appointed president instead. Although its raison d'être was
mostly social, Jung saw other applications. Jung felt his patients
needed a setting in which to put what they were gaining from
analysis to some practical use; he also wanted to see them in a less
artificial environment than a consulting room.

In many ways, Jung was experimenting with something that that enigmatic psychologist—or spiritual teacher, depending on your perspective—G. I. Gurdjieff was attempting at the same time in St. Petersburg and Moscow: putting people together to see how they would react in order to get past their personas or, as Gurdjieff called it, "false personality." Gurdjieff believed that self-transformation was hastened by the friction caused in groups and Jung seems to have had a similar idea. Indeed, one of Gurdjieff's most important disciples, Maurice Nicoll, who studied with Jung in Zürich, disappointed Jung when he abandoned "psychosynthe-sis" (Jung's early term) to enter Gurdjieff's *Prieuré* in Fontaineb-leau; on hearing of this, Freud is said to have remarked "Ah, you see what happens to Jung's disciples."[9] As with Rudolf Steiner, there are many similarities between Jung and Gurdjieff: both were physically strong, both had no qualms about sleeping with followers, both had a kind of "peasant" earthiness, both devel-oped a psychological typology, both were larger-than-life "man's men," both enjoyed cooking and hard physical labor, both had "psychic powers," and both aimed at getting past the surface per-sonality to one's "essence." At one point, Jung invented a game called "Alleluia," which members of the club were forced to play.[10] Forming a circle and then tying a large handkerchief into knots, they tossed this at each other, while shouting out some personal foible or embarrassing item about their target, who had to do the same, when tossing the handkerchief at another victim. Most of the people who came to Jung were shy introverts and hated it, as it forced them to act out of character, a transformative strategy Gurdjieff put to good, if sometimes excessive use.[11]

It's unclear how successful Jung's "silent experiment in group psychology that dragged on over forty years"[12]—as he once described the Psychological Club—was. Although it began as a forum for different ideas, it was only a matter of time before Jung's vision dominated. Members became annoyed at how the triumvirate—Jung, with Emma and Toni on each arm—entered the premises as if they owned it and resented the personality cult growing up around Jung. Jung wouldn't hide his boredom or disagreement with a speaker and would laugh out loud or audibly whisper his blunt assessment to Toni. It seemed he was unable to let someone else have the spotlight. His rudeness can be chalked up to the crisis, but his impolite and undemocratic ways carried on well after his "cure." On more than one occasion Jung stormed out of the club, infuriated at some criticism of his behavior or ideas; although he seemed unable to recognize it, he was becoming a second Freud, and in 1922, after a motion of censure against him was passed, he, Emma, and Toni resigned. They rejoined a few years later and gained complete dominance of the club. Most likely the club wouldn't have started without him, and whether we want to accept it or not, Jung *was* a highly dominant individual with a large ego and a genius to match, who, outside his consulting room (and often inside it), didn't suffer fools gladly. (He once remarked, "If I get another perfectly normal adult malingering as a sick patient I'll have him certified."[13]) But for someone concerned with individuating and achieving a higher degree of psychic maturity, he again comes across as spoiled.

Many outsider speakers lectured at the club. Hermann Hesse did, as did Martin Buber, the Jewish theologian, whose talk Jung boycotted because Buber had criticized his penchant for Gnosticism and focus on the Self rather than others, his "I and Me" rather than "I and Thou" dialectic. But it was mainly a sounding board for Jung's ideas, and it was this that led to accusations of a "Jung cult" sprouting up in Zürich. That for a while at least Jung saw the club as a means of injecting his ideas into society can be seen in a paper he wrote around the same time as "The Transcendent Function." "Adaptation, Individuation, Collectivity" is another important work from this period not published until decades later. Rather than the individual psyche, it addressed the individuating person's place in society, something for which the Psychological Club was a dry run.

Remembering his experience with Otto Gross, whose vision of cultural renewal, if not his aberrant lifestyle, Jung took to heart, Jung made clear that far from simply rejecting society's norms and "dropping out," "individuators" had a responsibility to create new values and achieve new levels of inner discipline. Although "individuation is exclusive adaptation to inner reality and hence an allegedly 'mystical' process," society has a right to "condemn the individuant if he fails to create equivalent values, for he is a disease."[14] Individuating means "stepping over into solitude, into the cloister of the inner self . . . inner adaptation leads to the conquest of inner realities, from which values are won for the reparation of the collective. Individuation remains a pose so long as no positive values are created. Whosoever is not creative enough must re-establish collective conformity . . . otherwise he remains an empty waster and windbag . . . society has a right to expect realizable values . . . "[15]

Jung's terminology sounds abstract, but his meaning is simple. It's not enough to withdraw from society and seek your own salvation, your own individuation. The individuator must return to society ("collectivity") to contribute his or her new insights, his or her new values, which must be at least equal to if not greater than the norm. Failing this, the individuating person must accept the norm and be, as Gurdjieff said, a good *obyvatel*, a good householder—basically someone who works hard and fulfills his obligations. "From the point of view of the possibility of evolution," Gurdjieff told his disciple Ouspensky, "a good *obyvatel* has many more chances than a 'lunatic' or a 'tramp,'"[16] Gurdjieff's names for the "misunderstood genius" of Jung's anti-artist rants. "Become who you are" isn't the same as "do your own thing" or "do what thou wilt," catchphrases often used to condone avoiding the responsibilities of life. Indeed, Jung believed that neuroses are attempts at avoiding life's tasks, methods of sidestepping its difficulties. Individuation means meeting these demands, not sinking below them and it is a common observation that Jungian therapy attracts highly successful people, not "tramps" or "lunatics." (Gurdjieff, too, drew from the best and brightest, not society's dregs.)

The next step, however, is crucial. After withdrawing into solitude and achieving a new unity (via the transcendent function), the individuator returns to the collective and *adds* to it. This is how society and civilization evolves; without this it grows stagnant and dies. This process of "withdrawal and return" was recognized by others. Nietzsche's Zarathustra returns from the mountains to preach in the marketplace. Hesse writes of it in *Steppenwolf*, when he remarks that "the vital force of the bourgeoisie resides by no means in the qualities of its normal members, but in those of its extremely numerous 'outsiders.'"[17] It plays an important part in the work of the historian Arnold Toynbee, whose enormous *Study of History* charts the rise, fall, or possible advance of civilizations through the efforts of a "creative minority." And the theme of the "outsider" who abandons society only to return after achieving greater self-integration is the central motif of Colin Wilson's huge body of work. Jung recognized that society advances only slowly, through the gradual integration of new insights gleaned through the often unrecorded work of individuals, whose attempts at self-transformation add incrementally to society's own growth. This is a theme he returned to in his late work *The Undiscovered Self*, written in 1957, which applies the insights of analytical psychology to the H-bomb threatened world of the Cold War years.

A better-known work to emerge from Jung's crisis was *Psychological Types*, published in 1921, and which no doubt benefited from Jung's observation of the members of the Psychological Club. Although the question of typology had a long history, of which Jung was at pains to inform his readers, reviewing at length the ideas of Nietzsche, Schiller, William James and others—as in *Symbols of Transformation*, Jung pours on the references—Jung's central impetus for the work appears to have been "thirty pages of his *Red Book*," at least according to an account given by the Dutch poet Roland Holst.[18] By now Jung's ideas on the introvert, extravert, and the four "functions"—thinking, feeling, sensation, intuition—have become part of common parlance: extraverts, we know, love parties; introverts stay at home. As often happens when specialized terminology becomes part of everyday speech, in the process they have lost much of their meaning, or have acquired so wide a use that whatever meaning they had originally has become clichéd. "Personality Tests" to determine your "type" using Jung's terminology are as common as newspaper horoscopes; probably the most popular is the Myers-Briggs Personality Test. Extravert and introvert seem anchored in Jung's experience of his No. 1 and No. 2; one face is turned toward the outer world, the other looks inside. Thinking, feeling, sensation, and intuition are different

modes of adaptation; in each of us one is dominant, with an auxiliary mode as a "second in command." As the terms suggest, thinkers adapt through thought, feelers through their feelings, sensation
types through the senses, and intuitives through hunches and sudden insights. Jung calls thinking and feeling rational functions, as
they operate through weighing pros and cons; sensing and intuition are irrational in the sense that they don't argue or give reasons ("I think this is true because . . . I feel it's good because . . .")
but simply are: one doesn't *decide* to smell a particular odor or
have a hunch. But as one function becomes hypertrophied, its
opposite or complement atrophies, and so to achieve balance, an
individual's "inferior" function needs to be strengthened.

It's also through the inferior function that the unconscious
enters consciousness; hence it's often the subject of active imagination. As the psyche is self-regulating, it invariably seeks to adjust
itself, as a thermostat does the heating. So when a thinker (whose
auxiliary function is either sensation or intuition) becomes too
obsessed with thought and disregards feeling, the unconscious
brings this to his attention, often to the thinker's dismay: irrational moods, sentimentality, and irritability are some of the unconscious' wake-up calls. In his thought a thinker may be as brilliant
as the sun, but his feelings are generally those of a twelve-year-old.
One classic example is the philosopher Bertrand Russell, who was
as brilliant as they come but who never outgrew an embarrassing
womanizing and was chasing skirts in his seventies.[19] (Having said
this, Jung comes to mind as well, and he himself recognized that
feeling was his weak spot).

It's a neat formulation and makes immediate sense and has a
pedigree going back to the ancients; Gurdjieff made use of something similar with his ideas on different "centers," the "intellectual,"

"emotional," and "moving," and on the different "ways," that of the yogi, the monk, and the fakir. Another similar typology, also based on spiritual dictation, is the poet W. B. Yeats' remarkable *A Vision*, which came to Yeats' wife in 1917, during experiments in automatic writing; Yeats is another occult figure who has much in common with Jung. The problem, as Jung soon recognized, is that people are not quite as clear cut as the classifications used to understand them, and that as soon as one starts to look more closely, the different types start to blend. Jung fine-tuned his different types until the initial insight was lost under a scaffolding of qualifications. No one is *only* a thinker, feeler, senser, or intuitive. And when we look at great works of art or thought, we see the functions producing something *more* than any one of them. Nietzsche, a philosopher who lived only for thought, famously said he wrote his books with his blood; his writings are filled with passion, and not the cold, dry reasoning we'd expect from a thinker. Another philosopher, vastly different from Nietzsche, Alfred North Whitehead, called propositions "lures for feeling" and said that a thought is an intense sensation. At certain levels of experience, the distinction between "functions" collapses. Differentiating types according to the preference they have for a particular function is a handy rule of thumb, but as with most things, stretching its application too far reveals its inadequacies.

By 1919, WWI was over and travel restrictions in Europe had ended. Jung took the opportunity to travel to London, to lecture to the Society for Psychical Research, which was founded in 1882 by Frederick Myers, Edmund Gurney, and other late Victorians with an interest in supernatural phenomena. Jung always had a warm affection for England. He made his first visit to London in 1903, shortly before marrying Emma. He felt at home there, took to dressing in an English style, became, as noted, fluent in English, and visited as often as he could. He even went in 1913, just before the start of his "visions." Jung's lecture to the SPR was on "The Psychological Foundations of Belief in Spirits." Its central theme harkened back to Jung's earliest work on Helly Preiswerk. Jung told the Society that apparitions (ghosts) and materializations were "unconscious projections" or, as he spoke of them to Freud, "exteriorisations." "I have repeatedly observed," Jung told his audience, "the telepathic effects of unconscious complexes, and also a number of parapsychic phenomena, but in all this I see no proof whatever of the existence of real spirits, and until such proof is forthcoming I must regard this whole territory as an appendix of psychology."

This sounds scientific enough, but a year later[20] when Jung was again in England, he encountered a somewhat more real ghost. Jung spent some weekends in a cottage in Aylesbury outside of London rented by Maurice Nicoll, and while there was serenaded by an assortment of eerie sounds—dripping water, knocks, inexplicable rustlings—while an unpleasant smell filled the bedroom. Locals said the place was haunted, and one particularly bad night, Jung opened his eyes to discover an old woman's head on the pillow next to his; half of her face was missing. Jung leaped out of bed, lit a candle, and waited until morning in an armchair. The house was later torn down. One would think that having already encountered the dead on their return from Jerusalem, Jung wouldn't be shaken by a fairly standard English ghost, but the experience rattled him. Yet his account of it only appeared thirty years later, in 1949, in an anthology of ghost stories.[21] When his lecture for the SPR was reprinted in the *Collected Works* in 1947, Jung added a footnote, explaining that he no longer felt as certain as he did in 1919 that apparitions were explicable through psychology, and that he doubted "whether an exclusively psychological approach can do justice to the phenomena . . ."[22] In a later postscript he again admitted that his earlier explanation was insufficient, but that he couldn't agree on the reality of spirits, because he had no experience of them—conveniently forgetting his experience in Aylesbury.[23]

A similar confusion surrounds Jung's experience with the *I Ching*, the ancient Chinese oracle, which he began to experiment with at this time and which, like horoscopes, became part of his therapeutic practice. Although Jung mentioned it here and there in his writing, it wasn't until 1949, again nearly thirty years later, in his introduction to the classic Wilhelm/Baynes translation, that he admitted outright to using it himself. And although he tried to explain the *I Ching's* efficacy through what would become his paranormal *deus ex machina*, synchronicity, Jung admits that the source of the oracle's insights are the "spiritual agencies" that form the "living soul of the book," a remark at odds with his quasi-scientific explanation.[24] This isn't to argue in favor of ghosts or spirits over "exteriorizations" or synchronicity, but to point out that even after his crisis, Jung's No. 1 and No. 2 were in good working order, the Herr Doctor Professor keeping things strictly scientific, while the mystic maintained a low profile. It would be some time before the "sage of Küsnacht" came out of the closet.[25]

England, however, wasn't the only spot on Jung's travel itinerary. In 1920 Jung began a series of journeys in order, he said, to see "the European from outside," and to acquire some firsthand experience of non-Western psyches. Given that he had two wives, five children, a large practice, and other responsibilities, Jung perhaps made a virtue of inclination and his trips may have been as much an opportunity to escape Küsnacht as anything else. His journey to North Africa wasn't planned; a friend, the businessman Hermann Sigg, told Jung he had to go to Tunis and asked if he would like to come. Jung immediately agreed. He had taken earlier unexpected holidays—as his father had, often alone—and it was a practice he would continue, often leaving his family and patients little notice.

Jung's remarks about how in North Africa he "felt cast back many centuries to an infinitely more naïve world of adolescents who were preparing, with the aid of a slender knowledge of the Koran, to emerge from their original state of twilight consciousness" may seem politically incorrect from our oversensitive perspective, but they highlight the core insight of the trip. Although Jung *knew* a great deal about mythology and mythological thinking, his own thinking was decidedly Western and rational—he described himself as a "thorough Westerner"[26]—and in many ways, Jung was a typical "left-brainer," with his detestation of "fantasy," his formality and punctuality, his precision and need to be "scientific." In his travels in North Africa, and later Taos and Central Africa, Jung was looking for signs of a consciousness not as differentiated from the unconscious matrix—what in the *Seven Sermons* he called "the Pleroma"—as ours, with its sharp distinction between conscious and unconscious. What Jung found in places such as Tunis, Sousse, Sfax, and the oasis city of Tozeur was a completely different sense of *time*. Coming from the land of cuckoo clocks and appointment books, this must have been a shock. Jung had entered a "dream of a static, age-old existence," a kind of perpetual *now*, a condition associated with the right brain, which lacks a sense of time; there was none of the incessant activity that characterized even a relatively small city like Zürich. Jung enjoyed the contrast, which gave him an opportunity to entertain criticisms of modernity, a practice that would become something of a habit in later years, but he also felt this timelessness was threatened. Thinking of his pocket watch, "the symbol of Europe's accelerated tempo," Jung worried that the "god of time" and its demon, progress, would soon "chop into bits and pieces"—hours, minutes, seconds—the "duration" he sensed here and which was the "closest thing to eternity."[27] ("Duration"—inner, psychological time as opposed to "clock time"— is most closely associated with the philosopher Henri Bergson, whose work Jung knew and with which his own has much in common.)

Western man, Jung saw, always wants to *do* something, to "get somewhere"; this kind of restlessness is characteristic of us all. A few years later, when Jung met the Pueblo chief Ochwiay Biano during his trip to Taos, he told Jung that the whites were always dissatisfied, and that this led to their cruelty. The kind of consciousness Jung encountered in North Africa was content with what *is*. At an oasis, Jung felt that "everything here was exactly the way it should be and the way it had always been."[28] Westerners usually feel this only after a few drinks or under the influence of drugs, hence their popularity. We find it inordinately difficult to relax, but what Jung found in North Africa was a consciousness that allowed the ego to *slow down* and sink into the warm embrace of the unconscious, as if after perpetually treading water, we suddenly discovered we could float. Yet, although Jung soaked up this temporal holiday, he knew that reverting to this "twilight consciousness" was no answer. The Africans he met seemed to lack an ego, and to be moved by impulse and emotion alone. They lacked the ability to reflect on their experience, to intend something, to will, to act *independently*. They lived and worked as a group, prompted by ritual, beating drums, and shouting. Western man paid heavily for his independence—the coin was alienation from the unconscious—but Jung knew it was indispensable. Yet the attraction to what Jung called "archaic man" remained and would become a central theme in his work.[29]

Count Hermann Keyserling came from an aristocratic Russian Baltic family. Before losing his fortune in the Bolshevik Revolution, Keyserling traveled around the world and wrote a book about his adventures, *The Travel Diary of a Philosopher*; it became a surprise bestseller. Keyserling had a deep interest in Eastern thought, and in 1920 he founded his School of Wisdom in Darmstadt, Germany, in order to synthesize the knowledge of East and West. A friend of Keyserling's attended one of Jung's seminars and suggested that Jung should lecture at the school. In 1922 he did and became a familiar figure there.

Keyserling's school became a meeting place for scholars and intellectuals dissatisfied with mainstream academia. Jung was branching out from his specialized area and entering broader streams of cultural and philosophical thought, a shift he began with his plunge into mythology, and someone he met at Darmstadt, became a close friend. The sinologist Richard Wilhelm had lectured on the *I Ching* and Chinese philosophy at the School of Wisdom, and Jung, who had been working with the oracle, was impressed by his insights. In 1923 Wilhelm lectured on the *I Ching* at the Psychological Club; Jung says that within two years a forecast Wilhelm made based on the oracle "was fulfilled to the letter and with unmistakable clearness."[30] Jung had already had some success using the *I Ching* with his patients. One man with a strong mother complex wanted to marry, but was unsure whether the woman was suitable. Concerned his patient would find himself under the thumb of another dominant woman, Jung asked the oracle. The reply was the hexagram Kou, "Coming to Meet." "The maiden is powerful," the *I Ching* said. "One should not marry such a maiden." One assumes Jung's patient didn't.[31]

Meeting Wilhelm produced its own synchronicity. In 1928, Jung painted a mandala featuring a golden castle, which struck him as Chinese, although he hadn't intended that. Soon after Wilhelm sent him the manuscript of *The Secret of the Golden Flower*, his translation of an ancient Taoist alchemical text, and asked Jung to write a commentary on it. Wilhelm's letter, Jung said, "broke through my isolation," and the text confirmed his ideas about the Self and mandalas, and triggered his insight into alchemy, which became the dominant theme of his later work. Jung's commentary is an extended application of his own ideas to Taoist thought— whether this does justice to Taoism or not is another matter, a consideration that applies to his remarks on Zen and Tibetan Buddhism as well[32]—and contains examples of the transcendent function and the clearest instructions on doing active imagination Jung ever wrote, although he again fails to use the term. Jung speaks of patients "outgrowing" problems that had destroyed others and achieving "a new level of consciousness." "Some higher or wider interest arose on the person's horizon, and through this widening of his view the insoluble problem lost its urgency." "What, on a lower level, had led to the wildest conflicts and panicky outbursts of emotion, viewed from the higher level of the personality, now seemed like a storm in the valley seen from a high mountain-top,"[33] which seems rather like Jung's experience during his crisis. Jung speaks of patients growing beyond themselves because of "unknown potentialities," and that this development was normal, the lack of it pathological—which suggests that many of us are abnormal. "Everyone must possess that higher level . . . and in favourable circumstances must be able to develop this possibility."[34]

What exactly those circumstances are, however, isn't clear; Jung speaks of "obscure possibilities" and "fate." And after concise instructions on how to practice active imagination—which he identifies with the meditation described in the text—Jung again warns that this way is "not without danger." "Everything good is costly, and the development of the personality is one of the most costly of all things,"[35] he tells us, something Jung knew from experience.

Jung's own individuation seemed to involve increasing detachment from his home and family, and in 1923 he began building what would become his famous "Tower" on land he had purchased near the lake at Bollingen. Just before starting work on it, he dreamed that the Wild Huntsman had ordered a monstrous wolfhound to capture a soul, and the next morning Jung learned that his mother had passed away. Before his mother's death, Jung had dreamed that his father came to him asking for marital advice, apparently unaware of Jung's own difficulties. Thinking his father was preparing for his wife's arrival, Jung took the dream as a premonition of his mother's death, but also as evidence of his belief that the dead need us, that we know things they do not, something the Seven Sermons argued as well.[36] It was a point he would make in his 1925 seminars; Jung told his students that in grasping the meaning of the union of conscious and unconscious, "we become aware of the ancestral lives that have gone into the making of our own lives," and that through this comes a "feeling of immortality." Individuation, in fact, leads to a "sense of the continuation of one's life through the ages" and gives "a feeling of eternity on this earth,"[37] a mystic insight Jung reserved for the initiated.

With his mother dead, Jung's last immediate tie to his past was gone, and Jung concentrated on realizing his self. The Tower, which Jung developed and expanded over the next thirty years, became a kind of mandala in stone, but also a kind of home for his ancestors; Jung believed that by building it, he was providing a resting place for their souls. When he showed his eldest daughter the spot, she was surprised and told him it was a place of the dead. Four years later, in 1927, while building an annex, Jung discovered the skeleton of a French soldier, killed in 1799; he took his daughter's remark as a sign she had inherited the Preiswerk blood.

It was a primitive place, and fed Jung's need to be close to the "archaic," a taste for which he developed in Africa. Jung's first instinct was to build a roundhouse, like an African hut; this later proved impractical and over the years the Tower grew and acquired more modern conveniences. At the start, however, it was absolutely basic. Jung learned to cut stone in a quarry and did most of the building work himself. Originally the Tower lacked electricity and running water. It was lit by candles and heated by a hearth, the stone floors had no carpets, and of course there was no telephone. In winter the front door froze over. Jung enjoyed the privileges of wealth but he also had a taste for simplicity, even the ascetic. He washed his own clothes in a tub by the lake and scrubbed himself down with a hard brush each morning. Toni Wolff, his only regular guest, was unused to this harsh regimen and resented having to chop wood and fetch and filter water from the lake; eventually Jung employed a water diviner who located a usable source for a well. Jung always needed solitude, and in the Tower he got it; in later years, to be invited to it was a honor. Barbara Hannah describes a visit in 1929.[38] She found Jung dressed in an Oriental robe, looking like an "old alchemist," and felt she had been transported back to the Middle Ages. Another guest described Jung throwing scraps to his dogs, as if he was a gothic lord; Jung's table manners in general were apparently barbaric and upset everyone around him, especially his family.

On Hannah's visit, Jung cooked some complicated stew in an enormous pot; he was a fanatical cook and didn't believe in conversation during a meal (a trait he inherited from his mother) and dinner was accompanied by large helpings of wine. Hannah didn't say a word and neither did Jung until he noticed how attentive she was to the food. "Oh, well," he told her, "you already know how to enjoy your food, that is *one* thing I shall not have to teach you." This is something a guru would say and increasingly people came to Jung in order to learn how to *live*, and not necessarily for a clinical neurosis. Jung famously said that about a third of his cases weren't suffering from some clinically definable illness, but from a sense of meaninglessness and aimlessness. Jung believed he could help them find some meaning. It had been his own quest, and understandably he felt he could help others in theirs. In a way, one could say Jung built his Tower so he would have a safe space for himself and some selected others to go crazy, without having to deal with the incomprehension of outsiders.

Most people who visited the Tower certainly felt it had an unusual atmosphere. Jung had some strange relationship with his pots and utensils; he spoke with them, believing they had souls, and required his guests to as well, and he insisted that the stove in his Küsnacht study was human.[39] He also felt the same about a bronze box that stored his tobacco, and even named it Habbakuk.[40] It isn't surprising to read that at the Tower Jung could immerse himself deeply in active imagination, often sitting for long periods in utter stillness, in a room set apart for this, where he painted his fantasies on the wall. He would see images and faces in stone and then slowly carve them; one stone in particular, a huge "perfect cube" Jung received from a quarry by mistake, became a favorite, and over the years Jung worked on it, carving on its surface alchemical, Greek, and Latin sayings.[41]

Yet the solitude Jung found at his Tower seemed not to settle the restlessness that characterized him in the 1920s and Jung was soon off on another journey, this time to New Mexico. In early 1925, using the excuse of a lecture tour, Jung traveled to the American Southwest with Fowler McCormick and a rich businessman, George Porter. Porter, like Medill McCormick, was another troubled soul, and in 1927 he blew his brains out, leaving Jung $20,000.

Jung was awed by the Grand Canyon, but the high point of the trip was a visit to the Pueblo Indians in Taos. Oddly, the novelist D. H. Lawrence, another student of the unconscious, was living there at the time, and apparently Jung had the same Indian guide as Lawrence. (It's probably beneficial they didn't meet; Jung considered Lawrence a Freudian who never outgrew his obsession with his mother.[42]) Here, as mentioned, Jung met Ochwiay Biano. Again Jung wanted to make contact with "archaic man" and he asked the Pueblo chief why he thought the whites were mad. Ochwiay told him it was because they think with their heads, while the Indians think with their hearts, a remark the esoteric Egyptologist René Schwaller de Lubicz would have appreciated.[43] Ochwiay's remark led Jung to a searing vision of Roman and Christian supremacy, bringing fear and suffering to their victims with "fire, sword, torture, and Christianity." Western civilization, Jung saw, had the "face of a bird of prey seeking with cruel intentness for distant quarry," a mea culpa regarding indigenous people well in advance of our own fashionable political correctness. One form of "thinking with the heart" impressed Jung deeply. The Pueblos performed a ritual that they insisted helped the sun in its daily course across the heavens. Jung, of course, knew that the sun was an average-sized star and that the earth moved around it, but in their hearts the Indians knew it was a god—*the* god—and that without their participation it would stop rising and then "it would be night forever."

It was this kind of connection to the world that modern consciousness lacked. For all the advances the West enjoyed, Jung saw that the Pueblos had a deeper, more fulfilling sense of themselves in the world; for them the world still had a soul, something which modern man had lost. Jung's love of the archaic and primitive and his own way of life at his Tower was a way of reconnecting the inner world with the outer, of re-establishing a participation between the two that the West had allowed to dwindle.

Jung's quest for the archaic led him to leave Europe again, only months after returning from America. In late 1925, on a second, more extensive trip to Africa, this time to Kenya and Uganda, Jung was again immersed in the timeless consciousness he experienced in Tunis. He began to feel as if he had lived there in a past life. On a train, riding into the dawn, Jung saw a tall figure standing on a cliff, leaning on his spear. It was a *déjà vu*, and Jung felt he had always known this primeval world, and that this dark-skinned man had been waiting for him for ages; curiously, the only other time he felt similarly was at the Burghölzli, when, with Bleuler, he witnessed paranormal phenomena. It seemed it was something he had known for centuries, a taste, again, of the collective unconscious. On this second trip, Jung had something like a mystical or metaphysical experience. He suddenly understood the *meaning* of self-consciousness, in an otherwise apparently oblivious universe. It was through our awareness of existence, Jung understood, that it gains meaning. On a game preserve on the Athai Plains, Jung saw huge herds of animals: antelopes, zebras, gazelles stretched endlessly to the horizon. He felt he witnessed "the stillness of the eternal beginning, the world as it had always been, in the state of non-being; for until then no one had been present to know that it was this world." Jung separated from his companions until they were out of sight and imagined he was utterly alone. He was trying to re-create the first moment of self-consciousness, when consciousness first recognized the distinction between itself and the world, when it could first regard the world *objectively*, detached from it, as an observer. "In an invisible act of creation," man had "put the stamp of perfection on the world by giving it objective existence."

It's a profound insight. Prior to the first human consciousness separating from the great surround and becoming aware that it *was aware*, all of creation was unknown. This is a peculiarly human ability; no animal can lift itself out of immediacy and regard the world as an *object. This* is the real act of creation; prior to it *no world existed*, regardless of any Big Bang or Genesis. For countless ages, the universe and everything in it might just as well not have existed, for there was no consciousness to recognize that it did. It was only with the rise of self-consciousness that anything like a "world" came into being. This puts a huge responsibility on consciousness; it was a creator of worlds.[44]

Yet a simple "archaic revival" wasn't an unalloyed benefit. One evening toward the end of their trip, Jung and his companions—who
by now included an Englishwoman, Ruth Bailey, who Jung met
while traveling and who became a lifelong friend—encountered a
local chief who demanded his tribe perform a dance in their honor.
Jung was enthusiastic, although he had heard reports of violence
in the area and the appearance of the chief's warriors wasn't reas-
suring. That evening sixty men appeared at Jung's camp, carrying
swords, clubs, and spears. Their women and children formed a circle around a fire. Jung noticed that his own Africans had fled, and
as the drumming began, Jung good-naturedly joined in—there
was a Dionysian side to Jung that enjoyed this kind of revelry.
But it soon seemed to be getting out of hand, and as the warriors
seemed more and more worked up, and brandished their weapons with greater ferocity, Jung asked the chief if it wasn't time to
stop. The chief refused and urged his dancers on, and Jung feared
how the proceedings would end; they were only a few whites with
a rifle or two between them and little ammunition. Fearing the
dance would turn into something more dangerous, Jung grabbed
his rhinoceros whip and cracked it loudly, laughing and shouting
obscenities in his *Schweizedeutsch,* then made gestures that it was
time to sleep. Jung had no idea how the tribe would react, but he
trusted his instinct and his own sheer strength of personality and
tried to outdo his company in wildness. The bluff paid off. The
chief laughed at the crazy white man and agreed it was time to
leave, too. Jung and the others relaxed and no doubt felt that on
this occasion, it was a good idea not to go native.[45]

But Jung still needed to find some connection to the past, and
strangely enough he would find it in Europe.

7. THE SHADOW KNOWS

By the 1930s, Jung was in his late fifties. He had established himself as one of the leaders of modern psychology, had published many books, had received many honors, and had passed through a tremendous personal crisis following the split with Freud. Through his patients, students, and the Psychology Club, his ideas were spreading, and if they weren't always understood, Jung's name was at least as familiar as Freud's. His personal life, too, had reached a workable if uncomfortable balance between his responsibilities as a husband and father and his need for a muse, and Jung enjoyed liberties and privileges not given to everyone: a mistress, a "fortress of solitude," frequent travel, a beautiful home, no financial worries. Yet something was missing, and Jung felt the need to ground his work in something more than his own discoveries. He wanted to anchor his psychology in history. Given that it was based on the idea that the collective unconscious and its archetypes were a kind of inherited repository of human experience, this idea made perfect sense. "Without history there can be no psychology, and certainly no psychology of the unconscious," he wrote.[1] But Jung also wanted to find some evidence that the kind of experience he had gone through had happened before, that the process of individuation had been known to others and wasn't peculiar to him. If indeed he had discovered some law of psychic growth that applied to everyone, there should be incidences of it in the past. The terminology would be different, of course, the images and symbols, too; but in the basic outline the similarity should be apparent.

Jung first thought he had found his antecedent in Gnosticism, and between 1918 and 1926 he studied the existing literature on the Gnostics. Jung had, in fact, begun his study of Gnosticism earlier, in 1912; he even wrote to Freud that the Gnostic Sophia contained an ancient wisdom that might come to light again in psychoanalysis, a remark that no doubt worried the master.[2] Jung had already become acquainted with Gnosticism through the work of G. R. S. Mead, who Jung knew and met on more than one occasion; Jung even traveled to London once to thank Mead personally for his translation of the Gnostic text known as the *Pistis Sophia*.[3] Most of the literature contemporary with the Gnostics, however, was written by the church fathers who were their sworn enemies, and so was less than unbiased. It wasn't until 1945 and the discovery of the Nag Hammadi Library in Upper Egypt that a substantial number of Gnostic texts were made available and researchers could read what the Gnostics had to say themselves.[4] Jung's link to Gnosticism was so significant that one of the Gnostic scrolls making up the library was purchased by the Jung Foundation in 1952 and named the "Jung Codex" in honor of the man many saw as a modern Gnostic.

Although Jung repeatedly disclaimed being anything of the sort (much as he disclaimed being a mystic or occultist, although he did tell Barbara Hannah that he felt the Gnostics were "friends"[5]) and some of his later interpreters have gone out of their way to agree,[6] others have seen Jung as reinterpreting Gnosticism for the modern world.[7] Not surprisingly the tag of modern Gnostic has led to some criticism, and the "official" scholars tend to see Jung and other "outsiders" as mystical poachers on their hunting grounds.[8] There are striking similarities between some elements of analytical psychology and Gnosticism, but in a broad immediate sense, Jung's Gnosticism is clear in the attitude he took toward the Judeo-Christian God. This was perhaps most apparent in his late, controversial work *Answer to Job* (1952), in which he takes the vengeful, vindictive God of the Old Testament to task over the question of evil. It is, in effect, an examination of God's "shadow" and comes to the remarkable conclusion that God himself is the source of evil and in that sense isn't omnipotent, all loving, or all good. He is capable of mistakes and, as Meister Eckhart said centuries earlier, needs man to complete Him.

The Gnostics had said that Jehovah wasn't the "true" god, but a kind of idiot demi-urge, or half-god (the phrase is Plato's) who out of either ignorance or hubris claimed to be the one true deity. The true God exists beyond creation, and we are separated from him by the powerful Archons, agents of the false god who deter us from union with the transcendental deity (Abraxas, incidentally, is one of the Archons and was discussed by Basilides of Alexandria). We do, however, contain in ourselves a spark of the original God, and union with the true deity can be achieved through gnosis, direct, immediate experience of spiritual reality. If you read "spiritual reality" as the unconscious and "gnosis" as active imagination—with which the meditative practices of the Gnostics have similarities—and the ignorant ego as a kind of "demi-urge" and the Archons as "complexes," then Jung's psychology can be seen as a modern form of Gnosticism. Jung, we recall, rejected the faith and belief of his father in favor of experience, and in his last years Jung made one of the most public Gnostic statements of all, during an interview for the BBC television program *Face to Face* in 1959. Asked by the presenter John Freeman if he believed in God, Jung replied "Believe? Hard to say. I *know*." You don't get more Gnostic than that.

In the end, however, Jung felt that the Gnostics were too distant in time from modern man for him to make a real connection with them, which is ironic, given the wide dissemination today of a kind of "popular Gnosticism" through the novels of Philip K. Dick and Thomas Pynchon and films such as *The Matrix* trilogy, *The Truman Show,* and *Dark City*, with their shared theme of a "false reality."9 It was, as we've seen, Richard Wilhelm who gave Jung the clue he needed. Jung had, of course, known about alchemy before; it was a theme he found in Goethe and he had read Herbert Silberer's fascinating *Probleme der Mystik und ihrer Symbolik* (*Problems of Mysticism and Its Symbols*, later published as *Hidden Symbolism of Alchemy and the Occult Arts*), which took a "constructive" view of alchemy. But, he said, he had forgotten Silberer's book by then. Yet once again Jung's dreams seemed to presage a major shift in his life. Once again Jung dreamed of a strange house and in one dream managed to enter it. Inside was a library, filled with works from the sixteenth and seventeenth centuries; the books contained strange images and symbols that Jung didn't recognize. In another dream, Jung found himself on the Italian front in WWI, driving in a wagon with a peasant. They passed over a bridge and through a tunnel and entered a beautiful sunlit landscape. Finally they entered the courtyard of an estate, and then suddenly, the gates closed, locking them inside. Then the peasant told him "Now we are caught in the seventeenth century." Resignedly, Jung accepted that he'd be there for some time.

He was. Jung spent the next several years studying alchemical works—the strange books he discovered in his dream library—and forging a link between alchemy and analytical psychology became the main effort of his last decades, culminating in his major late work *Mysterium Coniunctionis* (1955). After reading *The Secret of the Golden Flower*, Jung asked a rare bookseller in Munich to inform him when any alchemical works were available. Jung asked others for alchemical books as well, including the esoteric historian Manly P. Hall whose unique collection of alchemical works Jung drew on for his studies.[10] Jung was at first put off by the weird jargon and fantastic images crowding most alchemical texts, and anyone who has tried reading them wouldn't blame him. If alchemy means anything to most people, it's about turning lead into gold, an absurd practice that was pursued by many charlatans and mountebanks in the years before the rise of chemistry. That many people calling themselves alchemists did indeed ingratiate themselves with nobility—or wound up feeling their wrath—by promising to swell their coffers with miraculous gold is true, yet these "puffers," as they were called, were not true alchemists. Although the prejudice that it was all a lot of pre-scientific nonsense remains, anyone who takes the trouble to investigate it soon realizes that there was another side to alchemy and that this was its real character. Opinions differ on the details, but most serious students today recognize that alchemy was, and is, a spiritual pursuit, and that whether or not an actual outer physical transformation takes place during its operations, if these are carried out correctly, an inner spiritual one does. "*Aurum nostrum es non vulgi*" ("Our gold is not the vulgar gold"), Gerhard Dorn, one of Jung's favorite alchemists, said. The "gold" the true alchemists sought was inner transformation.

As Jung ploughed through his sixteenth- and seventeenth-century library, often putting aside a text as unreadable—one can imagine him reaching for Inspector Maigret instead—he gradually realized that this was what all the strangeness was about. Eventually Jung came to the conclusion that alchemy was about individuation, and today many books on Jungian therapy employ language one usually finds among alchemists; one example among many is Marie-Louise von Franz's *Alchemy: An Introduction to the Symbolism and the Psychology*.[11] Jung's investigations into alchemy led to massive tomes such as *Psychology and Alchemy* (1944) and *Mysterium Coniunctionis*, but in essence his take on it is summed up in an essay he wrote around the same time as "The Transcendent Function" and revised over the years, and which includes some of Jung's clearest remarks on the benefit of active imagination. In "The Relations Between the Ego and the Unconscious" Jung writes that "the secret of alchemy was in fact the transcendent function, the transformation of personality through the blending and fusion of the noble with the base components, of the differentiated with the inferior functions, of the conscious with the unconscious."[12]

This is Jung's favorite work: reconciliation of the opposites leading to some new, unknown development. In Jung it's the ego and the unconscious leading to the Self; in the alchemists it's the King and the Queen leading to alchemical gold. The alchemists, Jung concluded, were individuating—that is, practicing active imagination—but they didn't know it. Jung argued that during their complicated "operations," they unconsciously *projected* their inner images onto their materials, much as we see faces in a fireplace or camels in a cloud, and the whole procedure amounted to a version of Jung's own "confrontation with the unconscious."

Gerhard Dorn had told his fellow alchemists, "Transform your-self into living philosopher's stones." Clearly he didn't mean turn yourself into a lump of quartz. Along with gold, alchemists were in pursuit of the philosopher's stone, and Jung concluded that this was a name for what he called the Self.

Although more than anyone else Jung is responsible for mak-ing alchemy once again worthy of serious study, not everyone was happy with this interpretation. And not only other psychologists or historians of science, many of whom thought he was crazy, or so obsessed with his "discoveries" that he began to see corrobora-tion for them everywhere. Actual alchemists and students of eso-teric tradition thought he got it wrong. René Schwaller de Lubicz, who claimed to have cracked the secret of alchemical stained glass, thought little of Jung's ideas and maintained that there was a *real* physical transformation along with a spiritual one. Tradi-tionalist thinkers such as Titus Burckhardt and Julius Evola—whom Jung nevertheless quotes with approval in *Psychology and Alchemy*—also disagreed.[13] These and other students of alchemy complained that Jung simply "psychologized" alchemy and stripped it of its spiritual character, turning into something all-too-human. (A similar criticism later came from religious people who felt Jung had reduced God to an archetype.) The spiritual realities alchemy dealt with were *not* the same as the ego, the unconscious, the Self, etc. Even a psycho-spiritual alchemist who started out appreciating Jung's interpretation later admitted he was wrong. Israel Regardie, one-time student of Aleister Crowley and member of the Hermetic Order of the Golden Dawn, was at first a supporter of Jung's ideas, but then met a *real* alchemist who changed his mind. "It took no more than a few minutes," Regar-die writes, "to help me realize how presumptuous I had been to assert dogmatically that all alchemy was psycho-spiritual." "When Basil Valentine . . . [an alchemist of the early seventeenth century] says a coal fire, he was not referring to the inner fire or Kundalini. It is simply ridiculous to assume he is talking in symbols . . ."[14]

Having said this, to me at least there does seem to be a nice fit between the stages of the alchemical process and the trajectory of individuation. The alchemist starts with the *prima materia*, the basic matter—lead or some other ignoble stuff—and through a series of operations, transforms this into alchemical gold. Jung's *prima materia* is the un-individuated ego, beset by its neuroses, anxieties, and depressions. Like the *prima materia*, it goes through a dissolution, what the alchemists call the *nigredo*; for Jung this is the confrontation with the "shadow," one's "dark side." It would be too tedious to parallel the whole process—readers can find it in Marie-Louise von Franz's book mentioned earlier—but the outcome, if successful, in both alchemy and individuation is a union of opposites—the *coniunctionis* or transcendent function—leading to alchemical gold, the philosopher's stone, the elixir of life, or, in Jungian terms, the Self.

Yet while there do seem to be neat parallels, it's difficult to accept Jung's contention that the thousands of alchemists working over the centuries were all somewhat deluded about what they were doing, and that while they were practicing their art they were really "projecting" unconscious imagery onto their furnaces and retorts. If all they were doing was "projecting"—unconsciously locating unconscious material in the outer world, something, Jung said, we tend to do with our "shadow"—why were they trying to "make gold" in the first place? One doesn't need a fire and an alembic to see images; Leonardo da Vinci famously saw them in peeling paint on an old wall. Or if you need a fire, the one in your fireplace will do. No doubt the unconscious had something to do with the weird imagery that fills the alchemical landscape; but the alchemists seemed to have been speaking in allegory, and interpreting their images as one would a dream may not be the best way to approach them.

Which isn't to say that Jung's psychological approach to alchemy is valueless. Using the alchemical schema to give you some sense of what you're doing in analysis seems to work—and again, for Jung, if it works, it's real. As in the case with Taoism—in *The Secret of the Golden Flower*—Jung's interpretation may not be historically accurate but it is effective. Yet it's difficult to argue with people who feel that in this case, and in others—the archetypes are a good example—Jung takes the stencil of his psychology and places it over some past practice and says "Aha! There's evidence for my theory!" It would become a criticism Jung would have to face more and more.

Alchemy wasn't the only way Jung made contact with history in the 1930s. As early as 1918, in an important essay, "The Role of the Unconscious," written for a Swiss cultural magazine, in which he spells out the function of the collective unconscious, Jung presciently warned about the "blond beast," Germany, "prowling about in its underground prison, ready to burst out with devastating consequences."[15] By the 1930s, that "blond beast"— Nietzsche's phrase—had acquired a name, National Socialism, and its mouthpiece was one failed Austrian artist turned demagogue, Adolf Hitler. The "blond beast" was the result of Christianity's influence on the Teutonic psyche. By successfully splitting "the Germanic barbarian into an upper and lower half,"[16] Jung argued, Christianity had managed to civilize one side of the German people. But this left the other half, rooted in the collective unconscious, untouched, and the volcanic energies of the ancient Germans were repressed, creating a "dark side," not unlike the kind associated with Darth Vader (fans of the *Star Wars* films with a knowledge of Jung can detect the influence fairly easily). As Christianity's authority declined—as it had for the last few centuries—the beast grew more bold. And just as in the individual, repressed unconscious material can suddenly explode, so too in society. As he would argue in a later essay, assessing the origins of Nazism, for Jung, the phenomenon of National Socialism was the result of the ancient archetype of the Teutonic god Wotan bursting out of its psychic prison and taking over an entire people.[17]

Although warnings about the coming catastrophe in Germany could be found scattered in other of Jung's writings before the 1930s, this essay stood out—but not only because of its prophecy of what would become only too real twenty years later. It's a shame that while making some of his clearest statements about the collective unconscious, Jung also included remarks about racial differences that continue to haunt his reputation. Jung is at pains to establish that the collective unconscious is not the same as the Freudian personal unconscious, with its collection of "family quarrels" and "unhappy love affairs."[18] Instead it is "suprapersonal" and "comes alive in the creative man," revealing itself in "the vision of the artist, in the inspiration of the thinker" and the "inner experience of the mystic," working as "an all-pervading, omnipresent omniscient spirit."[19] Taking a potshot at Theosophy and Rudolf Steiner's Anthroposophy, Jung argues that the collective unconscious is the source of precisely "the same phenomena which the theosophical and Gnostic sects made accessible to the simple-minded in the forms of portentous mysteries"[20] and complains that these groups appropriate the term "unconscious" because they are "fond of scientific terms in order to dress their speculations in a 'scientific' guise."[21] (Untrue in Steiner's case as he makes little use of the idea of the "unconscious.") Yet while setting himself apart from these "non-scientific" dilettantes, Jung himself makes statements that his fellow "scientists" would only find mystical. Regardless of how civilized and modern we consider ourselves, Jung argues, we are "influenced in just as uncanny a fashion as the primitive" by the eruptions of the unconscious; the only difference is that the primitive speaks of "witchcraft and spirits," a theory Jung finds "very interesting and very sensible—actually more sensible than the academic view of modern sciences."[22]

Yet for a reader today, and for those in Germany in the 1930s, what stands out from Jung's essay are his remarks about the Jews. The danger of a "blond beast" doesn't arise with the Jew, Jung says, because he has a culture going back to antiquity, as well as the culture of the land he has adopted; he is the recipient of two cultures and hence is more "domesticated" (civilized) than the German, who acquired Christian culture only relatively recently. And having been a wanderer in different lands for many generations, the Jew lacks the roots in the earth that the German feels strongly; in fact this "chthonic quality is found in a dangerous concentration in the Germanic people."[23] To compensate for not living "wholly in the body," the Jew reduces everything to its "material beginnings" in order to "counterbalance" his excess of culture. He can, though, benefit from a bit of "primitivity"; hence the virtue of Freud's and Adler's "reduction of everything psychic to primitive sexual wishes and power drives."[24] These approaches, however, don't work with the German who has a "genuine barbarian" within him whose manifestation "is no comfort to us" and who takes things seriously "in the most unpleasant way." [25] The one-sided emphasis on goodness and morality that on the surface tamed the German barbarian has led to ominous rumblings below; and as the psyche always compensates for an imbalance, it is only a matter of time, Jung argues, before the beast is unleashed.

Some of Jung's remarks about Freud's and Adler's psychologies being beneficial solely to Jews—who can benefit by their "primitivity"—may have been prompted by Freud's attack on Jung in his history of the psychoanalytical movement published in the yearbook four years earlier. And however repellent it seems to us today, the "Jewish question"—like the "woman question"—was a hotly debated topic at the time; Rudolf Steiner, for example, wrote on it.[26] And we have to remember that when Jung made these remarks, Hitler was still a corporal in the 16th Bavarian Reserve Regiment, and that Jung is by no means celebrating the German "barbarian." Indeed, he hoped that WWI would alert Europe to the danger of the "blond beast"; sadly, it didn't. Yet it isn't difficult to see that Jung's remarks about Jews, as well as others about the "mystery" of "the soil,"[27] would be welcome to people eager to make clear distinctions between Aryans and Jews. Ironically, the people who took Jung's remarks most seriously were those within whom the "blond beast" was most ready to pounce. The fact that Jung had unwittingly helped corroborate Nazi accusations that psychoanalysis was a "Jewish science" and confirmed their belief that the Jews were parasites attracted charges of anti-Semitism and Nazi fellow traveling that are still heard today.

B y the 1930s, Jung's prestige in Germany had grown; prior to this, most of the professional recognition he received came from the United States and England. While this was gratifying, Germany was considered the scholarly nation par excellence, and Jung appreciated the attention. Jung's growing German fame was the result of two rather different sources. In 1930 Jung was elected vice president of the International General Medical Society for Psychotherapy, an organization based in Berlin that he joined in 1928. As he was in the psychoanalytic movement, Jung was a tireless promoter of the society's activities. The International Society arose in response to other well-established societies, such as the German Psychoanalytical Society and the Berlin Psychoanalytic Institute, both largely Freudian. The idea was to create a dialogue between followers of different schools. Many prominent psychologists joined—Karen Horney, Wilhelm Reich, and Georg Groddeck, for example—and its membership include practitioners from a wide ethnic and religious range. But one member would soon prove troublesome to Jung: Matthias Heinrich Göring, cousin of the soon-to-be infamous *Reichsmarschall* Hermann Göring, Hitler's second in command.

By 1933, Hitler was in power and all German professional societies were required to become *gleichgeschaltet*, "conformed" to Nazi ideology. As the International Society was based in Berlin, the Nazis were able to pressure its president, Ernst Kretschmer. Kretschmer, however, detested the Nazis, and refused to cooperate. Kretschmer was forced to resign and he urged Jung, who as vice president would automatically succeed him, to accept the presidency in order to prevent the society from becoming totally Nazified.[28]

Jung could be expected to resist Nazi demands to some extent for two reasons. In the first place he was Swiss, not German—which didn't prevent him developing a large German following through his work for the International Society. And secondly, by this time, he was seen by German psychologists as the answer to Freud.

In the years leading up to Hitler, many *völkisch* groups appeared in Germany; the English equivalent "folk" doesn't quite convey the blend of mythology, folklore, legend, and nationalism that the German term suggests. Jung's emphasis on history and myth, as well as his rejection of scientific materialism, made these groups sympathetic to his work, as opposed to Freud's which, along with being Jewish, was reductionist. Although much has been made of it,[29] Jung's own connection, if any,[30] to the *völkisch* movement is unclear. The only strong link is his friendship with the German indologist J. W. Hauer, who founded the German Faith Movement in 1932, a religious society aimed at replacing Christianity in German-speaking countries with an anti-Christian and anti-Semitic modern paganism based on German literature and Hindu scripture. Hauer, an ardent Nazi, hoped his movement would become the official religion of the *Reich*. Hitler, however, thought little of Hauer and laughed at his followers who "made asses of themselves by worshipping Wotan and Odin and the ancient, but now obsolete, German mythology,"[31] a remark that says much about Hitler's cynicism toward the *völkisch* ideology he neverthe-less exploited to gain power.

By 1936, Hauer's movement was banned. But before this he had developed a following both among those of a *völkisch* sensibility and those with a broader interest in myth or spirituality. Jung met Hauer at Count Keyserling's School of Wisdom in the late 1920s, where they discussed their common interest in yoga—although Jung disparaged Westerners adopting Eastern disciplines, he himself practice yoga regularly—and in 1930 Jung attended Hauer's lecture on yoga at a conference of the International Society in Baden-Baden. In 1931 Hauer lectured on yoga at the Psychological Club, and Jung was so inspired by this that in 1932 he broke off his own seminars on the active imagination visions of an American artist, Christiana Morgan (the "Visions Seminar"), in order for the Hindu scholar Heinrich Zimmer to lecture; later that year, Hauer and Jung gave joint talks on Kundalini yoga.

Yet even then their interests and lives were moving in different directions. As Hauer promoted his anti-Semitic neo-paganism with some success among some members of the Psychological Club, he nevertheless became increasingly marginalized in Jungian circles. In 1933 the Dutch socialite Olga Fröbe-Kapteyn began the famous Eranos conferences at her Casa Gabriella in Ascona, near the site of Monte Verità (see Chapter Three). *Eranos* is Greek for "banquet" or a "gathering" in which each guest contributes something; "potluck" might be a less formal translation. Fröbe-Kapteyn had originally planned for the auditorium she had built to be used by the Theosophist Alice Bailey, but Bailey declined, suggesting that the area was associated with black magic. When Fröbe-Kapteyn met Jung at Keyserling's School of Wisdom, he suggested the auditorium be used as a meeting place between East and West. Fröbe-Kapteyn agreed and in 1933 the yearly conferences began, with Jung lecturing on individuation. Over the years, scholars and thinkers such as Gershom Scholem, Mircea Eliade, Jean Gebser, Heinrich Zimmer, Karl Kerényi, Erich

Neumann, Joseph Campbell, and many others contributed to the gatherings, which continue today.[32] In 1934 Hauer spoke at Eranos on Indo-Aryan mysticism. Political discussion was banned, but at one point Hauer harangued the audience with a speech glorifying Nazism; Martin Buber, who was also speaking, turned the subject to Meister Eckhart, and Hauer was barred from further conferences, his name crossed off the founders list.[33] When he gave a similar speech at the Psychological Club, he was banned from there as well.[34] By this time Jung's books were banned in Germany and his name put on the Nazi hit list.[35]

In 1933 a German branch of the International Society was founded with Matthias Göring as president; needless to say it was *gleichgeschaltet* and Göring ensured that the rest of the society followed suit. Jung countered Göring by redrafting the society's rules, allowing Jewish members who had been forced to resign from the German branch to join as individuals. As editor of the society's journal, Jung made sure that work by Jewish members continued to be published, and that work by Jewish psychologists was reviewed. But as the journal was published in Germany, Jung had little hands-on control, and was enraged when Göring inserted a pro-Nazi statement in an issue in 1933, endorsing *Mein Kampf* as a core text for all psychotherapists and obliging all members to declare their loyalty to the Fuehrer. The statement was supposed to be included in only the German edition of the journal, but Göring overstepped Jung—something he did more than once—and Jung was furious to find his name among the statement's endorsers.

Earlier attempts to resign had been blocked by Göring, who wanted to make as much use of Jung as possible, and "English and Dutch representatives" also begged him to stay on,[36] but in 1939

Jung finally left the International Society and the journal. But that he accepted the position at all and remained as long as he did has been taken as evidence that he didn't want to get in the Nazis' bad books too early in the game. Jung, his critics say, was hedging his bets, and didn't want to be on the losing side. But Jung did speak out against Hitler some years before he left the society. In 1936 he condemned the Fuehrer as a "raving berserker" and a man "possessed" who had set Germany on its "course toward perdition."[37] And a year earlier, in his lecture series at London's Tavistock Clinic, Jung broke off his remarks to refer to his prophecy of 1918. "I saw it coming," he told his fellow psychologists, "I said in 1918 that the 'blond beast' is stirring in its sleep and that something will happen in Germany. No psychologist then understood at all what I meant . . ." Commenting on the power of the archetypes to overrun conscious decision, Jung called them "the great decisive forces."[38] They "get you below the belt and not in your mind, your brain just counts for nothing, your sympathetic system is gripped."[39] Remarks like these led to accusations that Jung gave people a way of avoiding responsibility for their actions: *they* didn't decide to become Nazis, the archetypes "made them do it." Yet they are remarkably similar to what the philosopher Jean Gebser, who had firsthand experience of Nazism, believed was at work: the "magical structure of consciousness," which Gebser characterized as a "vegetative intertwining of all living things," and which requires a "sacrifice of consciousness" and "occurs in the state of trance, or when consciousness dissolves as a result of mass reactions, slogans, or 'isms.'" Curiously, Gebser believed the "magical structure" was also responsible for synchronicities,[40] and in an interview in 1938, Jung himself said that "Hitler's power is not political; it is *magic*."[41]

But like many at the time, Jung initially believed that something good might come from the Nazi movement. After all, Germany had gone through more than a decade of national defeat, revolution, and an economic depression that makes our "credit crunch" look like a picnic, and Hitler seemed to offer strong leadership and a new beginning. In the 1918 essay where he speaks of the "blond beast," Jung remarked that the unconscious contains "all those forces which mere reasonableness, propriety, and the orderly course of bourgeois existence could never call awake; all the creative forces which lead man onward to new developments, new forms, and new goals," and he reportedly spoke of the Nazis as a "chaotic precondition for the birth of a new world,"[42] a gloss on Nietzsche's aphorism that "One must have chaos within oneself to give birth to a dancing star." Others have argued that Jung's medical training led him to take a "wait and see" approach, to not diagnose the condition too early, and that this is behind his apparent reluctance to damn the Nazis outright. Jung knew from experience that a crisis often precedes a cure.[43]

Yet whether out of hubris or naïveté, while criticizing the Nazis, Jung also allowed himself to be used by them. One of the most apparently damning pieces of evidence against Jung was an interview with him by Adolph von Weizsäcker, a former pupil, broadcast on Berlin Radio in 1933, soon after Jung accepted presidency of the International Society, and not long after the Nazis had secured power. Critics pounce on it as proof that Jung was at least a Nazi fellow traveler, and it is true that some of Jung's remarks pierce the cringe barrier, especially given his audience. Yet many who castigate Jung for this are highly selective in what they quote. Ronald Hayman, for example, who writes that "knowing what was required, Jung provided it," because, with Freud deposed, he "could become the leading depth-psychologist if he managed not to antagonise Germany's new rulers," omits to include any of Jung's remarks cautioning about the rise of Nazism.[44] When Weizsäcker asked what psychology's task was "in such a time of activity," Jung replied that "It is just because we live in an active and responsible time that we need more consciousness and self-reflection," otherwise we will be "unconsciously swept along by events." "Mass movements," Jung told his Nazi interviewer, "have the peculiarity of overpowering the individual by mass suggestion and making him unconscious. The political or social movement gains nothing by this when it has swarms of hypnotized camp followers." And when Weizsäcker remarked that "in Germany today psychology is suspect . . . precisely because it is concerned with the self-development of the so-called individual," and asked how "when the collective forces of the whole community have taken the lead in moulding our way of life, are we to assess the efforts of psychology," Jung replied that "the self-development of the individual is especially necessary in our time" and "only the self-development of the individual, which I consider to be the supreme goal of all psychological endeavour, can produce consciously responsible spokesmen and leaders."[45] Nazism, as is well known, had no use for individuals, and Jung's emphasis on the importance of individuals and their self-development was an outright attack on Nazi ideology. Most critics of Jung, however, fail to point this out.

Yet it has to be said that several of Jung's remarks at the time can easily be read as supporting Nazi ideas. In 1934, for example, Jung remarked that the Jews seem "never to have created a cultural form of their own," and needed a "host nation" in order to prosper.[46] He also spoke of the "old" Jewish psyche and the "young" German one, remarking that the "Aryan unconscious has a greater potential than the Jewish," a result of a "youthfulness that is not yet fully estranged from barbarism." Notwithstanding that these comments were made in the context of others about the "Eastern" and "Western" psyches and in the spirit of "objective" and "scientific" research and were not intended as criticisms of the Jews—and that Jews such as the philosophers Ludwig Wittgenstein and Otto Weininger had made similar statements themselves[47]—for Jung to make them at the time was at best insensitive, given that they could provide ammunition to Nazi racial hacks. Jung may have wanted to criticize psychoanalysis' "one size fits all" approach to the unconscious, but it didn't take hindsight to know it was not the best time to air these views.

Jung's personal attitude toward Jews is also frequently cited as evidence of his anti-Semitism, a bias his critics root in his jealousy of Freud.[48] Yet Jung made personal efforts to help many Jews, and counted Jews among his closest followers—Erich Neumann, Gerhard Adler, Jolande Jacobi, among others—and repeatedly voiced his respect for Freud.[49] But an atmosphere of ambiguity hangs around the affair, and although Jung did speak out against the accusations, denying he ever was a Nazi sympathizer or anti-Semitic, his clarifications never seem to have struck home, at least not with his critics, something his close friend and collaborator Jolande Jacobi remarked on. Counseling in 1946 against the publication of *Essays on Contemporary Events*, a collection of writings dealing with Nazism, Jacobi complained that "I do not quite understand . . . why you didn't proceed aggressively against Nazism when it was still hidden to the world what kind of devils were at work in it," and remarked that whatever subtleties his ideas about race may contain, his audience would not be in a position to appreciate them.[50] Jung did try to answer Jacobi's concerns, but in an interview given in 1949 for the *Bulletin of the Analytical Psychology Club of New York*, a privately published mimeographed newsletter, which, we can assume, didn't reach many readers. Responding to renewed accusations of Nazi sympathizing and anti-Semitism in the popular *Saturday Review of Literature*—the articles by Robert Hillyer were really about the poet Ezra Pound and Jung was dragged into them as a whipping boy—Jung explained that "it must be clear to anyone who has read any of my books that I have never been a Nazi sympathizer and I never have been anti-Semitic, and no amount of misquotation, mistranslation, or rearrangement of what I have written can alter the record of my true point of view." Jung explains how his remarks about Jews in 1934 were taken out of context, but admits that as the essay in which they appeared was to be printed in Germany, he had to write "in a somewhat veiled manner," in order for it to be clear that "an Aryan outside Germany stood for a scientific approach to psychotherapy," and not for its Nazification. And after explaining that his remarks are actually in many ways complementary about the Jews—which is clear to any unbiased reader—Jung explains how Göring and others "played double" with his name, putting it both on their "black list"—for remarks he made in support of Freud—and publicizing it "as a Swiss feather in their cap."

Yet Jung's most enlightening remarks about this dark time characterize his unenviable position. "It was impossible to fight the Nazi intolerance openly without endangering the position of all German doctors, and of German Jewish doctors in particular."[51] "One can say it was a foolish idealism which caused me to stand by, but it seemed unfair to all the people clinging to me to leave them in the lurch." He was not, he told his interviewer, "a rat which runs from a sinking ship," and so he stayed on until the outbreak of war and he was "of no further use."[52]

Jung's critics may not forgive him for what they see as his duplicity, but a letter from the eminent scholar of Jewish mysticism, Gershom Scholem, to Aniela Jaffé, shows that the people who counted could make amends with him. Scholem told the story of how, after the war, the Rabbi Leo Baeck, a survivor of the Theresienstadt concentration camp, who knew Jung from Count Keyserling's School of Wisdom, came to Zürich. Baeck had read Jung's remarks about Jews and about the possibility of something good coming out of Hitler and was dismayed; from what he knew of Jung, they made no sense; he would never think him anti-Semitic or pro-Nazi. Baeck avoided Jung and declined an invitation to Küsnacht, but Jung was determined to see him and one afternoon, Baeck found the psychologist at his hotel, where the two men had a lively and lengthy "confrontation," during which Jung explained his actions. In the midst of it Jung confessed that he had indeed "slipped up" when it came to his expectations about the Nazis. The phrase seems minimal for the context, but it satisfied Baeck. Scholem wrote that "they had cleared up everything that stood between them and were reconciled with each other once again." On the strength of that reconciliation, Scholem, who was undecided on going because of Jung's bad reputation, accepted his invitation to speak at the Eranos conference in 1947; Baeck also went to Casa Gabriella, and later stayed for two weeks at Küsnacht.

Jung would be the first to admit that he cast, if not a giant, at least a considerable shadow, and in his encounter with the Nazis, it may have come to the fore. Yet in recent years, new information about Jung's activities during the last years of WWII offers a different perspective on his relations with the Third Reich. As Deirdre Bair reveals, in 1942 Jung was involved in two aborted German plots to oust Hitler from power.[53] In the first he was asked by one of Hitler's physicians to go to Berchtesgaden, Hitler's Bavarian stronghold, to observe the Führer. A group of high-ranking officers were concerned about his increasingly erratic behavior and they wanted an impartial assessment, from a psychologist still respected in Germany. Although Jung had resigned from the International Society, the Nazis still made use of his ideas when it was convenient for them to do so. What Hitler's doctor didn't tell Jung was that the concerned officers wanted his assessment in order to convince other wavering officials and military personnel to join their plot to seize power and end a war they knew they would lose. If Jung concluded Hitler was cracking up, the officers would see it as their patriotic duty to take command and arrange an honorable surrender. Jung declined, giving ill health as an excuse, but his real reason was that he knew being a "respected" psychologist in Nazi Germany was no honor, and any visit there would only work against him. One wonders, though, what might have happened had Jung granted the request and declared Hitler incapacitated. In the second plot Jung was a more knowing conspirator.

Again in 1942, he was approached by Wilhelm Bitter, a German psychiatrist and analytical psychologist. Bitter knew Jung and had worked with him before the war, and had commiserated with him about the difficulties involved in dealing with the Nazi government and the detrimental influence it had on psychoanaly-sis in Germany. Bitter owned a summerhouse in Switzerland but hadn't visited it since the war began, being kept in Berlin by the Nazis. While working at the Berlin Psychoanalytic Institute, Bit-ter was approached by General Walter Schellenberg, later head of German Intelligence, and asked to use his Swiss contacts to discover what the outside world thought of Nazism. Schellenberg himself had come to the conclusion that National Socialism was a mistake, and Bitter agreed, and remarked that only an uncondi-tional surrender could save Germany from being overrun by the Soviets (both men, we should remember, were taking a consid-erable risk by being so frank). Bitter then found himself with a travel pass to Switzerland, ostensibly for health reasons, but with the secret assignment of making any Swiss contacts that could help secure a Nazi capitulation.

Schellenberg knew of Jung and when he heard that he had refused to diagnose Hitler, he asked another psychologist, Max de Crinis, whom Bitter had worked with and who had sent him on to study with Jung, to do it. The plan was to have Hitler declared incapable of command, and to declare an armistice on the West-ern Front. This would allow the Germany army to concentrate on defeating the Soviets. Winston Churchill, the British prime min-ister, had made it clear that he was as concerned about a Commu-nist Europe as he was about a Nazi one, and Schellenberg and the others believed their idea would appeal to him. Jung was pulled into the plot because of his comments about Russia in an inter-view he gave in 1938 to an American journalist, H. R. Knicker-bocker. A *gleichgeschaltet* version of the interview had been widely read in Germany, but in the uncensored original, Jung remarked that Hitler reminded him of some of his psychotic patients, who were so obsessed with their inner voices that they were deaf to anything else. The only way to save Western democracy, Jung said, was to turn Hitler's fantasies to the East. "Let him go to Russia, Jung said, "that is the *logical* cure for Hitler."[54] Like Churchill, Jung had fears of a Soviet Europe, and no doubt would have liked both dictatorships to destroy each other.

When Bitter made contact with Jung and told him of the plan—he had by this time received permission to attend bi-monthly sessions of the Teaching Institute for Psychotherapy at the University of Zürich—Jung was interested, but said he first wanted to run it past some people, whose political acumen he respected; one of these was his life-long friend Albert Oeri, then editor of the *Baseler Nachrichten* and a representative in the *Nationalrat*, the Swiss federal parliament. Jung is also believed to have recruited other Swiss physicians and businessmen in the plot. It was known that Jung had many important friends and acquaintances in England, including William Temple, the archbishop of Canterbury, who would be able to bring word of it to Churchill. But with the mail stopped because of the war, Jung had no way of reaching anyone in England. A Swedish "agent" was initially chosen to be the go-between, but when he was caught, Jung needed a plan B.

A British citizen living in Switzerland would be ideal, Jung thought, and he turned to Barbara Hannah; though born in England she had lived in Zürich since 1920. Jung invited her to Bollingen, and after swearing her to secrecy and mentioning than neither Emma nor Toni was aware of Jung's involvement, told her of the plan and of the part she could play. As a British citizen wishing to return home, she would be under no suspicion traveling to England, and as her father was a dean in the Anglican Church, she could have access to the archbishop. Although Hannah hadn't any intention of leaving Zürich—she knew she wouldn't be able to return while the war was on—she saw the wisdom in this and agreed. But this plot, too, fizzled out. When Hitler's doctors suggested that de Crinis examine him, he refused and exploded in rage. Bitter's name came up several times in the ensuing rant about "defeatists." Hearing this, Bitter understandably fled Germany and remained in Switzerland until the end of the war.

Even more remarkable was Jung's work with the OSS agent Allen W. Dulles, who went on to become the first civilian and longest serving director of the CIA, as well as a member of the Warren Commission investigating the assassination of John F. Kennedy.[55] Working with the Office of Strategic Services, Dulles arrived in Bern, Switzerland, in November 1942. The OSS needed a good Swiss intelligence operative and Dulles was their man. Although neutral, Switzerland was rife with espionage, and agents doubling as foreign diplomats wheedled information from each other over cocktails and hors d'oeuvres. Dulles was one of these, and his assignment was to create a Swiss anti-Nazi network. Dulles' contact was Gerald Mayer, the press attaché at the American Embassy, whose job was to prepare the groundwork for Dulles and to help him recruit new agents. As the Germans had a large delegation in Zürich, Mayer moved between both cities and got to know the Americans living in them. One individual living in Zürich seemed an unlikely, hence potentially profitable possibility. Mary Bancroft was in a decidedly open marriage with a French-Swiss diplomat; a part-time journalist, her German was good enough to write articles on Switzerland for American papers, and ones on America for Swiss publications. Mayer commissioned her to write more of these, and edited them to show that Swiss neutrality was only government policy, and didn't reflect the real beliefs of the Swiss people who were, he believed, on the Allies' side. Mary was also a patient of Jung's and a member of the Psychological Club, although a not particularly well-liked one; her sexual indiscretions had made her the topic of gossip and it took Toni Wolff's imprimatur to keep other members from throwing her out. Mayer had asked Mary to use her Jungian expertise to analyze speeches by Hitler, Göring, and Goebbels, and came to the conclusion that she could be of use to Dulles. When Dulles and Bancroft met at the Baur au Lac in Zürich, Dulles came to that conclusion, too. Mary was also convinced; always on the lookout for new sexual conquests, she agreed to work with Dulles, both as an agent and as a mistress.

One of the German agents in Zürich was Hans Bernd Gisevius. Ostensibly a low-level consul in the German delegation, he was actually a senior agent in the *Abwehr*, the Nazi military intelligence service. The head of the *Abwehr*, Rear Admiral Wilhelm Canaris, was a leader of the secret German resistance against Hitler. He was later executed just weeks before the end of the war at the Flossenbürg concentration camp. Among other offenses, he was implicated in the failed assassination attempt on Hitler on July 20, 1944, depicted in the 2009 film *Valkyrie*. (Canaris was relieved of his position in the *Abwehr* in 1944 and replaced by Schellenberg, which shows how riddled the German high command was with anti-Hitler sentiment.) Even before the war, Canaris had turned against the Nazis and had recruited like-minded individuals among his agents. One of these was Gisevius, whose mission in Switzerland was to find Allied support for the assassination plot. It should be recognized that neither Gisevius nor Canaris nor Schellenberg was a traitor, in the usual sense; they were "good

Germans," who saw that Hitler was a madman who would destroy their country if he wasn't removed from power. Dulles recognized this and knew he had to move cautiously.

Gisevius was writing a book that he wanted to be published in English and German simultaneously. It was both a memoir and an account of the decisions made by the military and the Nazi government during his time as an intelligence agent and would serve as evidence that it was Hitler, and not Germany, who was responsible for the war and its atrocities. Dulles heard of the book and saw that it could be used as a way of getting to Gisevius. Dulles convinced Gisevius that Mary was a highly skilled typist and translator and would be of inestimable service in preparing his book for publication. He asked Mary if she would be willing to do a bit of typing and translating as part of secret mission, and to report anything that Gisevius told her that contradicted what he said to Dulles. The fact that Dulles impressed on her that the fate of five thousand lives—those of other agents—were at risk unnerved her, but when he said their romance could work as a cover for the operation, she agreed.

When she was contacted by "Doctor Bernhard"—Gisevius' code name—and saw the thousand-plus hand-written pages of his manuscript, she had second thoughts. This was no occasional work and she realized her German probably wasn't up to it. Mary had been in and out of analysis with Jung for some time and was not an easy customer. But now, feeling the pressure of the five thousand lives, she went back to him for help. Jung convinced her that disciplining herself to complete the work was the best thing for her, and assured her that anytime she needed him, he would be there. Encouraged, she asked another of Jung's patients, Mary Briner, to help, and soon both women were talking to Jung about the work. Jung would offer his insights and interpretation of Gisevius' remarks on Nazi officials, providing a psychological analysis. Mary Bancroft began to speak about Jung to Dulles and this got Dulles thinking.

Dulles knew of Jung through his wife, who had an interest in psychoanalysis and had trained as an analyst in Zürich before the war. He also knew of the reports of Jung's Nazi fellow traveling. He had these checked and found they were unsubstantiated. Eventually Dulles and Jung met and began an "experimental marriage between espionage and psychology" involving the "psychological profile" of political and military leaders. Dulles was so impressed by Jung's insights that he urged his OSS chiefs to pay great attention to his analyses, especially of Hitler, who Jung had cautioned wouldn't shy from suicide if things got desperate. By this time, Hitler was living in an underground bunker in East Prussia, and required anyone wanting an interview to be disarmed and X-rayed. This is how Jung became "Agent 488," his code name in Dulles' OSS reports. Dulles was convinced that Jung's assessments of Nazi and Fascist leaders "showed a deep antipathy to what Nazism and Fascism stood for," and in later life, Dulles remarked that "Nobody will probably ever know how much Professor Jung contributed to the Allied cause during the war." When asked for details, Dulles demurred, saying the information was "highly classified for the indefinite future," which meant that Jung's "services would have to remain undocumented."

By the end of the war, Jung's ideas were reaching the top brass of the Allied hierarchy when General (later President) Dwight D. Eisenhower turned to reading Jung for insight into how to convince the German populace that defeat was inevitable and surrender the only option.[56] In a letter to Dulles, Jung wrote that

Eisenhower's proclamations to the Germans were the best means of doing this, because they appealed to what was best in them, their idealism and decency, which had long been crushed by Nazi propaganda. Dulles told Jung that he would pass his letter on to Eisenhower, who would appreciate it. Even before the war, Jung's essay "Wotan," in which he argues that Germany, a "land of spiritual catastrophes," had been overwhelmed by the archetype of the ancient god, became required reading among some diplomats in the British Foreign Office, who used it as a basis for negotiations with the Nazi government. It was even distributed by British diplomats to important Germans they hoped to influence.[57]

For different reasons Jung himself couldn't mention these items while rebuffing charges of Nazi sympathies, but now that they are public knowledge, they do much, I think, to counter the accusations that have plagued his reputation for three quarters of a century.

8. ARCHETYPES
FROM OUTER SPACE

Although dealing with Dr. Göring and the International Society kept Jung busy, Nazi bureaucracy and charges of anti-Semitism weren't the only things on his mind. In 1933 he traveled to Egypt and Palestine, after earlier lecturing in Cologne and Essen. He also began lecturing at the Federal Polytechnic in Zürich, a post he would keep until 1941, and made the acquaintance of the physicist Wolfgang Pauli, with whom he would later collaborate on his major statement on synchronicity. In 1934 Jung started his controversial seminars on Nietzsche's *Thus Spoke Zarathustra*, which lasted until 1939; Nazi hacks had appropriated Nietzsche and given him a bad name, so to lecture on him at this time was suspect. That same year Jung was asked by the novelist James Joyce, a resident of Zürich, to treat his daughter Lucrezia, who had been diagnosed as schizophrenic, and had already seen twenty doctors. Joyce had little love for Jung, and asking for his help was an act of desperation. In 1932 Jung had written a critical essay on *Ulysses* in which he wondered how anyone could get through the book "without fatal attacks of drowsiness." An earlier essay on Picasso showed that Jung was no lover of modern art. A year later Joyce withdrew Lucrezia from Jung's care, saying she was a mere girl, "yung and easily freudened."

She was eventually institutionalized and Jung himself probably wasn't optimistic about the case and may have taken it only out of a sense of pride. Strangely, the writer Samuel Beckett, who was Joyce's secretary for a time, attended Jung's Tavistock lectures in 1935, brought by his therapist Wilfred Bion; the lectures impressed Beckett, whose impenetrable writings Jung would no doubt have classed with Joyce's as a "work of Anti-Christ."[1] Yet although Jung may have had little time for modern literature, his name was entering a broader stream of popular culture. In the 1936 film *The Petrified Forest*, which made Humphrey Bogart a star, a world-weary Leslie Howard roams the Arizona desert, with a copy of *Modern Man in Search of His Soul* (1933) in his rucksack.

Eranos kept Jung busy, too, with lectures on the archetypes (1934), dream symbolism (1935), alchemy (1936), "The Visions of Zosimos," a Greek-Egyptian alchemist circa 300 AD (1937), the mother archetype (1938), and rebirth (1939). The 1930s were Casa Gabriella's heyday and Jung was the dominant figure, often holding informal talks on the grounds after the official lectures were over, sitting on his favorite wall, his acolytes clustered around him. On one occasion, Jung's Dionysian character escaped from his Swiss primness, and an after-lecture party had neighbors complaining about the noise. The Barrel had hoisted quite a few and insisted no one be sober, and "plunging in now here, now there, he sparkled with wit, banter, and drunken high spirits."[2]

Jung lectured elsewhere, too, less vociferously perhaps, but with no less honor. In 1936 he took part in Harvard's Tercentenary Conference, and in 1937 gave the prestigious Terry Lectures at Yale, later published as *Psychology and Religion* (1940). After battling hard to prevent it being held in Germany, in 1938 Jung chaired a congress of the International Society in Oxford, where he received an honorary degree. Earlier that year Jung's taste for travel was renewed with a trip to India, where he received honorary doctorates from the universities of Calcutta, Benares, and Allahabad. Although Jung had studied a great deal of Indian philosophy and discussed it with Heinrich Zimmer, he "studiously avoided all so-called 'holy men,'" and during the voyage to the sub-continent he read Gerhard Dorn's *Theatrum Chemicum* from cover to cover.

Jung wasn't impressed by the Hindu psyche, which, he believed, aimed at *nirvana*, a condition Jung characterized as a kind of psychic "emptiness." It sought freedom from inner images, but he wanted to grasp them more firmly. Again, whether or not Jung's remarks about Indian philosophy, which have been criticized, tell us more about Jung's vision than anything else, he did come to see the Buddha as a more complete embodiment of the Self than Christ, in the sense that he lived a fuller life. Jung was deeply impressed by his visit to the stupas of Sanchi, where Buddha had delivered his "Fire Sermon," teaching that liberation comes through inner detachment from the mind and the senses. Yet from many of his remarks in *Memories, Dreams, Reflections*, the major events of the trip were a case of dysentery and a dream about the Holy Grail: Jung's body may have been in India, but his soul was still in Europe. Nevertheless, in 1938 Jung wrote a commentary to a Swiss publication of W. Y. Evans-Wentz's classic edition of *The Tibetan Book of the Dead*. As in his comments on Taoism, Jung's remarks may again tell us more about analytical psychology than Tibetan Buddhism, but in many ways this is irrelevant. Jung the Westerner was becoming the key modern link to Eastern thought, a conduit for the Eastern spirituality that would explode into popular consciousness in the 1960s. Without Jung's imprimatur on Taoism, Zen, the *I Ching*, and Tibetan Buddhism, the impact these would have had is debatable, and many people received their first taste of the "wisdom of the East" through Jung's interpretations.

Jung's personal life changed a great deal, too. Although she was still a fixture in it, Toni Wolff began to drift toward the margins. Age may have contributed—Jung turned 60 in 1935—but the main reason was her lack of interest in alchemy. Toni showed no passion for it and was troubled that Jung gave it so much attention. Although there was no sexual connection, her place as *soror mystica* and helper was taken by the eighteen-year-old Marie-Louise von Franz, who first met Jung in 1933, when she was invited to the Tower by Toni's nephew, who knew her from the Zürich Free Gymnasium; Jung wanted to make contact with Swiss youth and asked him to bring some of his friends around. Like Barbara Hannah, von Franz was unsettled by her first visit, and asked to cut a cucumber, she sliced her finger instead. Jung impressed her with story about a patient who believed she lived on the moon. Although at first skeptical, she later realized that Jung wanted her to see that "what happens psychically is real, and what happens outwardly is only secondary," an insight she said would take ten years to assimilate.[3] Von Franz threw herself into alchemy, searching out hard-to-find texts for Jung and making translations from Latin and Greek; she soon became one of Jung's most articulate interpreters and collaborators, and in 1948 was instrumental in founding the C. G. Jung Institute in Zürich, a center for Jungian studies that continues today, with branches in many major American cities.

Two events at the end of the 1930s marked a break in Jung's life. One was the death of Freud. Whether wished for or not, with Freud gone, and Adler, too (he died in 1937), Jung was the last survivor of the triumvirate "Freud, Jung, and Adler," and was unquestionably the most famous living psychologist. His long obituary for his former master in the *Baseler Nachrichten* joined praise with criticism: Freud was at once a "singular human being" and a "man possessed," remarks that could easily apply to Jung himself. Yet although Freud had remained for many the standard against which Jung's achievements were gauged, he had long lost any vital significance for Jung. More pressing for him and for everyone else in Europe was the outbreak of WWII.

Hitler had already annexed Austria—Freud died in exile in London after fleeing the *Anschluss* in 1938—and had been handed Czechoslovakia on a platter. On September 1, 1939, he invaded Poland; two days later Britain and France declared war on Germany. Although Switzerland was neutral, the Swiss had reason to believe Hitler would grab them, too: the German-speaking Swiss were Aryans—at least in Nazi eyes—and Hitler had used that as an excuse to occupy new *Lebensraum* elsewhere. And as in Austria, many Swiss themselves saw the Fuehrer as a savior, and, sadly, not a few of these were members of the Psychological Club (it later initiated a quota on the number of Jewish members it would accept). The country was put on alert and Jung himself was particularly concerned. He knew his name was on the Nazi *Schwarze Liste* ("black list") and what that meant. Friends suggested he flee to America, where he had wealthy patrons and could write his own ticket. But Jung was too rooted in the Swiss soil to run. He also had a large family to think of, and his patients. His health was also bad. He had never fully recovered from the amoebic dysentery he got in India, and at age sixty-five (as he would be in 1940) he was not as robust as before; photographs from the 1940s on show an increasingly frail Jung. Jung was too old for military duty, but he was drafted as a physician and found the work exhausting. Like everyone else, the Jungs suffered some deprivations—at one point they were growing their own food in their garden— and understandably the war seemed to throw Jung into a negative frame of mind, both about his own work, and about the age in general; in 1940 he told a correspondent, "I loathe the new style, the new Art, the new Music, Literature, Politics, and above all the new Man."⁴ (In another letter he asked "Why in hell is Man unable to grow up?"⁵) Travel was curtailed, and many of Jung's foreign followers had to leave, including the Americans Paul and Mary Mellon, whom Jung had met at Eranos, days before war was declared, and who would later be responsible for the Bollingen Foundation and seeing Jung's *Collected Works* into print.

By the end of June 1940, France had fallen and the threat of a Nazi invasion of Switzerland subsided, but, as mentioned in the last chapter, Jung soon found a new identity in his undercover work for the Allies. Jung's tenure as a secret agent and his dealings with the Nazi machine threw him into the front lines of the "outer world." Whether it was a compensatory reaction or not, an accident in 1944 led to his deepest plunge into the inner one since his crisis. On February 11, taking his daily walk, the sixty-eight-year-old Jung slipped on some ice and broke his fibula. Ten days later, in hospital he suffered a myocardial infarct caused by embolisms from his immobilized leg. Treated with oxygen and camphor, Jung lost consciousness and entered what seems a combination near-death and out-of-the-body experience or, depending on your perspective, delirium. Jung found himself floating a thousand miles above Earth. The sea and continents below—he could see Ceylon (now Sri Lanka) and India—shimmered in blue light and Jung could make out the Arabian desert and snow-tipped Himalayas. Jung felt he was on the verge of leaving orbit, but then, turning to the south, a huge black monolith came into view. It was a kind of temple, and at the entrance Jung saw a Hindu sitting in a lotus position. Inside, tiny lights filled innumerable niches, much like the "sacred flame" Jung had kept going in the "fire wall" of his youth. Jung felt that the "whole phantasmagoria of earthly existence" was being stripped away; it wasn't pleasant, and what remained was an "essential Jung," a core of his experiences, that gave him at once a sense of emptiness and fullness, much like the Pleroma he spoke of in the *Seven Sermons*. Jung knew that inside the temple he would meet all the people to whom he really belonged. The mystery of his existence, why he came into being, his fate, his purpose in life, would be answered. Jung was about to cross the threshold when from below, rising from the direction of Europe, he saw the image of his doctor in the archetypal form of the King of Kos, the site of the temple of Asclepius, the Greek god of medicine. Jung's doctor told him that his departure was premature; many were demanding his return and he was there to ferry him back. Jung was immensely disappointed at the news, and once he heard it, the vision ended.

Jung experienced the reluctance to live that many who have been "brought back" encounter; it took him three weeks, he says, to resign himself to it. All during that time everything earthly repelled him. After his vision in space the "real" world seemed like a prison; he had sloughed off all that was trivial and useless and now he had to take it seriously again. But what troubled Jung most was seeing his doctor in his archetypal form; he knew this meant that he had sacrificed his life to save Jung's. Jung tried to explain but his doctor no doubt thought he was still delirious. On April 4, 1944—a date numerologists can delight in—Jung sat up in bed for the first time since his heart attack. On the same day, Jung's doctor came down with septicemia and took to his bed; he never left it and died a few days later. Jung's visions continued, and paranormal events surrounded the experience. He thought his nurse was an old Jewish woman and that he was involved in a kabbalistic ritual, a mystic marriage of Tiphereth and Malkuth, sephiroth of the Tree of Life. At midnight he would wake and, for an hour, enter a mystical state. The beauty and power of these midnight hours were indescribable.

Jung was convinced that what he experienced weren't simply hallucinations caused by his illness, but that he had been granted a vision of reality. It was "utterly real" and had a "quality of absolute objectivity." In essence he had passed outside time, and past, present, and future existed simultaneously in some way our limited rational minds cannot explain, but which mystics have experienced throughout the ages. Critics argue that once again Jung was making grandiose statements based on his pathology. Perhaps. But the experience had a palpable effect on Jung. It changed him, and in that sense, if in no other, it was real. I for one will go further and accept that Jung *did* enter some extraordinary state of consciousness and that, like mystics and sages before and after him, he had broken through to the *real* world. For one thing, the depression and pessimism that overcame him during the war vanished; as had happened after his crisis, Jung was humbled and felt an acceptance of things "as they are," an unconditional affirmation of life. He even remarks that before his heart attack—he would have another in 1946 and suffer from tachycardia for the rest of his life—he felt that something in his attitude was "wrong" and implies that his unconscious somehow orchestrated his illness to get him back on track.

The experience was certainly real enough to allow the scientist in Jung to take something of a back seat for the remaining seventeen years of his life. Although, as we know, Jung had *always* believed in the reality of the "other" world, whether he spoke of spirits or archetypes, after his visions he seemed less hesitant than in his earlier remarks about it. Jung had, it seems, a kind of conversion experience, or at least a brush with the infinite so moving that he no longer cared so much about being seen as a scientist or not. The painful process of having everything trivial torn from him must have seen to that. It was, in a way, a "wake-up call," and Jung came away from it with a sense of what really mattered, something many people experience after a close encounter with death. If Jung had played at being alchemist and mystic relatively unobserved within the safe confines of his Tower, it was now time to go public. The "sage of Küsnacht" had arrived.

One of the first products of his mystical awakening was, as we've seen, his commentary on the *I Ching* and the public announcement that the celebrated Herr Doctor Professor used the ancient Chinese oracle. A more baffling result was his strange book *Aion*, which appeared in 1951. As early as 1940, Jung was talking about the Age of Aquarius. In a letter to H. G. Baynes dated August 1940, Jung alludes to a vision he had in 1918 in which he saw "fire falling like rain from heaven and consuming the cities of Germany." Jung felt that 1940 was the crucial year, and in his letter he says that it's "when we approach the meridian of the first star in Aquarius." It was, he said, "the premonitory earthquake of the New Age."[6]

Jung had been studying astrology for nearly thirty years and was familiar with the phenomenon of the precession of the equinoxes, the apparent backward movement of the sun through the signs of the zodiac, due to a wobble in the earth's axis. One complete cycle takes roughly 26,000 years, and by acting as a backdrop to sunrise at the vernal equinox, each sign gives its name to an "age"—known as a "Platonic month"—which lasts roughly 2150 years. Subtitled "Researches into the Phenomenology of the Self," *Aion* focuses on Christ as a symbol of the Self, but in the familiar wealth of references and allusions, Jung presents a remarkable notion: that the individuation of Western civilization as a whole follows the path of the "Platonic months." *Aion* is, in fact, an essay in the evolution of consciousness, using the astrological ages as symbols of the collective unconscious, a kind of "precession of the archetypes." Fish symbolism surrounds Christ because Christ was the central symbol of the Age of Pisces, the astrological sign of the fish. Previous ages, of Taurus and Aries, produced bull and ram symbolism. The coming age is that of Aquarius, the Water Bearer, something many of us have heard about for some time. Depending on your method of calculation, it has either already started or will do so sometime this millennium.

In conversation with Margaret Ostrowski-Sachs, a friend of Hermann Hesse, Jung admitted that he had kept this "secret knowledge" to himself for years, and only finally made it public in *Aion*. Jung wasn't sure he was "allowed" to, but during his illness he received "confirmation" that he should. The Aquarian age would "constellate the problem of the union of opposites."

The "real existence" of evil would have to be acknowledged; it could no longer be understood as the mere absence of good, as was the official Christian stance. This would come about not through politics or any collective effort but through the "individual human being, via his experience of the living spirit," that is, the unconscious.[7] As an example of how the archetypes work on the collective consciousness, Jung notes the then recent papal decree making the Assumption of Mary, Christ's mother, part of Christian dogma. This was of enormous importance for Jung; it showed that Christianity recognized the need to include the feminine in the Godhead, something it had lacked and which had weakened its appeal. The idea that Mary didn't die but was taken, body and soul, to heaven, had been accepted for nearly a century, but it wasn't made part of divine revelation until Pope Pius XII's decree on November 1, 1950. The masses demanded it and their insistence was, Jung writes, "the urge of the archetype to realize itself."[8]

The archetypes would realize themselves in other ways, too. In one of his last books, *Flying Saucers: A Modern Myth of Things Seen in the Sky* (1958), Jung argued that whatever their *physical* reality—and Jung seemed to be of two minds on this[9]—the strange circular flying shapes that had been reported for the last decade (contemporary UFO sightings began in 1947, when Kenneth Arnold, a pilot from Washington state, made his famous report) were "projections" of the modern psyche's need for meaning, an expression of a mass hunger for wholeness. They were, in short, mandalas from outer space. By the late 1950s, the Cold War was close to defrosting in a nuclear meltdown, and the split between the US and USSR had created a kind of global schizophrenia. In his patients, Jung discovered mandalas emerging from the unconscious as a sign of, and stimulus to, a new whole-ness. Now the global unconscious was projecting these unearthly circular shapes as both a wake-up call for planetary wholeness and a means of achieving it—meditation on the mandala is, we know, an aid in individuation. Western consciousness was having its own nervous breakdown and its psyche was trying to compensate.

But just as mandalas herald a new development in the indi-vidual psyche, these mass sightings suggested that a collective shift in human consciousness was on the way. UFO sightings were so significant that, referring to his prophecy of the "blond beast," Jung felt "compelled, as once before . . . to sound a note of warn-ing." "My conscience as a psychiatrist bids me fulfill my duty and prepare those few who will hear me for coming events which are in accord with the end of an era," he told his readers. "As we know from ancient Egyptian history, they are symptoms of psy-chic changes that always appear at the end of one Platonic month and at the beginning of another. They are, it seems, changes in the constellation of the psychic dominants, of the archetypes or 'Gods' as they used to be called, which bring about . . . long-lasting transformations of the collective psyche. This transformation started . . . in the transition of the Age of Taurus to that of Aries, and then from Aries to Pisces, whose beginning coincides with the rise of Christianity. We are now nearing that great change . . . when the spring-point enters Aquarius . . ." Ten years later the Fifth Dimension (whose name suggests the mystical character of the 1960s) had a hit song from the musical *Hair* echoing Jung's ideas, and millions of people all over the world believed it was "the dawning of the Age of Aquarius."

Yet Jung's concern about his scientific reputation hadn't completely vanished. Making such pronouncements, he knew, put him the category of interpreters of "signs and portents," made him, in fact, a kind of modern Nostradamus, whom he had written about in *Aion*. Yet, even if it meant putting his "hard-won reputation for truthfulness, trustworthiness and scientific judgement in jeopardy," he would risk it in order to help "all those that are unprepared by the events in question and disconcerted by their incomprehensible nature," an act he calls a "thankless task."[10]

In one sense he was right; the old charge of mystic and charlatan resurfaced, and for some the "sage of Küsnacht" was little more than a "journalists' oracle," pontificating on things cosmic and cranky in the interviews "to which he so gladly submitted," and of which there were many.[11] Jung could still be stung by the accusation that what he was doing wasn't science, and the proof is in his major statement on what is arguably the most influential idea he bequeathed to the coming age, synchronicity.

Although Jung had spoken about it in lectures and mentioned it briefly in other writings, it wasn't until 1952 that he produced a detailed account of what he called "meaningful coincidences." *Synchronicity: An Acausal Connecting Principle*, written in collaboration with the physicist Wolfgang Pauli, was based on Jung's last Eranos lecture, given in 1951. For anyone hoping to find a clear, unambiguous statement about the idea, it's a frustrating work. Jung's most important remark on it *can* be found, but it is embedded in some of his most tortuous Herr Doctor Professor prose, and it leaves us no nearer to an explanation for this baffling phenomenon. In order to account for the strange character of synchronicities—the uncanny juxtaposition of the outer world and the inner one—Jung concludes that "either there are physical processes which cause psychic happenings, or there is a pre-existent psyche which organises matter." Simply put, either what's "outside" affects what's "inside," or vice versa. To which I think we can add a third possibility, which Jung hints at but never declares outright: that synchronicities are, as Colin Wilson suggests, "a kind of nudge from some unknown guardian angel, whose purpose is to tell us that life is not as meaningless as it looks,"[12] a form of the "spirit hypothesis." From my own experience, this is an idea worth considering.

Most UFO researchers rejected Jung's notion that flying saucers were a "projection" of the unconscious, without, however, rejecting UFOs. Likewise, most devotees of "meaningful coincidence" found Jung's attempt to account for it in terms of archetypes, quantum physics, statistical analysis, mathematics, J. B. Rhine's experiments with ESP, astrology, and so on rather baffling, *without* rejecting synchronicity. I've recorded "meaningful coincidences" for nearly thirty years—I have several notebooks full of them— and I'm as convinced of their reality as I am that of the desk I'm sitting at. But Jung's attempts to map out an "acausal connecting principle" strike me as an example of his once again placing the stencil of the archetypes on a phenomenon and saying "Aha!"

Arthur Koestler, who, like Jung, risked the loss of scientific credibility when he began writing seriously about parapsychology, pointed out that Jung's notion of an "acausal" principle is effectively meaningless, as Jung "kept relapsing into spurious causal explanations to make the a-causal principle work."[13] Similarly,

Koestler points out that Jung coins a term, synchronicity, that, with its link to "synchronous" clearly implies simultaneity (secret agents "synchronize" their watches), then goes out of his way to explain "that it does not mean what it means," an example, Koestler says, of the "obscurity" that runs through much of Jung's writing.[14] "It is painful," Koestler lamented, "to watch how a great mind, trying to disentangle itself from the causal chains of materialistic science, gets entangled in its own verbiage."[15] Other writers, equally open to the reality of synchronicity, complain that Jung lumps practically *all* paranormal phenomena under its banner. As with the archetypes and the collective unconscious, it became a kind of one-size-fits-all means of explaining a host of different experiences, a tendency that has only increased by *synchronicity*'s adoption into common usage (nowadays, whenever anything "weird" happens, people often say "Wow, what a synchronicity.") Of the examples of synchronicity Jung gives, only one meets the requirement of "meaningful coincidence," while the rest can be accounted for by ESP, telepathy, precognition, astrology, and other paranormal abilities. Readers unfamiliar with parapsychology came away from the book with the idea that the remarkable results J. B. Rhine was getting at Duke University with his experiments in ESP were examples of synchronicity. Ones that were familiar with it shook their heads when Jung chalked up an example of precognition or telepathy to his all-purpose "acausal principle."

The one example of "pure" synchronicity Jung provides makes clear that the essential ingredient is *meaning*: what is "outside" *must* have a meaningful relation to what is "inside" for it to be a true synchronicity, no matter how remarkable the coincidence. Jung tells the by-now well-known case of one of his patients, an infuriatingly rationalistic woman whose hyper-intellectualism made her treatment difficult. One day, as she was recounting a dream about a golden scarab, Jung heard a knocking at the window. Opening it, a golden-green scarab flew into the room. Jung's patient was stunned at the coincidence, her rationalism cracked, and he was able to get on with therapy. In this case there is a clear *meaningful* connection between the inner—the woman's dream— and the outer—the real-life scarab—that resulted in a change in her outlook, a kind of mini-transcendent function. Jung mentioned a similar case to Esther Harding, a leading American Jungian. Trying to get a woman who insisted on interpreting any expression of sex in her dreams symbolically to accept its more visceral reality, Jung got nowhere until "two sparrows fluttered to the ground at her feet and 'performed the act.'"[16] Again, there is a clear correspondence between the inner and outer. But in another case of coincidence that Jung cites, the meaningful element seems missing. Jung recounts the tale of M. de Fortgibu and the plum pudding, which turns up in practically every account of synchronicity, and was first recorded by the French scientist Camille Flammarion. When he was a boy, M. Deschamps was given a plum pudding by M. de Fortgibu. Ten years later, he saw some plum pudding in a Paris restaurant and asked for it, only to discover that it had just been ordered by M. de Fortgibu. Many years later, he was invited to a dinner at which plum pudding would be served. Remarking on his curious history with the rare delight, he mentioned that all that was needed now was for old M. de Fortgibu to appear—at which, a senile M. de Fortgibu, who had come to the wrong address, walked in . . .

Undoubtedly this is one of the most remarkable cases of coincidence on record—and there are others of equal force—but unless some information appears to suggest that the repeated link of plum pudding and the two men was in some way *meaningful*—which is not apparent from what is known—I have to chalk it up to something other than synchronicity, unless, of course, M. Deschamps' guardian angel was trying to teach him something which escapes us, which is perfectly possible. It is this element of immediate personal meaning that gives synchronicities their uncanny, unsettling aspect, as if some intelligence outside ourselves *knows* what we're thinking. Jung's talk of a universal "acausal ordering principle," as if synchronicities were an expression of an impersonal "force" in nature like gravity, seems besides the point, and is again a manifestation of his lingering need to sound scientific.

With his UFO book, Jung wanted to reach a wider, popular audience, something he hoped to do by agreeing to the John Freeman interview on *Face to Face*, and to the autobiography. He knew he didn't have many more years to live, and he felt the need to get his message across. Illness plagued his last decades, and he had already seen the people closest to him move on. Toni Wolff died in 1953; she was sixty-four. Jung claimed ill health kept him from attending her funeral, but their relationship had cooled, and although she continued to see him, he found her visits taxing. The major blow came in November 1955 when Emma Jung died from cancer. She had been suffering for the last few years but had kept the illness a secret until it was impossible to hide. Ever practical, she spent her last days preparing for her departure and arranging for Jung to be taken care of after her death. Ruth Bailey, whom Jung had met in Africa, had become a close family friend and had visited Küsnacht regularly. Years earlier she promised

Emma that, whether Jung or she died first, she would come and care for the survivor. When Emma slipped into unconsciousness and quietly died, Jung was shaken. The loss was great, and Jung fell into a depression that so incapacitated him that his children were concerned about his mental health; when Jung realized this, he broke down sobbing. Years of Swiss propriety prevented his children from making any outward show of affection—Jung's relation to them all was difficult at best—and it was left to Bailey to comfort the old sage. She remained at Küsnacht as Jung's companion until his own death.

With Bailey living with him, Jung's spirits began to revive, and one of the first signs of returning life was the stone he carved for Emma, with the inscription *O vas insigne devotione et obedientia*, "Oh vase, sign of devotion and obedience." One last gesture of gratitude toward his wife of fifty-two years, who had endured and given so much, was to ask Marie-Louise von Franz to complete Emma's book on the Holy Grail, left unfinished at her death. She did, and *The Grail Legend* appeared in 1960.

Jung said that after Emma's death, he felt an obligation to become what he is.[17] For someone who spent a lifetime doing that, this seems an odd statement, but in practice it meant that Jung added a new story to the Tower, one that represented his ego, his personality. He spent more time there and in his own way was preparing for death. When he carved the names of his ancestors on some stones he was, in a way, making ready to join them. In 1955 Jung told an interviewer for the London *Daily Mail*, "At my country retreat I do as I please. I write, I paint—but I spend most of the time just drifting along with my thoughts." At eighty, he had already outlived other gurus such as Rudolf Steiner and Gurdjieff, and in his old age the frail Jung still carried an inner solidity and alertness that made him like a force of nature, something that comes through in the *Face to Face* footage. Yet long ago he had recognized that the second half of life was a preparation for death, and now he was coming to terms with his own insight.

Yet although he believed that with his visions of 1944 he reached a "completed individuation,"[18] to Ruth Bailey and to others, Jung was often a querulous old man. Aniela Jaffé felt his wrath when he complained at length over minor typing mistakes. Although Emma had left more than enough to meet his needs, and his own earnings were considerable, the elderly Jung became frantic over money and took to hiding it around the house. The depression that came over him during the war returned, and Jung, one of the most famous men in the world, felt that his work was ignored and frequently complained that "only a few heaven-inspired minds" understood him.[19] Always a fussy chef, Jung was enraged when, against his instructions, Ruth Bailey added two tomatoes to a stew. His torrent of abuse continued until she threatened to leave him. When she came to care for him, he warned her that he was capable of getting into rages, but added that she should take no notice of them. Yet having the sage of Küsnacht bellowing at her over lunch must have been difficult to ignore. Jung calmed down, and like a repentant child explained: "All you have to remember is not to make me angry," no mean feat and a remark that suggests Jung was used to being humored.

Perhaps if Jung had more male friends his last years could have been less fretful. But he never had much luck with male friendships, and at one point he complained to Margaret Ostrowski-Sachs that "I seldom get to have a conversation with an adequate partner." Women, he said, understood him, "but with women their home, their husband, and their children always come first."

But when talking with a man, "one listens to the reverberation from the cosmic spaces of the spirit."²⁰ His last male friendship, with the English Dominican Father Victor White, had given Jung much pleasure and stimulation, but it had broken down over Jung's *Answer to Job*, an answer White, as a Christian priest, could not accept. Although White initially embraced Jung's exercise in the problem of evil, he soon saw that the psychological truths it advanced clashed with the theological truths of his faith, and White eventually came to criticize both the book and Jung heavily, a volte-face that hurt Jung deeply. In 1959, one late visitor to Küsnacht, the writer and Chilean diplomat Miguel Serrano, importuned Jung with questions about dreams and alchemy and the relations between the sexes. Jung told him that "nothing is possible without love, not even the processes of alchemy," but after speaking "as though he were in a trance" about "a Flower, a Stone, a Crystal, a Queen, a King," and a woman who "died eight years ago"—a possible reference to Toni Wolff, although the dates are off—Jung remarked that "nobody understands what I mean" and added "I am very old. . . ."²¹ Jung didn't know it at the time, but one wonders how he would have reacted to the fact that Serrano had been a member of the Chilean Nazi party, was a rabid anti-Semite, and would later achieve international notoriety as the central architect of "esoteric Hitlerism."²² Perhaps knowing Jung's troubles with the "blond beast," Serrano saw fit to keep this information to himself.

Jung had, he thought, said all he had to say, and the *Collected Works*, which began to appear in 1953, showed that was quite a bit. Yet Jung must have felt some sense that the new decade would be his, and that the real conduit of his teaching would be with popular readers, not the intellectuals. In 1960 a French book on the occult, *The Morning of the Magicians*, was a surprise bestseller—a success later repeated in its English translation—and sparked the "magical revival" that spanned that decade and continues into our own time. A grab bag of speculation on a number of esoteric themes, among *The Morning of the Magicians'* many chapters, several were on alchemy. If Jung knew of the book, he would have been gratified. And although Jung would have disliked the hippies—he was of a rather conservative bent and would have found "flower power" sadly naïve—he must have felt that in some way, the world he would soon be leaving would be one more open to his ideas.

In fact, Jung's unconscious knew this, and told him so. After the *Face to Face* interview, Jung was approached by an English publisher with the idea of writing a book aimed at the "average reader." It was a shame, the publisher told him, that while Freud's ideas were widely known, Jung's, which were of equal if not more importance, were still fairly obscure. Jung considered the idea but demurred, saying he had never popularized his work in the past, and that in any case he was too old to do it now. Soon after, however, Jung dreamed that he was in a public place, addressing masses of ordinary people who listened to him attentively and *understood* what he said. For someone who complained at length that he was "an increasingly lonely old man writing for other lonely men,"[23] this was a rather different perspective, and Jung knew that, once again, the psyche was seeking to compensate for a too one-sided conscious attitude—his own. The many letters Jung received from "average" viewers of *Face to Face* suggested that hundreds of "ordinary" people were interested in him and his ideas, and that he was perhaps wrong in thinking that a popular book was a bad idea, and was simply indulging in negative thoughts.

Jung changed his mind and the product was *Man and His Symbols*, which contains his last work, the long essay "Approaching the Unconscious." Ten days after finishing it, Jung took to his bed with his final illness. With essays by Marie-Louise von Franz, Aniela Jaffé, Jolande Jacobi, and Joseph Henderson—all high-ranking Jungians—in *Man and His Symbols*, Jung not only encapsulated his basic ideas for the average reader, but he also handed the torch on to his followers. As an introduction to Jungian thought, it's excellent, and I still remember the excitement I felt years ago, reading it as a teenager. The importance of dreams; the problem of types; the work of the functions; the power of the archetypes; the need for myth; the one-sidedness of consciousness and the need for the unconscious to compensate; the significance of symbols—all the central ideas of his life's work are there, along with concerns about overpopulation, H-bombs, totalitarianism, "mass man," and the loss of the individual in modern society. As he argued in *The Undiscovered Self*, Jung told the "average" reader that any possibility of avoiding disaster "must begin with an individual." "It might be any one of us. Nobody can afford to look around and wait for someone else to do what he is loath to do himself." And what must the individual do, given that all our conscious, rational, scientific efforts seem to only land us deeper in the mire? He must "ask himself whether by chance his or her unconscious may know something that will help us."[24] The basic message of Jung's last work is the one that cost him his friendship with Freud: that the unconscious is not some dark basement full of unwanted, disreputable things, but a living, creative, and often wise partner *with* consciousness in the business of a becoming fully actualized human being, a partner who frequently knows more than we—our conscious egos—do, and who speaks to us in symbols, those remarkable products of the transcendent function.

Jung spoke to the coming decade when he declared that "the meaning of life is not exhaustively explained by one's business life, nor is the deep desire of the human heart answered by a bank account,"[25] anticipating the appetite for "dropping out" of the rat race that would characterize the 1960s. But more important, he emphasized that the growth of consciousness, the work of individuation—the two are the same—was a historical, evolutionary process that stretched back into the past and ahead into the future. "The mind," he told his readers, "has grown into its present state of consciousness as an acorn grows into an oak or as saurians developed into mammals. As it has for so long been developing, so it still develops, and thus we are moved by forces from within as well as by stimuli from without."[26] Our task, he said, is to understand the forces from within, in order to meet the challenges from without.

The work exhausted Jung, but he knew he had made the right decision. And although there was still an enormous amount to do, he had made a decent start. "The really complex and unfamiliar part of the mind, from which symbols are produced," was, he knew, "still virtually unexplored," and almost fifty years after Jung's death, this still remains true, although, to be sure, some headway has been made. "Man's greatest instrument, his psyche, is little thought of, and is often directly mistrusted and despised." Yet "a beginning has been made" and the "results are encouraging" and "seem to indicate an answer to many so far unanswered questions of present-day mankind."[27] That beginning, of course, was Jung's work, and it still goes on today.

Visitors found Jung enfeebled in his last days. He was, after all, a man like other men, and sickness, age, and the weight of life take their toll on all of us. On the day he died, June 6, 1961, the Barrel said to Ruth Bailey, "Let's have a really good red wine tonight." He had been in and out of consciousness often and when he entered a coma that afternoon, there was no King of Kos to bring him back to Earth. Writing of his sister Trudi's death many years earlier—she died in 1935—Jung said, "What happens after death is so unspeakably glorious that our imagination and feelings do not suffice to form even an approximate conception of it."[28] This was a decade before his own aborted journey to the afterworld, and Jung does not tell us how he knows. But one suspects he is right, and wonders who he met in that orbiting Hindu temple, where all those people to whom he really belonged were waiting for him.

EPILOGUE:
AFTER JUNG

I t's now nearly half a century since Jung's death, and while the mainstream scientific acceptance he craved is still far from forthcoming—although, to be sure, some of his followers have worked hard at building bridges between the mainstream and Jung's ideas[1]—the popular appeal that Jung recognized in his last years has grown enormously. Jung's remarks about "ordinary people" being the real readers of his books, quoted in the Introduction, may seem disingenuous, especially when we consider the difficulty of those books, and Jung's mantra-like insistence that he was a scientist. But Jung must have known that banging his head against the scientific wall was pointless, and that what was important was getting his ideas across to a broad audience. The *Face to Face* interview, *Man and His Symbols*, and, most of all, *Memories, Dreams, Reflections* were all aimed at doing just that. Whether it was hubris, his ego, or, as he said, his "conscience as a psychiatrist" that compelled him, in his last years Jung felt the need to speak on matters of global consequence, and it's difficult to come away from his last books and interviews without feeling that, put simply, he was convinced that in order for there to be a better world, practically everyone had to start individuating.

On the face of it, that's not bad advice, although the kind of "Jung cult" envisioned by Richard Noll, consisting of a world-wide movement headed by an elite corps of individuated initiates, exists only in the pages of his books. Clearly, Jung centers do exist in many major cities around the world, where people are trained in Jung's approach to psychotherapy, his ideas on the psyche are argued and discussed, and Jungian psychology is promoted. But as Anthony Storr remarked, "the idea of a universal Jungian church cannot really be sustained," pointing out that in London alone "there were four incompatible groups all owing some allegiance to Jung."² Jung didn't sprout a system like Scientology or a devotional movement like that of Bhagwan Shree Rajneesh or a spiritual technique like Transcendental Meditation. And although there are similarities between some of his ideas and those of Gurdjieff and Rudolf Steiner—as well as similar personal characteristics—Jung didn't hand down a "teaching" in the way that these equally important thinkers did. Which is not to say that some of those who followed Jung didn't set him up as a guru and seek to align their lives with the letter, and not only the spirit, of his "law."

What Jung did leave behind was an immense body of work and enough ideas and, perhaps even more important, enough ambiguity about them, to keep a few generations of students busy for quite some time. Again, the comparison with the philosopher Heidegger is apt. Generally speaking, thinkers whose work is clear and precise do not produce "schools," as their clarity obviates the need for interpreters. Jung's obscurity alone did not, of course, guarantee the Jungians who came after him; the importance of his ideas was responsible for that. But it did provide them with a huge task of clarification and dissemination.

Emma Jung's and Toni Wolff's contribution to Jung's work has been noted, but it was those of his surviving immediate circle who developed what is broadly known as Jungian thought. And as this book, I think, has made clear, most of these intimates were women. Jung, of course, did have male followers. Erich Neumann's major work, *The Origin and History of Consciousness* (1949), applied Jung's ideas on individual psychology to the history of human consciousness, and his writings on art, creativity, and the Great Mother brought Jungian themes into a wider, philosophical and cultural context. Sadly, Neumann's premature death in 1960 at the age of fifty-five cut short a promising life and a fruitful field of development. Another important male follower of Jung was Carl A. Meier, Jung's assistant and later first president of the C. G. Jung Institute in Zürich. Meier was at Jung's side during the dark days of the 1930s and was a prolific interpreter of his thought. Yet after his disassociation with the Jung Institute in 1957, Meier dropped out of view and he remains relatively obscure in the Jungian archives, undeservedly, as his many writings show; he died in 1995 at the age of 90. Certainly these were not Jung's only male followers, but they were two of the most important.

Yet the Jungian word was spread most effectively by the "Valkyries," as a book on the subject refers to the clutch of women who surrounded the great sage.[3] Jolande Jacobi (d. 1973), Aniela Jaffé (d. 1991), and Barbara Hannah (d. 1986) all produced several significant books, lectures, and articles about either Jung or his ideas. Jung once remarked that "The systematic elaboration of my ideas, which were often just thrown out, is a task for those who come after me, and unless it is accomplished there will be no progress in the science of analytical psychology."[4] The Valkyries who survived Jung took this injunction to heart.

Among her other books, Jacobi's *The Way of Individuation* (1965) is an excellent step-by-step exposition of Jung's ideas on the process of individuation, and her anthology of Jung's remarks, *Psychological Reflections* (1953), is a helpful gathering of the pith of Jung's insights, something for which those, like myself, who stumble through the rough terrain of Jung's books are thankful. Barbara Hannah's *Jung, His Life and Work* (1977), which I've drawn on for this book, provides firsthand reminiscences of working with Jung, and her *Encounters With Soul* (1981) offers an in-depth account of active imagination throughout an analysis; she also wrote extensively on the archetypal symbology of animals, and the creative process. Along with being Jung's amanuensis and coauthor of his "so-called autobiography," in *The Myth of Meaning* (1970) Aniela Jaffé explored Jung's existential insight that the most common cause of neurosis in the modern world was a sense of meaninglessness, and her *Apparitions: An Archetypal Approach to Death, Dreams and Ghosts* (1978) carried on Jung's fascination with the spirit world. Her *C. G. Jung: Word and Image* (1979), which I first read many years ago and went back to for this book, is a beautiful introduction to Jung's life and world, containing, as mentioned, several images from his uncanny *Red Book*. She was also one of the first to ask whether Jung was a mystic, as her collection of essays *Was Jung a Mystic?* shows.

All three women carried the Jungian torch into new areas and made valuable contributions to the Jungian canon. But the Valkyrie most associated with systematizing and clarifying the many ideas that Jung just "threw out" was Marie-Louise von Franz (d. 1998), who came to Jung as a teenager and stayed, first with him and then with his work, for the rest of her life. Von Franz lectured extensively on Jung's work, trained analysts at the C. G. Jung Institute in Zürich (of which she was a founder), and developed Jung's ideas in a number of areas: alchemy, synchronicity, death, dreams, mythology, and active imagination, adding her insights to the entire Jung corpus. Many people know of her through a remarkable series of films, *The Way of the Dream* (1987), made with her student, Fraser Boa. And von Franz, Jaffé, Hannah, and others who knew Jung, along with some footage of Jung himself, can also be see in Mark Whitney's extraordinary film *Matter of Heart* (1985). Von Franz is perhaps most known for her work on fairy tales, and her many lectures on the subject were published in a series of books: *Problems of the Feminine in Fairy Tales* (1972); *An Introduction to the Interpretation of Fairy Tales* (1973); *Shadow and Evil in Fairy Tales* (1974); and *Individuation in Fairy Tales* (1977).

Von Franz's work reached a wider audience when it was discussed in the poet Robert Bly's influential essay *A Little Book on the Human Shadow* (1981). As did Joseph Campbell, when his *Power of Myth* television interviews with Bill Moyers in 1988 brought Jungian ideas into millions of living rooms, Bly became a household name when his riposte to the excesses of feminism, *Iron John* (1990), which drew on fairy tales and Jungian themes, became a bestseller and inaugurated the Men's Movement. Clarissa Pinkola Estés, a poet and Jungian analyst, did something similar for the feminine side in the equally bestselling *Women Who Run With the Wolves* (1992). Both brought back into common usage the notion of soul, which, agreeing with Jung, both believed modern man—and woman—had lost.

Soul is a central theme of perhaps the most well-known apostate of Jungian psychology, James Hillman. Hillman got his analyst's diploma from the Jung Institute in Zürich in 1959 and went on to become its first director of studies, a position he held until 1969, when he left following a scandal involving a student—along the lines of Jung's with Sabina Spielrein—which triggered a personal crisis.[5] He then went on to become editor of Spring Publications, a publishing house devoted to Jungian studies and Hillman's own brand of Jungian thought, "archetypal psychology." Hillman is notorious for his criticisms of psychotherapy—in 1993 he coauthored *We've Had a Hundred Years of Psychotherapy—And the World's Getting Worse* with the journalist Michael Ventura—and for his "re-visioning" of Jung's ideas, specifically on the centrality of the Self, proposed in his work *Re-Visioning Psychology* (1975). Aligning himself, at least for a time, with post-modern notions of deconstruction and de-centering, Hillman proposed a more fluid, shifting notion of the psyche, one not aimed, as Jung's is, at achieving "wholeness" or integration, but in allowing multiple "selves" to coexist in a kind of psychological polytheism.

Hillman has also been a strong critic of medical, pathological models of the psyche, and has argued that the soul needs to be taken out of the hands of the doctors, and given back to artists and poets, a theme Jung may well have sniffed at. Indeed, Hillman draws on art and beauty as essential elements of human psychology to a degree Jung would have found scandalous. Whereas von Franz's work clarified, codified, and systematized Jung's ideas—in many ways playing Ouspensky to Jung's Gurdjieff—Hillman broke the mold and threw "Jungian studies" into something of a crisis, allowing for new, fresh approaches which more than likely will guarantee its survival. When a thinker's work has reached the "re-visioning" and "post" stage, as Jung's has, with books such as Andrew Samuels' *Jung and the Post-Jungians* (1986) and *Jung and Film: Post-Jungian Takes on the Moving Image* (2001) by Chris Hauke (taken at random from amazon.com), you can be assured it will be around for some time. Jung has stimulated feminists, anthropologists, ecologists, occultists, and many others to argue with him, and this can only be a good thing, as it helps keep the ideas alive.

The broader world of the self-help genre has also proved open to Jungian themes, a New Age imprimatur that more academic Jungian scholars, such as Sonu Shamdasani, are wary of. Shamdasani is general editor and cofounder of the Philemon Foundation, whose mission is to "make the complete body of Jung's work available in editions that meet the highest standards of scholarship and do justice to the true measure of this major creative thinker."[6] Shamdasani has also recently been appointed professor in Jung History at the Wellcome Trust Center for the History of Medicine at University College London, a position that Jung, if he is at all aware of earthly things in his archetypal form, is undoubtedly pleased with. Along with the occult cachet that has attached itself to Jung's name, Shamdasani would no doubt like to purge it of its associates with pop psychology. In the self-help boom of the 1980s and '90s, Robert A. Johnson took Jung's ideas about the shadow, the anima, the animus, and others and turned them into bestsellers with his books *He: Understanding Masculine Psychology* (1989), *She: Understanding Feminine Psychology* (1989), and *We: Understanding the Psychology of Romantic Love* (1983). Indeed, Jung's ideas seemed heaven-sent for the burgeoning literature on relationships and self-development. Post-Jungian ideas weren't left out, as the success of Thomas Moore's *Care of the Soul*

(1992), based on James Hillman's work, shows; Moore even rated an appearance on *Oprah*. Hillman himself reached best-sellerdom in 1997 with *The Soul's Code: In Search of Character and Calling*.[7] Jung may have been exaggerating in his last years when he said that his readers were "ordinary people." Today, however, he's right on target, and mystic or not, he'll be with us for a while.

Undoubtedly the most significant recent development in Jungian studies is the publication of his *Red Book*,[1] which, at the time of writing—late October 2009— has already sold out its first printing, and is encroaching upon some best-seller lists. Touted as the most "influential unpublished work in the history of psychology,"[2] and a work of psychology "in a literary and prophetic form,"[3] the unfinished book, which Jung considered his most important, but which he kept hidden from the world, as did his family, has created a sensation in the publishing trade far beyond anything Jung himself would have imagined. No doubt this is mostly due to the work's strange history, which makes people not particularly interested in Jungian ideas nevertheless fascinated with it. To Jungians themselves, it is rather like the effect discovering the Dead Sea Scrolls or the Nag Hammadi texts had on Christians, or how an alchemist would feel if he actually stumbled upon the fabled Emerald Tablet of Hermes Trismegistus, or if readers of H. P. Lovecraft unearthed a copy of the legendary *Necronomicon*. The title of Sara Corbett's long *New York Times* article—a journal not usually generous toward Jung—about the book's publication, "The Holy Grail of the Unconscious," captured the significance the event has for the Jungian community.⁴ Whether *The Red Book* actually is that magical vessel, readers will have to decide for themselves. Personally I have no doubt that many now believe a new sacred text has been bequeathed to them. And that, I suspect, may have been one of the reasons why Jung kept it under wraps.

The Red Book contains Jung's record of his "confrontation with the unconscious," and is an elaboration and amplification of the material he first recorded in his *Black Books* as he followed his psyche down the rabbit hole of the archetypes (see Chapter Five). Also known as *Liber Novus* ("The New Book"), *The Red Book* is, by any standards, a remarkable work, and comments likening it to the Celtic *Book of Kells* or William Blake's illuminated texts are apt.

Jung began recording his fantasies and active imaginations in 1913, and although his "creative illness" reached its end in 1919, Jung continued to add to and tinker with *The Red Book* until roughly 1930, when he locked it away in a cupboard in Küsnacht, where it more or less remained until 1984, when Jung's family transferred it to a Zürich bank vault. Its folio-sized pages, bound in red leather, burst with fantastic images and intricate, perhaps even obsessive calligraphy, and tell a sometimes fascinating, sometimes disturbing story of Jung's inner journey to meet "the spirit of the depths" in order to unseat the "spirit of the times," and to serve "the inexplicable and the paradoxical" in order to produce "the supreme meaning" and "the God yet to come." Serpents, dragons, giants, the dead, and other, less identifiable creatures abound, and the inner Jung finds himself in some unusual situations, including incest, murder, and cannibalism. As it was started around the same time as Jung's *Seven Sermons to the Dead*, readers won't be surprised to find the same sometimes poetic, sometimes

bombastic language—the language, Jung said, of the archetypes—
and depending on your tastes, this can either enchant you or put
you off. Jung is believed to have been re-reading Nietzsche's *Thus
Spake Zarathustra* when he began *The Red Book*, and for anyone
familiar with Nietzsche, his influence is obvious, both in *The Red
Book*'s style and in its message. Yet Nietzsche's mock-biblical prose,
often full of humor and grace, is never as heavy-handed as Jung's.[5]

For Jung, *The Red Book* was the source of everything that followed, and the ideas he is famous for today—the collective unconscious, the archetypes, individuation—all emerged, he said, from
the slime and egg shell of this strange birth. Stylistically the book is
often reminiscent of Nikos Kazantzakis' quasi-prophetic *The Saviours of God* (1922) and the more hermetic *Nature Word* (1963) by
the esoteric Egyptologist R. A. Schwaller de Lubicz, which, like *The
Red Book*, recounts "conversations" with inner figures.[6] However,
although certainly a fascinating, often powerful work, *The Red
Book*'s literary merits are debatable. It's translators' suggestion that
Jung "chose not make a name for himself in this literary manner,"
can be read as somewhat presumptuous, as there is no guarantee
that Jung would have found literary acclaim with the work had
he chosen to publish it. But its literary worth isn't what makes
it important, and the work *The Red Book* is most reminiscent of
is Swedenborg's *Spiritual Diary* (1745–1765), the literary merits of
which are frankly limited. Like Jung, Swedenborg entered "waking
dreams"—active imaginations—and recorded his experiences and
conversations with the denizens of heaven, hell, and an intermedi-
ary realm he called the "spirit world" over a number of years. Jung,
we know, read Swedenborg, and along with Nietzsche, Swedenborg's influence can be seen, especially in Jung's remarks on the
nature of hell. For Jung "the way to your beyond leads through

Hell and in fact through your own particular Hell . . . Everything odious and disgusting is your own particular Hell,"⁷ and at one point Jung laments that "I perish on a dung heap."⁸ Swedenborg taught that we each create our own hell through the choices we make in life, and his depiction of the hellish realms after death, full of ordure, squalidness, and unspeakable stenches, is as off-putting and repulsive as Jung's. The central theme of *The Red Book* is that one has to find one's own way and live one's own life. If nothing else, Jung's account shows how difficult that can be.

Most people who buy *The Red Book*, however, will do so more for Jung's paintings than the tale. Jung repeated that he was *not* an artist almost as often as he insisted that he *was* a scientist, but anyone who spends any time gazing at the entrancing images that practically leap out of *The Red Book* will find it difficult to agree with him. Personally I don't think it matters whether Jung was a scientist or not—his work is important whatever you like to call it—but that he was an artist *The Red Book* makes undeniable. What becomes more interesting is Jung's insistence that he wasn't. As I think I've made clear in this book, Jung did this because he felt allowing the artist in him equal time would detract from his scientific reputation, and perhaps even pull him away from what he believed was his life's calling. This says as much about Jung's insecurities as it does about our own sensibilities, hypnotized into accepting that only science "counts" in any "serious" way. Jung vacillated over publishing *The Red Book* and finally decided not to, not only because the mysticism filling its pages would ruin his shaky scientific standing. It would also show he was the very thing his crafty *anima* accused him of being: an artist (again, see Chapter Five).

The amount of care and precision that Jung brought to his paintings and calligraphy reminds me of the laser-like attention some Zen masters applied to their parchments. Yet there is little of Zen calm in these pages. The colors, figures, and abstract images—mostly mandalas—seemed tightly held together, poised in an only temporary balance, like some psychedelic pop-up book, ready to spring out and confront the reader in a kind of graphic high-definition 3D. Jung remarked about his stone carvings, which also belie his "I'm-not-an-artist" declarations, that in them he tried "to give form to something that seems to be in the stone and makes me restless. It's nothing for show, it's only to make these troublesome things steady and durable."⁹ The same applies to *The Red Book*, and one comes away from it with a sense of a terrific energy just barely kept under control. The mandalas especially give the impression of a need to achieve an order that must be repeatedly renewed. Order and—I can think of no better word—tidiness were important to Jung, both in his inner world and his outer one. Visitors to Bollingen were admonished to put everything back where they found it. This was because, without modern lighting, Jung often had to find his way around his Tower in the dark, and he could do this only if everything was "in its place." Creating *The Red Book*, Jung was finding his way around another kind of darkness, and the mandalas show a drive to have everything "just right" in the house of Jung's soul.

Curiously, when I think of artists whose work Jung's paintings remind me of, a few names come to mind. The Belgian James Ensor, who influenced the German Expressionists and the Surrealists, and the Swedish Theosophist and Anthroposophist Hilma af Klint, immediately suggest themselves, as does the work of Lady Frieda Harris, who designed Aleister Crowley's famous Thoth Tarot Deck. As Jung had no use for modern art—he once turned down a request to write about Paul Klee—and even less for Theosophy, Anthroposophy, or Crowley, he probably was ignorant of Ensor, Klint, and Harris, although he may have been aware of Wassily Kandinsky's and Piet Mondrian's work—both of whom studied Theosophy and Anthroposophy. Their attempts to go beyond "art" in order to reach the spiritual reality behind the physical world seem very much in line with Jung's contentions that the images captured in *The Red Book* are spontaneous products of the unconscious. Other artists, too, suggest this themselves, such as the Russian mystic and painter Nicholas Roerich, and the psychedelic pop artist Peter Max, and the similarities between Jung's mandalas and Navajo sand paintings are also striking. Yet another artist I was reminded of may have been known to Jung, and not because he was a famous painter.

In 1895, at the age of thirty, Adolf Wölfli, a Swiss farm laborer, was admitted to the Waldau Clinic in Berne, Switzerland, where he remained the rest of his life; he died in 1930. Wölfli was psychotic and suffered hallucinations, but sometime after his admission he began to draw, eventually producing an enormous number of works. These attracted the attention of his doctor, Walter Morgenthaler, who wrote a book on Wölfli, *Ein Geisteskranker als Künstler* (*A Psychiatric Patient as Artist* 1921). Wölfli later became associated with Art Brut, but he is most known as one of the earliest examples of "outsider art," art created by mentally unstable individuals (the term was later expanded to include self-taught, folk, and "naïve" artists). Crammed with dizzying cascades of abstract design, one of the trademarks of Wölfli's work is his "horror vacui," the need to fill the entire surface of a work with detail, something associated with Islamic art, psychedelic art, and, interestingly, the *Book of Kells.* That Jung's mandalas, figurative paintings, and calligraphy squeeze a terrific amount of detail on to the page suggest a similar sensibility, and that he produced much of *The Red Book* during a time of psychic stress suggests that the pages of his hidden magnum opus would guarantee him a place among other "outsider artists." It was perhaps some recognition of this that kept him from either finishing *The Red Book* or publishing it.

Jung's attitude toward *The Red Book* shared the ambivalence he showed toward his mystical and occult interests. On the one hand it was a sanctum sanctorum, its pages reserved for only those closest to him, such as Toni Wolff. On the other hand, Jung is said to have often left it out, open on his desk, when seeing patients, and would point out a dream image or account of a fantasy, when trying to help them deal with their own inner journeys. Although he didn't publish a limited edition for friends and followers, as he did with the *Seven Sermons to the Dead*, Jung did send out feelers concerning *The Red Book*'s publication, asking colleagues if they thought it was a good idea. Here Jung's caution borders on calculation. One can't imagine William Blake, an "outsider artist" long before Adolf Wölfli, asking friends if he should publish *Milton, The Marriage of Heaven and Hell,* or his other illuminated (in more ways than one) texts. But then Blake was never of two minds about who or what he was. Blake, as is well known, was considered quite mad during his lifetime, and it was only after his death that his genius was really recognized.

After Jung's death, his son Franz took over running the house at Küsnacht, and as Jung had left no instructions about *The Red Book*, Franz left it in the cupboard where Jung put it. By many accounts, Franz's attitude toward the book was somewhat less appreciative than that of its new readers, and the family's attitude in general toward pilgrims in search of a glimpse of the mystical tome was, at least according to *The Red Book*'s editor, Sonu Shamdasani, "get lost."[10] *The Red Book* has been advertised as being seen until now by only a handful of people outside the Jung clan. As synchronicity would have it, I met one of those shortly before the book's UK publication. David Tresemer, author, among other books, of *Star Wisdom & Rudolf Steiner*, remembers visiting Küsnacht as a psychology graduate student during a seminar on Jung and Hermann Hesse in 1971. At one point Franz Jung "unlocked some kind of door or cabinet and produced with a flourish what he called *The Red Book*." The students asked if they could open it and Franz said, "Sure, I don't care." "There ensued an odd combination of behaviour," Tresemer told me in an e-mail. "Some people pored over these pages and whispered to each other, while Jung's son made comments that were slighting of Jung, more than a little too loud, trying to ignore the marvel in front of him. . . . I was most impressed by the juxtaposition of disdain and awe in the room. I glanced at the book a bit, and felt a few things. First: 'This is in an artistic code that cannot be cracked on its own, and this man who has brought it out is hardly likely to tell us the code, even if he knows.' Secondly, the dominant feeling in the room was this man's eclipse by his own father. . . . He had brought out a treasure, and it pained him to yet again have all attention go to someone who was dead. Thirdly, the aura of the book itself emanated to me, an aura of care, of attention to detail, to the task of making art from one's own life experience. Fourthly, when the page of The Shadow [a cloaked figure wearing a top hat, standing before a Mondrian-like wall that seems to be trying to become a mandala; my interpretation] was pointed out, I felt, 'This is not for me to see—this is another man's shadow, and meant to be locked away.' Then I wondered what was the purpose of this book. . . . And what would happen to it. When it was withdrawn again, the room felt much calmer emotionally."[11]

I include David Tresemer's account to show that *The Red Book*, while a treasure to many, was a kind of embarrassment for Jung's family, who were fiercely private and possessive of Jung's legacy, while at the same time somewhat dismissive of his status as a "sage." They seemed not to know what to do with *The Red Book*, and given that Jung himself allegedly considered it to be his most important work, to have left no instructions about it is simply baffling. (The idea that a thinker would leave the fate of the foundation of his life's work to chance is beyond me.) After moving it from the cupboard to a bank vault, the Jung clan kept a strict off-limits policy about *The Red Book* until 1997, when Franz Jung died. It was then that *The Red Book*'s editor, Sonu Shamdasani, approached the family with the idea of bringing out a scholarly, fully edited edition. Shamdasani's main bargaining chip was the fact that, although locked away in a Swiss bank, typed copies of Jung's text did exist, and that if he had gained access to them, others would, too. Given that Jung's reputation had recently been rocked by Richard Noll's damning *The Jung Cult*, Shamdasani convinced the family that excerpts from *The Red Book* were bound to emerge, and that the only way to avoid misrepresentation was to bring out an authorized version. They eventually agreed; Shamdasani was given complete access to *The Red Book*, and the Philemon Foundation, dedicated to advancing a new era in Jungian scholarship, was created to finance the project.

Shamdasani's achievement is unquestioned, and *The Red Book* is one of the great works of scholarship—Jungian or otherwise—of the century. He practically lived with the book for nearly a decade, and his long introduction and more than 1000 footnotes—in true Jungian fashion, making as many connections as possible—places Jung's strange work in its historical and cultural context. No doubt he is correct when he says that with *The Red Book*'s publication, there will be a "before and after" in Jung studies. But will it really "wipe out all the biographies"?[12] This seems doubtful, and is rather like saying it will "wipe out" all of Jung's previous books. Equally debatable is the idea that *The Red Book* is "nothing less than the central book in his [Jung's] oeuvre," and the "single most important documentary source" for his life.[13] Again, this is like saying that the work of Jung scholars who lacked access to *The Red Book* is practically worthless, a situation that Jung himself—who for all his bluff unconcern very much wanted to be understood—would have abetted by holding the work back. And while it is true that all of Jung's later psychology emerged from *The Red Book*'s pages, that psychology is familiar to readers of Jung's other works. It is undeniably fascinating to wade through the "primordial soup," as it were, out of which Jung's system emerged, but the soup doesn't necessarily tell us substantially more about the ideas themselves. In this way *The Red Book* is like other notebooks of men of genius: in them we can see the process through which their mature works came to being. No one, however, thinks that Nietzsche's notebook, published after his death as *The Will to Power*, is "the central book in his oeuvre," although his sister and some Nazi hacks argued that it was,[14] just as no one, I think, prefers Blake's sketches for his illuminated paintings to the finished product. Again, this isn't to diminish the importance of *The Red Book*, merely to affirm the importance of Jung's other works.

Although this is the first time the full work has been available for scholars and general readers, some of its content has appeared before. As mentioned, Aniela Jaffé's lovely tribute to Jung's life, *C. G. Jung: Word and Image*, contains several of the paintings from the book, and a few appeared in *Memories, Dreams, Reflections*. Even during Jung's own life, some stray pages saw print. In *The Secret of the Golden Flower*, Jung offers some mandalas from

The Red Book as examples "made by patients."[15] Jung was already taking a chance with his commentary to this work, making some of his most explicit statements about active imagination, the practice behind *The Red Book*, although, as mentioned, Jung never uses the term (see Chapter Six). But he didn't seem confident enough to admit that the mandalas were his. Curiously, it was the synchronicity of receiving the manuscript of *The Secret of the Golden Flower* soon after painting what was to be his last mandala, "The Castle," that prompted Jung to more or less close *The Red Book*. "The Castle" is one of the mandalas included in *The Secret of the Golden Flower* as being done by a patient.

It was at this point, Shamdasani argues, that Jung adopted his "allegorical method," in which, "rather than write directly of his experiences, he commented on analogous developments in esoteric practices, and most of all in medieval alchemy."[16] Yet this seems rather like a replay of Jung's tactic when writing his dissertation about the séances with Helly Preiswerk: rather than admit his own direct, personal involvement, he chose the safer route of writing in a detached manner, almost in the third person. Commenting on what medieval alchemists were doing, Jung could avoid telling his readers what *he* was doing. (And of course for Jung, the alchemists *were* doing what he was doing: active imagination.) But William James (Chapter Four), for example, who had just as valuable a scientific reputation as Jung, had no problem writing about his own experiences, which included experimenting with nitrous oxide, investigating mediums, entering spontaneous mystical states, even having a "creative illness" like Jung's, among others.[17] Both men liked and admired each other, yet James comes across as a much more "open" character, willing to put his reputation on the line, and ignoring what anyone thought about it. (Perhaps his being American had something to do with it.) For all Sham-dasani's explanations, there remains something unsatisfying about Jung's "indirect" communications, and his "allegorical method" may go someway to account for the difficulty of later works, such as *Psychology and Alchemy* and *Mysterium Coniunctionis*, in which the Herr Doctor Professor effect is unremitting.

The fact, too, that Jung's psychology grew out of the experiences recorded in *The Red Book* is no secret. He tells us this in *Memories, Dreams, Reflections*. And when Shamdasani remarks that Jung's reason for beginning *The Red Book* was that he had become disillu-sioned with scientific rationalism, one has to ask: when was he ever *not* disillusioned with it, remembering his lectures to the Zofingia society on metaphysics and the paranormal, his love of Goethe and Schopenhauer, his interest in spirits, visions, and dreams, his child-hood growing up with a mother who channeled another identity, and his own experiences of his No. 2 personality? Jung was a roman-tic who *never* embraced scientific rationalism, and if his parents had more money and could send him to another university, he might never have become a psychologist; his first choice, remember, was archaeology. There was no "conversion experience" for Jung that made him abandon scientific rationalism. Clearly, when he entered the world that produced *The Red Book*, Jung plunged headfirst into deep waters he had already waded in and tried to touch bottom. What he did while there is essentially what Swedenborg did nearly two centuries before him and what Rudolf Steiner was doing at the same time: inducing visionary states and trying to draw meaning and insight from them. The result is a remarkable work that Jun-gians and non-Jungians alike can marvel at. It is also provides more evidence—perhaps the most fascinating—of the strange ambiva-lence Jung the scientist showed toward Jung the mystic.

ACKNOWLEDGMENTS

Although a writer sits at his desk alone, many people help to put him there. I would like to thank Dr. Michael Neve, for help in obtaining research material; Mike Jay, for his invariably illuminating remarks; David Bennett, for arranging a private tour of the Freud Museum; and Ivan Ward, for opening its doors and allowing privileged access to its Otto Gross exhibition. Gottfried Heuer's remarks on Gross and his relationship with Jung were particularly helpful, as was the material on Gross on his website http://www.ottogross.org/english/documents/BiographicalSurvey.html. I'd also like to thank David Tresemer, for sharing with me his memories of *The Red Book* and of his visit to Jung's home in Küsnacht. My thanks also go to Jonathan Stedall, for use of his film *Laurens van der Post at 80*, which contained many helpful remarks about Jung, and to Richard Tarnas, for kindly giving me a tour of Casa Gabriella, and introducing me to John von Pragg and Robert Hinshaw of the Eranos Foundation. My friend James Hamilton allowed me to bend his ear to no end discussing several aspects of the book, and my friends John Browner, Lisa Yarger, and their daughter Greta, were of inestimable value in helping me research elements of the book while in Munich. My editor, Mitch Horowitz, is to be thanked for his sensitive appreciation of the writer's life. I would also like to thank the staff of the Camden Library, the British Library, and the Wellcome Library, without whom much of this book could not have been written, and my thanks also go to David Sutton and Val Stevenson of *Fortean Times,* for their swift reply to calls for help. Lastly, my warm thanks go to my sons, Maximilian and Joshua, and to their mother, Ruth, for doing their best to keep me Jung at heart.

NOTES

INTRODUCTION: THE UNDISCOVERED JUNG

1. R. I. Evans, *Dialogue with Carl Jung* (New York: Praeger Publishing, 1981), p. 147.

2. Originally published in German as *Wandlungen und Symbole der Libido*, and first translated into English in 1916 as *The Psychology of the Unconscious*. With his first major work, Jung began a pattern that would continue throughout his career and provide his biographers and critics with not a few headaches. Jung frequently subjected his books, articles, lectures, and even interviews to significant revisions, refashioning them at times into practically new works. This tinkering can be seen as an example of Jung's contention that his whole oeuvre was only a "work in progress." Yet, as we will see, in cases like that of his most well known work, the "so-called autobiography" *Memories, Dreams, Reflections*, how much is actually *echt* Jung is debatable.

3. C. G. Jung, *Analytical Psychology: Its Theory and Practice* (London: Routledge and Kegan Paul, 1982), pp. 44–45.

4. Ibid., p. 110.

5. Quoted in Vincent Brome, *Jung: Man and Myth* (London: Scientific Book Club,, 1979), p. 286.

6. Anthony Storr, *Jung* (Glasgow: Fontana/Collins, 1982), p. 51.

7. Stephan Hoeller, *The Gnostic Jung and the Seven Sermons to the Dead* (Wheaton, IL: Quest Books, 1982), p. 3.

8. Storr, 50.

9. Ibid., 58.

10. C. G. Jung, *Collected Works, Volume 7* (London: Routledge and Kegan Paul, 1977), p. 218.

11. Ibid., 215.

12. Ibid., 218.

13. See Richard Noll's *The Jung Cult* (Princeton, NJ: Princeton University Press, 1994) and *The Aryan Christ* (New York: Random House, 1997).

14. See, for example, Sonu Shamdasani's devastating *Cult Fictions* (London: Routledge, 1998).

15. Ibid.

16. Hoeller, p. xiii.

17. Ibid., pp. 26, 31.

18. Colin Wilson, *Superconsciousness* (London: Watkins Publishing, 2009), p. 145.

19. Hoeller, 31–32.

20. *C. G. Jung Speaking*, edited by William McGuire, translated by R. F. C. Hull (London: Picador, 1980), p. 398.

21. Aniela Jaffé, ed., *C. G. Jung: Word and Image, Bollingen Series* (Princeton, NJ: Princeton University Press, 1979), p. 6.

CHAPTER ONE: MEMORIES, DREAMS, REFRACTIONS

1. Quoted in Gerhard Wehr, *Jung: A Biography* (Boston: Shambhala, 1987), p. 1.

2. Some words of clarification regarding *Memories, Dreams, Reflections* are in order. When Jung agreed to reminisce with Aniela Jaffé, it was under the impression that she would be considered the book's author; he was giving her material firsthand, but essentially the book would be a biography. The idea of an "official" biography had come up before, and Jung had avoided it. Now, with pressure from Kurt Wolff, and others, Jung agreed. After his initial resistance, Jung began to take an interest, and his "remembrances of things past" began to excite him. When Jaffé reported to Wolff that Jung had actually started writing some chapters himself, Wolff was excited, too; he knew that a book about his life by Jung himself would sell more than a biography of him. Jung, however, maintained that the author of the book would be Jaffé, and six months before he died, he even signed a declaration expressly stating this. One reason Jung did this was that he wanted to provide for Jaffé after his death; she would no longer be his secretary, but as author, she would receive considerable royalties, a point not lost on Jung's heirs. Jung's other non-negotiable stipulation was on a posthumous publication. Given some of his remarks during his sessions with Jaffé, this may have seemed a reasonable decision. In actuality, more than anything else, it was the source of the confusion that followed.

Before he died Jung realized that Jaffé had made changes to his original remarks, that she was, in his coinage, "auntifying" (*Tantifizierung*, "auntification" is how he expressed it) his earthy and often outspoken language in order to make it more acceptable to conventional readers. She made him sound, he said, like a maiden aunt. People who knew Jung remarked on his immediacy and "peasant" gruffness, which came across in conversation and lectures, but which was absent in his Herr Doctor Professor prose. When he started the project in 1957, Jung was still a formidable taskmaster, and Jaffé would never have thought to take liberties with his language. But Jung was already eighty-two and tired easily, and by 1960 he had little strength left to resist her suggestions. To give one example, one of the most significant events in Jung's youth was his vision of a huge turd falling from heaven and smashing the roof of Basel Cathedral. In the "Protocols," the name given to the original conversations with Jaffé, Jung expresses this with concrete brevity: God shat on the cathedral and the turd was so enormous that the roof collapsed. But what he says in *Memories, Dreams, Reflections* is "God sits on his golden throne, high above the world—and from under the throne an enormous turd falls upon the sparkling new roof, shatters it, and breaks the walls of the cathedral asunder." The idea is the same, the content hasn't been corrupted, but anyone who knew Jung well would know that he wouldn't express himself in this way, at least not in conversation.

Another source of "auntification" was Jung's own family. Like Jaffé they objected to father's rude speech and added their own euphemisms to hers. They were also protective of their privacy; the idea that Jung, as a renowned scientist and thinker, somehow belonged to the world escaped them, and they were determined that anything to do with the family would be severely edited. This meant that many passages about Emma, his parents, his sister, and his mistress were cut, as were reminiscences about his relationship with men, with people like Hermann Hesse, and the indologist Heinrich Zimmer. This gave an already highly introverted account an even more extreme sense that its author was, if not oblivious to, certainly not focusing on, his relations with other people.

Some of the people involved in producing *Memories, Dreams, Reflections* tried to prevent Jaffé and Jung's family from completing "auntifying" the book; Jung's translator, R. F. C. Hull for one. But when Jung died and Kurt Wolff soon followed, there was no one to stop them. Later, Jaffé herself felt pressure from the family, who thought it inappropriate that she should receive such a huge cut of the profits. Legal squabbling colored the months leading up to publication in 1962, and Deirdre Bair's exhaustive account makes for some sad reading.

Although the German and English editions differ considerably, both suffered from the "auntifiers," and the book that introduces most people to Jung is a curious blend of Jung, Jaffé, and Jung's family. This is not to say that it is a fraud or a work of fiction. Jaffé was a dedicated student of Jung; she was one of the many who clustered round him at the Eranos conferences in Ascona, Switzerland, in the 1930s. She was a serious interpreter of his work and produced significant books of her own. But as with many followers of a teacher, she and not a few of her colleagues were often more "Jungian" than Jung and wanted to project the right *image* of him for the future. Whether she has done Jung and the many readers of the book a disservice is debatable. The book has been out for half a century now, and the Jung that most people know is the Jung it presents.

3. Deirdre Bair, *Jung: A Biography* (London: Little, Brown, 2004), p. 592.
4. C. G. Jung, *Memories, Dreams, Reflections* (London: Fontana Paperbacks, 1989), pp. 389–90.
5. Ronald Hayman, *A Life of Jung* (London: Bloomsbury, 1999), p. 221.
6. Wehr, p. 1.
7. Albert Oeri in *C. G. Jung Speaking*, edited by William McGuire and R.F. C. Hull (London: Picador, 1980), pp. 25–31.
8. Brome, *Jung: Man and Myth*, p. 21.
9. A nonpartisan biographical comparison between Jung and Steiner remains to be written. See however Gerhard Wehr's *Jung & Steiner: The Birth of a New Psychology* (Great Barrington, MA: Anthroposophic Press, 2002), pp. 48–76. Briefly, both spent a great deal of time alone as children, both came from poor families, both had early psychic experiences, both had a peculiar relationship with the dead, both felt themselves to be "outsiders," privy to secrets no one else understood, both thought of themselves as scientists, both went through what the historian of psychology Henri Ellenberger called a "creative illness," both gathered many female followers, and both exhibited behavior that the psychiatrist Anthony Storr termed "schizotypic," not full-blown schizophrenia, but sharing some of its characteristics.
10. Wehr, p. 17. Samuel Preiswerk wrote a Hebrew grammar that circulated as far as America; he also argued for the resettlement of Palestine by Jews decades before Theodor Herzl proposed the idea.
11. See Jean Gebser's magnum opus *The Ever-Present Origin* (Athens, OH: Ohio University Press, 1984), p. 70.
12. Jung, *Memories, Dreams, Reflections*, p. 24.

13. That Jung was recalling a dream he had eight decades ago might suggest that his account of it must have been embellished over the years, and the idea that a four-year-old boy would dream of a huge ritual phallus hidden below the earth is in itself difficult for some to accept. But Jung was not the only "mystic" to have a peculiarly vivid early dream life. "From my earliest years," the Russian esoteric philosopher P. D. Ouspensky wrote, "the world of dreams attracted me, made me search for explanations of its incomprehensible phenomena and try to determine the interrelation of the real and unreal in dreams. . . . When still a child I woke on several occasions with the distinct feeling of having experienced something so interesting and enthralling that all I had known before, all I had come into contact with or seen in life, appeared to me afterwards to be unworthy of attention and devoid of interest." Clearly, Ouspensky's own early experiences of dreams, which he calls "the most interesting first impressions of my life," (P. D. Ouspensky, *A New Model of the Universe* [New York: Alfred A. Knopf, 1969] p. 242) do not corroborate Jung's later ideas about them; but they do suggest that it is not impossible for a young boy to have the kind of dreams Jung says he had.

14. C. G. Jung, "Civilization in Transition" in *Collected Works, Volume 10* (Princeton, NJ: Princeton University Press, 1970), par. 803.

15. Jung's distinction between self and persona seems remarkably similar to Gurdjieff's distinction between "essence" and "personality." See P. D. Ouspensky, *In Search of the Miraculous* (New York: Harcourt, Brace and Co., 1949), pp. 161–65.

16. Jung, *Memories, Dreams, Reflections*, p. 376.

17. Ibid., p. 46.

18. Again, the link with Steiner is noteworthy; Steiner, too, was a strong hypnagogist. For hypnagogia in general and in particular Steiner's use of it, see my *Secret History of Consciousness* (Great Barrington, MA: Lindisfarne, 2003), pp. 85–94.

19. William James, "The Energies of Men" in *On Vital Reserves* (New York: Henry Holt, 1922), p. 14.

20. Henri Ellenberger, *The Discovery of the Unconscious* (London: Fontana Press, 1994), p. 664.

21. Jung, *Memories, Dreams, Reflections*, p. 49.

22. Gurdjieff's exact nationality, like his date of birth, remains a debated point. See my *In Search of P. D. Ouspensky* (Wheaton, IL: Quest Books, 2006), pp. 83–84.

23. Jung's own later "bullying treatment" gave him a reputation of being insensitive; as Colin Wilson writes, "Jung's own superabundant vitality

seems to have blunted the fine edge of human sympathy that is necessary to be a good psychiatrist" (*C. G. Jung: Lord of the Underworld* [Wellingborough: Aquarian Press,1984], p. 37). Yet anyone familiar with the Gurdjieff "work" will see a clear parallel with William James and Jung. Gurdjieff often forced his pupils to make "super efforts," with the result that many of them hit their own "second wind." They became, Gurdjieff said, connected to the "Great Accumulator" and were pumped full of new energy (P. D. Ouspensky, *In Search of the Miraculous*, pp. 233–37). This, in essence, is what happened to Jung.

24. Ibid., p. 58.

25. Ibid., p. 91.

26. Curiously, Hegel's famous "dialectic," in which thesis meets antithesis to produce a new thesis, transcending both, is in many ways similar to Jung's notion of the "transcendent function" discussed in Chapter Five.

27. C. G. Jung, *Analytical Psychology: Notes of the Seminar Given in 1925* (London: Routledge, 1992), pp. 134–35.

CHAPTER TWO: AN UNHAPPY MEDIUM

1. Jung, *Memories, Dreams, Reflections*, p. 108.

2. Ibid., pp. 95–96.

3. *The Freud/Jung Letters*, edited by William McGuire (London: Hogarth Press and Routledge and Kegan Paul, 1974), p. 95.

4. Others have suggested other possibilities. Ronald Hayman believes Jung's "submission" happened at an earlier age, around the time of his fainting fits (Hayman, *A Life of Jung*, p. 20). Jolande Jacobi believed it was when he was eighteen (Ibid.). Deirdre Bair (Bair, *Jung: A Biography*, p. 71) suggests it may have been a Catholic priest who was a friend of Paul Jung; Naomi Goldberg (Goldberg, *Returning Words to Flesh: Feminism, Psychoanalysis, and the Resurrection of the Body* [Boston: Beacon Press, 1990], p. 131) posits Paul Jung himself. Colin Wilson suggests the chemist as the individual in question (Wilson, *C. G. Jung: Lord of the Underworld*, p. 22). Jung was still young enough at the time to have been physically dominated by an older man; by the age of eighteen, he would have been too big to submit involuntarily. It does remain unclear, however, what exactly Jung's "submission" entailed. It is clear, though, that Jung's decision to pursue science came after this holiday. The chemist clearly served as a role model, and Jung's later shame may have been at realizing his hero had a rather base interest in him.

5. Jung, *Memories, Dreams, Reflections*, p. 23.

6. Ibid., p. 116.

7. Colin Wilson, *Afterlife* (New York: Doubleday, 1987), pp. 73–108.
8. Brome, p. 63.
9. Jung, *Memories, Dreams, Reflections*, pp. 125–27.
10. C. G. Jung, *Letters*, edited by Gerhard Adler (London: Routledge and Kegan Paul, 1973), pp. 180–82. It was discrepancies like these that alerted critics to the problems with *Memories, Dreams, Reflections*. In his letter, written in 1934, Jung is remembering incidents of forty years past; in his conversations with Aniela Jaffé, another twenty-three years or more are tacked on. Jung's letters weren't published until more than decade after *MDR* had appeared, and it is unclear how much access to them Jaffé had, although as his secretary one would think it would be considerable. Jung was a prodigious correspondent; his letters to Freud alone fill a hefty volume, so it is understandable that several decades after writing it, he may have forgotten about his account of the knife and table in his letter to Rhine, although given that it is one of the key items in his argument in support of the paranormal, one might think it warranted a better memory. Yet, although Jung does give differing accounts, the differences are not great enough to suggest, as some have, that nothing happened at all (Hayman, p. 49).
11. Wehr, p. 72.
12. Ibid. Helly Preiswerk's niece, Stephanie Zumstein-Preiswerk, published an account of her aunt's activities as a medium, *C. G. Jung's Medium* (Munich: Wissenschaftshistorische Sammlungen der ETH Bibliotek, 1975).
13. Bair, p. 48.
14. Ibid., p. 49.
15. Ibid., p. 51.
16. See Colin Wilson, *Mysteries* (London: Watkins Publishing, 2006), pp. 203–234; also Wilson Van Dusen, *The Presence of Other Worlds* (London: Wildwood House, 1975), pp. 117–38.
17. Jung, *Analytical Psychology: Notes of the Seminar Given in 1925*, p. 36.
18. Hayman, p. 60.
19. Ibid., p. 61.
20. Ibid., pp. 50–51.

CHAPTER THREE: INTRUDERS IN THE MIND

1. Quoted in Ellenberger, pp. 667–69.
2. Bair, p. 59.
3. Jung, *Memories, Dreams, Reflections*, p. 135.
4. Wilson, *C. G. Jung: Lord of the Underworld*, p. 35.
5. Quoted in Wehr, p. 81.

234 NOTES

6. Jung, *Memories, Dreams, Reflections*, p. 134.
7. Bair, p. 57.
8. Hayman, p. 75.
9. Maslow tells the story of a young woman during the Depression who suffered from a general sense of meaninglessness and apathy that affected her so badly she had even stopped menstruating. She was an intelligent college graduate, but was supporting herself and her entire family by working as a manager in a chewing-gum factory. The job was well paid and the money was welcome, but it was clear that she was wasting her potential on it. She wanted to do graduate studies in psychology, but couldn't, as she had to keep the job in order to keep her family out of the poorhouse. Although she told herself she *should* be happy— millions were out of work—she wasn't, and it affected her whole life. Maslow's "cure" was to suggest she take night classes. She did, and the anomie disappeared. The need to "self-actualize"—Maslow's version of "individuation"—is so great in some people that repressing it, even for the noblest of reasons, is a kind of living suicide. Quoted in Colin Wilson *New Pathways in Psychology* (New York: Taplinger Publishing Company, 1972), pp. 22–3.
10. *C. G. Jung Speaking*, p. 236.
11. Bruno Bettelheim, Commentary in Aldo Carotenuto's *A Secret Symmetry: Sabina Spielrein Between Freud and Jung* (London: Routledge and Kegan Paul, 1984), p. xxxviii.
12. Jung, *Analytical Psychology: Notes of the Seminar Given in 1925*, p. 8.
13. *The Freud/Jung Letters*, p. 289.
14. Jung, *Memories, Dreams, Reflections*, p. 172.
15. Martin Green, *Mountain of Truth: The Counterculture Begins, Ascona 1900–1920* (Hanover and London: University Press of New England, 1986); see also my *Politics and the Occult: The Right, the Left, and the Radically Unseen* (Wheaton, IL: Quest Books, 2008), pp. 136–38.
16. For Gross, Schwabing, and Monte Verità see Richard Noll's *The Jung Cult* (London: Fontana Press, 1996); for Schwabing see David Clay Large, *Where Ghosts Walked: Munich's Road to the Third Reich* (New York: W. W. Norton, 1997), pp. 3–42.
17. In *Memories, Dreams, Reflections*, pp. 165–66, Jung writes that "in the course of his practice a doctor will come across people who have a great effect on him, too. He meets personalities . . . whose destiny it is to pass through unprecedented developments and disasters. Sometimes they are persons of extraordinary talents, who might well inspire another to give his life for them; but these talents may be implanted

in so strangely unfavourable a psychic disposition that we cannot tell whether it is a question of genius or of fragmentary development. Frequently, too, in this unlikely soil there flower rare blossoms of the psyche which we would never have thought to find in the flatlands of society." This strikes me as a reference to Gross, and possibly Sabina Spielrein, too, neither of whom is mentioned in the book.

18. Like Jung, Freud was of two minds about at least one paranormal phenomenon, telepathy, "officially" rejecting it while maintaining a long personal and "closet" professional fascination with it. He was also of a more superstitious cast than he publicly admitted; in 1905, he "sacrificed" a treasured antiquity as an offering to the gods when his daughter Mathilde suffered a dangerous illness. In the 1920s, to close associates Freud maintained that he was not one who "right off rejects the study of the so-called occult psychological phenomena as unscientific," but this was a confession reserved for his intimates alone. A paper on "Psychoanalysis and Telepathy" was kept confidential, and an article in 1922, "Dreams and Telepathy," though published, left its readers unclear as to where the master actually stood on the matter. He told them that in it they would "learn nothing about the riddle of telepathy," nor discover whether he believed in it or not, and if he "awakened" in them the impression that he was "secretly" in favor of its reality, he regretted it, as he had "no opinion" on it and knew "nothing about it." Why bother then to write about it, especially as, to the end of his days, Freud maintained an attitude of strict scientific materialism? One suggestion is that, as with psychoanalysis itself, Freud was willing to explore areas of thought that went against the mainstream. Yet if that is so, why then did he not come out openly in support of unbiased experiment in the subject, and why then was he perpetually on guard against psychoanalysis being too closely associated with the occult? In 1925, by which time he had engaged in informal telepathic explorations with his daughter Anna, Freud advised Sándor Ferenczi *against* reading a paper on these experiments to the next psychoanalytical congress. Freud maintained that his fascination with telepathy was a personal matter—like his Jewishness and passion for cigars—and that it was "unessential" for psychoanalysis. Yet his doublethink about it suggests some part of him recognized its authenticity, while his adamant rational (and professionally prudent) side denied it, a conflict that would inform his relations with Jung (Peter Gay, *Freud: A Life for Our Times* [London: Little Books, 2006], pp. 443–45). For a brief but amusing picture of Freud as a "closet" Kabbalist—an idea presented in

David Bakan's *Sigmund Freud and the Jewish Mystical Tradition* (New York: Schocken, 1958)—see Frank Tallis' entertaining thriller, *Darkness Rising* (London: Arrow Books, 2009).

19. Ibid., p. 173.
20. Ibid., pp. 178–79.
21. Ibid., 159–60.
22. *C. G. Jung Speaking*, p. 184.
23. Ibid., p. 395.
24. "Mana" is a Melanesian term Jung adopted in several places in his work to indicate exceptional personal power, or the supernatural power emanating from spirits or sacred objects.
25. *C. G. Jung: Letters, Volume 1: 1906–1950*, edited by Gerhard Adler (London: Routledge and Kegan Paul, 1973), p. 9. It's possible that Jung got the idea of a psychosynthesis from the Italian psychologist Roberto Assagioli (1888-1974), whom Jung met in 1909 and whose work he admired. Like Jung, Assagioli was a disciple of Freud who took the spiritual dimension of human nature seriously, and he developed a system based on it, which he called psychosynthesis. See Roberto Assagioli, *Psychosynthesis: A Manual of Principles and Techniques* (New York: Viking, 1971).
26. Ibid., p. 10.
27. When Freud refused to give Reich his "training analysis"—an initiatory rite for practicing psychoanalysts, an idea that Jung was the first to propose—Reich had a breakdown which required hospitalization. See Colin Wilson, *The Quest for Wilhelm Reich* (New York: Anchor Press, 1981), pp. 90–95; for Tausk, pp. 67–68; for Silberer, pp. 72–73.

CHAPTER FOUR: METAMORPHOSES OF THE LIBIDO

1. Bair, p. 191.
2. *C. G. Jung Speaking*, p. 146.
3. Bair, p. 165.
4. For an interesting study of Freud's limitations when it comes to art see Anthony Storr's *The Dynamics of Creation* (New York: Atheneum, 1972).
5. Hayman, p.113.
6. Jung, *Memories, Dreams, Reflections*, pp. 179–80.
7. Jed Rubenfeld's 2007 best seller *The Interpretation of Murder* gives a fictional account of Freud and Jung's time in New York. Its portrayal of Jung, however, never rises above caricature.

8. Friedrich Nietzsche, *Human All-too-Human*, translated by R. J. Hollingdale (Cambridge: Cambridge University Press,, 1986), p. 17.

9. Bair, p. 184. I am indebted to Ms. Bair's chapter on Honegger and Schwyzer for my account here.

10. Space does not allow me to tell Honegger's full story; interested readers can find a detailed account in Bair. There they can also find an impartial assessment of the arguments for and against the idea that Jung stole Honegger's work. Bair, I think, refutes the charge that Jung was an intellectual thief, but readers can make up their own minds. See also "Appendix: The Honegger Papers," pp. 641–47.

11. Bair, p. 199.

12. Bair, p. 191.

13. Anthony Storr, *Jung* (Glasgow: Fontana/Collins, 1982), pp. 37–8.

14. *The Freud/Jung Letters*, p. 517.

15. Jung, *Memories, Dreams, Reflections*, p. 189.

16. Ibid., p. 524.

17. *The Freud/Jung Letters*, pp. 525–27.

18. Ibid., p. 533.

19. Ibid., p. 526.

20. Ibid., pp. 534–35.

21. I can't help but see a similar dynamic in the equally dysfunctional relationship between Gurdjieff and his most brilliant follower, P. D. Ouspensky. See my *In Search of P. D. Ouspensky*, 2nd edition (Wheaton, IL: Quest Books, 2006).

22. Ibid., p. 539.

23. Ibid., p. 540.

24. Ibid.

CHAPTER FIVE: TRANSCENDENT FUNCTIONS

1. Quoted in Hayman, p. 163.

2. Sonu Shamdasani, Introduction to C. G. Jung's *The Red Book* (New York: W. W. Norton & Co., 2009), p. 198.

3. C. G. Jung, "The Transcendent Function," in *Collected Works, Volume 8* (London: Routledge and Kegan Paul, 1981), p. 86.

4. Jung, *Analytical Psychology: Notes of the Seminar Given in 1925*, p. 43. Gerhard Wehr points out that Margarete Susman, a Jewish journalist living in Zürich at the same time as Jung, had similar premonitions. Wehr, p. 168.

5. Ellenberger, p. 673.

6. Jung doesn't specify the type of yoga he practiced, but it may have been a variant of the *savasana* asana of Hatha yoga, as Jung once recommended this to a patient suffering stress. Although many believe yoga first came to the West in the 1960s, it was familiar to many Europeans and North Americans as early as the late 19th century, through the proselytizing work of Swami Vivekananda, a disciple of Ramakrishna. See C. G. Jung, *The Psychology of Kundalini Yoga: Notes of the Seminar Given in 1932 by C. G. Jung*, edited by Sonu Shamdasani (London: Routledge, 1996), p. xxv.

7. See my article at http://www.forteantimes.com/features/profiles/167/august_strindberg.html. Also see my *A Dark Muse* (New York: Thunder's Mouth Press, 2005), pp. 201–7.

8. Jung, *Analytical Psychology: Notes of the Seminar Given in 1925*, p. 27.

9. Jung, *Symbols of Transformation, Bollingen Series* (Princeton: Princeton University Press, 1976), pp. 7–33.

10. Franz Jung, quoted in Linda Donn, *Freud and Jung: Years of Friendship, Years of Loss* (New York: Collier Books, 1990).

11. Images from *The Red Book* can be found in Aniela Jaffé's *C. G. Jung: Word and Image* (Princeton, NJ: Princeton University Press, 1979) a beautifully illustrated introduction to Jung's world.

12. Jung, *Memories, Dreams, Reflections*, p. 207.

13. Jung, *Analytical Psychology: Notes of the Seminar Given in 1925*, p. 38.

14. Ibid., p. 45.

15. Ibid., p. 46.

16. Ibid., p. 95.

17. One of the most important remarks Jung made in the 1925 seminar is that in ancient times—the times of the Upanishads and Tao Te Ching—"*thought happened* to people in a strangely direct and immediate way so as to give the impression of being given to the mind rather than made by it" (Ibid., pp. 74–75). Jung shares this insight with Rudolf Steiner and Jean Gebser, but also with the Princeton psychologist Julian Jaynes, who argued that until around 1250 BC human beings did not possess a self-reflective ego. They were not self-conscious in the way we are and did not think in the way we do. Thoughts *came* to them, Jaynes argues, and they believed these were the voices of the gods. Jaynes argues that these voices were produced by the right cerebral hemisphere and that in ancient times the right and left brain were separated—"bicameral"—and that only in relatively recent times did they begin to operate simultaneously, as they do today. For Steiner and Gebser's take on this, see my *A Secret History of Consciousness* pp. 245–48.

18. Aldous Huxley, *The Doors of Perception and Heaven and Hell* (London: Grafton Books, 1987), pp. 69–70.

19. Readers can find a good description of active imagination in therapeutic practice in Marie-Louise von Franz's *Shadows and Evil in Fairytales* (Dallas: Spring Publications, 1980), pp. 74–8. For the transcendent function, see p. 224.

20. Jung, "The Transcendent Function," p. 67.

21. Von Franz, *Shadow and Evil in Fairytales*, p. 77.

22. Jung, *Letters 1906–1950*, p. 460.

23. "Report on a Method of Eliciting and Observing Certain Symbolic Hallucination-Phenomena," collected in *Organisation and Pathology of Thought*, edited by David Rapaport (New York: Columbia University Press, 1951).

24. C. G. Jung, *Mysterium Coniunctionis*, Bollingen Series (Princeton, NJ: Princeton University Press, 1977), p. 555.

25. Jung, "The Transcendent Function," p. 82.

26. Jung, *Memories, Dreams, Reflections*, p.212.

27. Ibid., p. 210.

28. Bair, p. 223.

29. Ibid., p. 277.

30. Jung, *Memories, Dreams, Reflections*, p. 212.

31. Ibid., p. 210.

32. Wilson, *C.G. Jung: Lord of the Underworld*, p. 153.

33. Brome, p. 169.

34. Hoeller, pp. 8–9.

35. It is also available, along with selections of Jung's writings on Gnosticism, in *The Gnostic Jung*, edited by Robert Segal (London: Routledge and Kegan Paul, 1992).

36. Jung, *Letters 1906–1950*, p. 34.

37. Hoeller, pp. 183, 189.

38. Ibid., p. 574 n.6.

39. Jung, *Memories, Dreams, Reflections*, p. 220; Bair, p. 291; Hayman, p. 183.

40. See http://www.cgjungpage.org/junghistory/jung-history-volume1-issue2 .pdf

CHAPTER SIX: THE JUNG CULT

1. Ellenberger, p. 673.

2. Anthony Storr, *Feet of Clay* (New York: Free Press, 1997), p. 85.

3. Hermann Hesse, *Steppenwolf* (New York: Henry Holt, 1929) p. 83.

4. Hoeller, p. 4.

5. Bair, p. 322.

6. Brome, p. 170.

7. Bair, p. 248.

8. Barbara Hannah, *Jung: His Life and Work* (London: Michael Joseph, 1976), p 118.

9. James Moore, *Gurdjieff: A Biography* (Dorset, England: Element Books, 1991), p. 178.

10. Bair, p. 312. Also Hannah, pp. 194–95.

11. The classic book on Gurdjieff's Russian period is of course P. D. Ouspensky's *In Search of the Miraculous*. For more on Gurdjieff's tactics, see my *In Search of P. D. Ouspensky*, pp. 115–16.

12. Foreword to Toni Wolff's *Studies in C. G. Jung's Psychology* quoted in Sonu Shamdasani, *Cult Fictions* (London: Routledge, 1998), p. 25.

13. Brome, p. 202.

14. C. G. Jung, "Adaptation, Individuation, Collectivity" in *Collected Works, Volume 17* (London: Routledge, 1991), p. 451.

15. Ibid., p. 452.

16. Ouspensky, *In Search of the Miraculous*, p. 362.

17. Hesse, *Steppenwolf*, pp. 70–71.

18. Hoeller, p. 6.

19. Colin Wilson, *The Misfits* (London: Grafton Books, 1988), pp. 215–17.

20. Or possibly during that trip; the dates are somewhat confused. Hayman, p. 229.

21. Fanny Moser, *Spuk* (Baden bei Zürich: Gyr-Verlag, 1950).

22. Jung, *Collected Works, Volume 8*, p. 316.

23. Again, in a letter of 1946 to Fritz Kunkel, a psychotherapist, Jung admits that "metapsychic phenomena could be explained better by the hypothesis of spirits than by the qualities and peculiarities of the unconscious." Jung, *Letters Volume 1: 1906–1950*, pp. 430–34.

24. C. G. Jung, Foreword to Richard Wilhelm's *The I Ching or Book of Changes* (Princeton, NJ: Princeton University Press, 1977), p. xxv.

25. Jung took a less psychological approach to ghosts on other occasions. In his Preface to the German edition of Steward Edward White's classic *The Unobstructed Universe*, after careful qualifications, Jung remarks that there is "not a single argument which could disprove the existence of ghosts." Quoted in Aniela Jaffé, "C. G. Jung and Parapsychology" in *Science and ESP* edited by J. R. Smythies (London: Routledge and Kegan, 1967). He had also affirmed the existence of spirits in his

Zofingia lectures, and in 1951, he admitted to Anthony Storr a belief in witchcraft. See Storr, *Feet of Clay*, p. 101.

26. C. G. Jung, "Commentary" in *The Secret of the Golden Flower*, translated by Richard Wilhelm (New York: Harvest/HBJ, 1962), p. 81.

27. Jung, *Memories, Dreams, Reflections*, pp. 267.

28. Ibid., p. 268.

29. See especially the essay "Archaic Man," in C. G. Jung, *Modern Man in Search of a Soul* (New York: Harvest Books, 1933).

30. Jung, "In Memory of Richard Wilhelm," in *The Secret of the Golden Flower*, p. 142.

31. Apropos of this particular case, I can't resist telling a story that, I think, exemplifies perfectly Jung's notion of synchronicity. A few years ago, while waiting for a bus, I was reading Jung's account of this case, and, thinking of my own marital difficulties—which resulted in a divorce—I wistfully regretted that I didn't have Jung and the *I Ching* to consult on the marriage. No sooner had I thought this than my ex-wife stepped off a bus that had just arrived. She didn't live in that neighborhood, didn't usually visit it, and we were not in the habit of seeing each other. Oddly, several other incidences of a similar nature occurred between us, but these will have to wait for another occasion.

32. See Jung's Commentary in W. Y. Evans-Wentz's classic edition of the *Tibetan Book of the Dead* (London: Oxford University Press, 1970) and his introduction to D. T. Suzuki's *Introduction to Zen Buddhism* (London: Rider, 1948).

33. Jung, *The Secret of the Golden Flower*, p. 91.

34. Ibid., p. 92.

35. Ibid., p. 95.

36. Vincent Brome found the idea of a marriage continuing after death "bizarre." Jung, however, would have come across the idea in Emanuel Swedenborg; in *Conjugial Love*, one of Swedenborg's last books, he describes how in heaven soul mates are reunited. See my *Into the Interior: Discovering Swedenborg* (London: Swedenborg Society, 2006), pp. 23–24.

37. Jung, *Analytical Psychology: Notes of the Seminar Given in 1925*, p. 144.

38. Hannah, pp. 199–200.

39. Miguel Serrano, *C. G. Jung and Hermann Hesse: A Record of Two Friendships* (New York: Schocken Books, 1966), p. 98; *C. G. Jung Speaking*, edited by William McGuire (London: Picador, 1980), p. 147.

40. Aniela Jaffé, *From the Life and Work of C. G. Jung* (Einsiedeln: Daimon Verlag, 1989), p. 145.

41. Again, I can't resist noting another synchronicity, one that came while I was researching this book. My family and I were on holiday in Munich during Halloween, and we brought a pumpkin home to carve a jack o' lantern. Earlier in the day I watched *C. G. Jung at the Bollingen Tower Retreat*, an excellent documentary about Jung's stone carvings, made in 1951. In it Jung tells the story of receiving the stone by mistake, and explains that he kept it because it seemed a "perfect cube." That evening, while carving the pumpkin, my older son Joshua pulled out a piece he had just cut. He held it up to me and said "Look at this! A *perfect* cube!" He had never used those words before and I hadn't heard the story of Jung's cube until that day.

42. See Richard Boyle "If Crowley had met Lawrence and Lawrence had met Jung . . ." http://sundaytimes.lk/070225/Plus/012_pls.html

43. See my "René Schwaller De Lubicz and the Intelligence of the Heart" in *The Inner West*, edited by Jay Kinney (New York: Tarcher/Penguin, 2004), pp. 264-77.

44. Marie-Louise von Franz has addressed this idea in her remarkable *Creation Myths* (Boston: Shambhala, 1995); see also my *Secret History of Consciousness*, pp. 103–10.

45. Peter Gabriel's song "The Rhythm of the Heart" on his 1982 album *Security* is based on this incident. Gabriel was not the only rock musician inspired by Jung's ideas; in 1983 the Police released their last album, *Synchronicity*, named after Jung's term for an "acausal connecting principle." The group got the idea from Arthur Koestler's *The Roots of Coincidence*; fans of Koestler's work, they took the name of an earlier album, *The Ghost in the Machine* (1981) from the title of one of Koestler's books.

CHAPTER SEVEN: THE SHADOW KNOWS

1. Jung, *Memories, Dreams, Reflections*, p. 232.

2. Hoeller, p. 16.

3. *G. R. S. Mead and the Gnostic Quest*, edited by Claire Goodrick-Clarke and Nicholas Goodrick-Clarke (Berkeley: North Atlantic Books, 2005), p. 31.

4. The story is told brilliantly in Elaine Pagels' *The Gnostic Gospels* (London: Penguin, 1990).

5. Hoeller, p. 16.

6. Notably Robert Segal; see his introduction to *The Gnostic Jung*.

7. Notably Stephan Hoeller; see above.

8. Stephan Hoeller, Introduction to G. R. S. Mead's *The Hymns of Hermes* (Boston: Weiser Books, 2006), p. 21.

9. For an excellent account of Gnostic themes from ancient times to the present, see Richard Smoley's *Forbidden Faith: The Gnostic Legacy* (San Francisco: Harper SanFrancisco, 2006).

10. Hall's remarkable esoteric collection is on display at the fascinating library of his Philosophical Research Society in Los Angeles. See http://www.prs.org/

11. Marie-Louise von Franz, *Alchemy: An Introduction to the Symbolism and the Psychology* (Toronto: Inner City Books, 1980).

12. C. G. Jung, *Collected Works, Volume 7* (London: Routledge and Kegan Paul, 1977), p. 218. In the same essay apropos of active imagination, Jung writes: "Continual conscious realization of unconscious fantasies, together with active participation in the fantastic events, has . . . the effect firstly of extending the conscious horizon by inclusion of numerous unconscious contents; secondly of gradually diminishing the dominant influence of the unconscious; and thirdly of bringing about a change of personality" (Ibid., p. 217).

13. See Titus Burckhardt's *Alchemy: Science of the Cosmos, Science of the Soul* (Louisville: Fons Vitae, 1997) and Julius Evola's *The Hermetic Tradition* (Rochester: Inner Traditions, 1995).

14. Israel Regardie, *The Philosopher's Stone* (St. Paul: Llewellyn Publications, 1970), p. iv.

15. C. G. Jung, *Collected Works, Volume 10* (London: Routledge and Kegan Paul, 1974), p. 13.

16. Ibid.

17. C. G. Jung, "Wotan" in *Essays on Contemporary Events* (Princeton, NJ: Princeton University Press, 1989).

18. Jung, *Collected Works, Volume 10*, p. 17.

19. Ibid., p. 10.

20. Ibid., p. 16.

21. Ibid., p. 3.

22. Ibid., p. 11.

23. Ibid., p. 13.

24. Ibid.

25. Ibid.

26. See my *Rudolf Steiner*, p. 61.

27. Ibid., p. 12.

28. Bair, p. 439.

29. In Noll's *The Jung Cult* for example.
30. In *Cult Fictions* (p. 83) Sonu Shamdasani argues persuasively that, contrary to Noll's sensational claims, the influence of Theodore Flournoy and Pierre Janet on Jung was much greater than that of the *völkisch* zeitgeist of Munich and Monte Verità.
31. Petteri Pietikainen, "The Volk and Its Unconscious: Jung, Hauer, and the 'German Revolution,'" in *Journal of Contemporary History* 35, No. 4, p. 527.
32. In August 2009, while researching this book, I had the pleasure of visiting Casa Gabriella, during a stay in Intragna, in Switzerland, near Ascona. I was given a tour by Richard Tarnas, author of *The Passion of the Western Mind*, and saw the rooms Jung and Emma stayed in, the hall in which he lectured, and the garden where his "informal" talks occurred. Having already read a great deal about Eranos and Monte Veritá, it was something of a thrill to see these places, as it were, "in the flesh."
33. Bair, p. 792, n. 20.
34. Ibid., p. 469.
35. Jung, *Essays on Contemporary Events*, p. 79.
36. *C. G. Jung Speaking*, p.198.
37. Jung, *Essays on Contemporary Events*, pp. 16–17.
38. C. G. Jung, *Analytical Psychology: Its Theory and Practice*, p. 181.
39. Ibid., p.184.
40. See my *Secret History of Consciousness*, pp. 241–45.
41. *C. G. Jung Speaking*, p. 126.
42. Cyprian E. Blamires and Paul Jackson, eds. *World Fascism: A Historical Encyclopaedia* (Santa Barbara: ABC Clio, 2006), p. 358.
43. See http://pandc.ca/?cat=carl_jung&page=jung_nazis
44. Hayman, pp. 312-13.
45. "An Interview on Radio Berlin" in *C. G. Jung Speaking*, pp. 76–77.
46. C. G. Jung, "The State of Psychotherapy Today" in *Collected Works, Volume 10*.
47. Wittgenstein's comments can be found in his *Culture and Value*, translated by Peter Winch (Chicago: University of Chicago Press, 1980), pp. 18–19; for Weininger, see his *Sex and Character* (London: William Heinemann, 1906); also my *Dedalus Book of Literary Suicides: Dead Letters* (Sawtry, Cambs: Dedalus 2008), pp. 192–99.
48. Hayman, p. 314.
49. *C. G. Jung Speaking*, p. 197.

50. Bair, p. 512.
51. *C. G. Jung Speaking*, p. 197.
52. Ibid., p. 198.
53. Fuller accounts of the following can be found in Bair, pp. 481–95, whose chapter I have gratefully drawn on for the material here.
54. *C. G. Jung Speaking*, p. 132.
55. Among other questionable achievements, during his directorship, Dulles initiated the CIA's Project MK-Ultra, which investigated the use of psychedelic drugs as weapons of mind control, and was responsible for "turning on" 1960s radicals like Allen Ginsberg and Ken Kesey. Thus Dulles, like Jung, was indirectly responsible for the "mystical" character of that decade. On Project MK-Ultra, see Martin A. Lee's and Bruce Shlain's fascinating *Acid Dreams: The Complete Social History of LSD* (New York: Grove Press, 1992).
56. Bair, p. 494.
57. Ibid., p. 482.

CHAPTER EIGHT: ARCHETYPES FROM OUTER SPACE

1. Jung, *Mysterium Coniunctionis*, p. 324.
2. Wehr, p. 273.
3. Von Franz and others' reminiscences of Jung can be found in the 1985 documentary *Matter of Heart*; the DVD also includes the 1959 *Face to Face* interview and an unfinished documentary *C.G. Jung at Bollingen*.
4. Jung, *Letters, Volume 1: 1906–1950*, p. 286.
5. Ibid., p. 297.
6. Jung, *Letters, Volume 1: 1906–1950*, p. 285. Exactly when talk of a coming "age of Aquarius" began is difficult to pin down. Jung was certainly one of the earliest and undoubtedly the most prestigious person to speak of it, but he had predecessors. In 1937 the French esotericist Paul Le Cour published *Ere du Verseau*, "The Era (or age) of Aquarius," which predated Jung's earliest written remarks by three years. Le Cour himself based his comments on an article by the English writer and mystic Edward Carpenter, "The Symbolism of the Equinox," published in a French journal *L'Astrosophie* in 1929, and Carpenter's work borrowed from that of the arcane scholar Gerald Massey, whose *Lectures* (1900) discuss the transition from the age of the Fishes to that of the Water Bearer. A channeled work, *The Aquarian Gospel of Jesus the Christ*, by Levi H. Dowling, appeared in 1908. There had, of course, been mention of a "new age" earlier than this, but not of a specifically Aquarian

one. The popular idea of an Aquarian age spread through the '60s counterculture through Gavin Arthur's astrology column in the *San Francisco Oracle*. Arthur knew Carpenter in the late 1920s (Arthur was in his sixties during the "summer of love") and, like Jung, he marked 1940 as a year in which the "planet had entered a new age of culture" (see my *Turn Off Your Mind*, pp. 337–40).

7. C. G. Jung, *Aion* (Princeton, NJ: Princeton University Press, 1979), p. 87.

8. Ibid.

9. In August 1959, the celebrated pilot Charles Lindbergh visited Jung at the Bollingen Tower, where, among other things, they discussed UFOs. To his "astonishment," Lindberg found that "Jung accepted flying saucers as factual" and "didn't seem in the least interested in psychological aspects," nor in any "factual information relating to the investigation of flying-saucer reports," information which, Lindbergh, a skeptic, believed demolished any case for their "real" existence. See "A Visit from Lindbergh" in *C.G. Jung Speaking*, pp. 364–67. Lindbergh came away from the meeting wondering why "the Old Wizard just didn't open his mind to me on the subject of flying saucers."

10. C. G. Jung, "Flying Saucers: A Modern Myth of Things Seen in the Sky" in *Collected Works, Volume 10*, pp. 311–12.

11. Peter Gay, *Freud: A Life for Our Time* (London: Little Books: London, 2006) pp. 197–98.

12. Wilson, *Jung: Lord of the Underworld*, p. 116.

13. By "acausal" Jung simply wants to point out that the link between what is "inside" and "outside" is one of *meaning*, not cause and effect. In Chapter Six, note 31, I tell the story of a synchronicity involving my ex-wife. If a "causal" connection was involved, either I somehow unconsciously caused her to get on the bus at exactly the right time in order for her to exit it at precisely the moment I was thinking of her or she somehow unconsciously caused me to read the passage about Jung, the *I Ching*, and his patient at precisely the time and place where I would run into her. Both of these possibilities involve difficulties with time, as either of us would have had to start the process well in advance of the synchronicity taking place—I would have had to unconsciously *will* her to decide to come to that part of town, etc., which seems implausible at best, as it would entail my having a detailed knowledge of bus routes and an awareness of traffic on that particular day that I simply did not possess, not to mention the difficulties in explaining how I could will her to do this at all. If I merely thought of my ex-wife

and then saw her coming off the bus, some form of telepathy *could* have been involved, but the fact that I was also reading about a case of synchronicity (the *I Ching*) involving a dubious marriage, complicates this. Likewise the case in note 39; if the link was causal, I somehow "made" my son say "a perfect cube" when he did, which seems absurd. In both cases, however, there is a *meaningful* link between the outer event and the inner one, and it's this that generates the mystery.

14. Arthur Koestler, *The Roots of Coincidence* (New York: Random House, 1972), pp. 100, 95.
15. Ibid, p. 98.
16. *C. G. Jung Speaking*, p. 183.
17. Jung, *Memories, Dreams, Reflections*, p. 251.
18. Ibid., p. 327.
19. *C. G. Jung Speaking*, p. 215.
20. Quoted in Wehr, p. 275.
21. Serrano, pp. 60–61.
22. See Joscelyn Godwin, *Arktos: The Polar Myth in Science, Symbolism, and Nazi Survival* (Kempton, IL: Adventures Unlimited Press, 1996).
23. Quoted in Wilson, *C. G. Jung: Lord of the Underworld*, pp. 122–23.
24. C. G. Jung, *Man and His Symbols* (New York: Dell Publishing, 1968), pp. 91–92.
25. Ibid., p. 93.
26. Ibid., p. 71.
27. Ibid., pp. 93–94.
28. Quoted in Brome, p. 227.

EPILOGUE: AFTER JUNG

1. See, for example, the work of Anthony Stevens, especially his *Archetype Revisited: A Natural History of the Self* (London: Routledge, 2002), which links Jung's ideas to evolutionary psychology and animal ecology.
2. Storr, *Feet of Clay*, p. 96.
3. Maggy Anthony, *The Valkyries: The Women Around Jung* (Shaftesbury: Element, 1990).
4. Quoted in Jolande Jacobi, *The Way of Individuation* (New York: Harcourt, Brace & World, 1967), p. vii.
5. Thomas B. Kirsch, *The Jungians: A Comparative and Historical Perspective* (London: Routledge, 2000), p. 20.
6. https://philemonfoundation.org/mission/
7. Moore's relationship to Hillman's work, which, like Jung's, is not a model of clarity, is in some ways similar to von Franz's to Jung's.

For an interesting take on this see http://www.nytimes.com/1995/ 04/23/magazine/how-the-soul-is-sold.html?sec=health&spon= &pagewanted=all

POSTSCRIPT: *THE RED BOOK*

1. C. G. Jung, *The Red Book*, edited by Sonu Shamdasani, translated by Sonu Shamdasani, John Peck, and Mark Kyburz (New York: W. W. Norton & Co., 2009).
2. https://philemonfoundation.org/projects/red_book/
3. Ibid.
4. http://www.nytimes.com/2009/09/20/magazine/20jung-t .html?pagewanted=all
5. Jung himself recognized his debt to Nietzsche, or at least one of his inner figures did. At one point, while Jung was wrestling with doubts about the project, a voice told him "Nietzsche did this better than you." C. G. Jung, *The Red Book*, p. 235 n. 65. A parallel reading of *The Red Book* and *Thus Spake Zarathustra* would highlight many echoes. For example, on p. 231 Jung writes, "You seek the path? I warn you away from my own. It can also be the wrong way for you." Zarathustra tells his followers, "I now go away alone, my disciples. You too now go away and be alone!" and "You had not yet sought yourselves when you found me" (Friedrich Nietzsche, *Thus Spake Zarathustra*, translated by R. J. Hollingdale [London: Penguin, 1969], p. 103). Jung's remarks on the cold, empty space of solitude (p. 245) are an encapsulation of Zarathustra's sermon "Of the Way of the Creator" (pp. 88–91). These are just a few examples. In pointing this out I am not saying that Jung "stole" from Nietzsche; one would be hard pressed to find an important thinker or writer in the decades following Nietzsche's death (1900) who *wasn't* influenced by him. Yet the parallels, not only stylistically, but also in the "teaching" found in *The Red Book*, with Nietzsche's own philosophy, are too evident to ignore. For a brief account of the similarities between Nietzsche and Jung, see Anthony Storr's *Music and the Mind* (London: HarperCollins, 1997), pp. 150–55.
6. Another work which deals with this theme, although in a more literary way, is Owen Barfield's novel *Unancestral Voice* (London: Faber & Faber, 1965), in which the hero becomes aware of the Meggid, a "voice that spoke within the mind." Meggid most likely derives from Maggid, a Hebrew name for preacher.
7. C. G. Jung, *The Red Book*, p. 264.
8. Ibid., p. 275.

9. Letter to Don Stacy, September 1, 1952 in *C. G. Jung Letters, Volume 2: 1951–1961* (London: Routledge and Kegan Paul, 1976), p. 83.

10. http://www.nytimes.com/2009/09/20/magazine/20jung-t .html?pagewanted=all. This ambivalence haunts accounts of how Jung's family reacted to his "night sea journey." In the Preface to *The Red Book*, Ulrich Hoerni, Jung's grandson, remarks that Jung's "children . . . were not informed about his self-experiment and they did not notice anything unusual" (p. vii). Yet this differs from the account in *Memories, Dreams, Reflections* of the "haunting of Küsancht" and Franz Jung's remarks about living with a man who kept a loaded pistol by his bed (Chapter Five).

11. Personal correspondence with the author, October 12, 2009.

12. http://www.nytimes.com/2009/09/20/magazine/20jung-t.html?page wanted=10&_r=2&emc=eta1

13. Sonu Shamdasani, Introduction to Jung's *The Red Book*, p. 221.

14. See Walter Kaufmann's Introduction to Friedrich Nietzsche's *The Will to Power*, translated by Walter Kaufmann and R. J. Hollingdale (New York: Random House, 1967) pp. xiii-xxiii.

15. C. G. Jung, "Commentary" in *The Secret of the Golden Flower*, p. 137.

16. Sonu Shamdasani, Introduction to Jung's *The Red Book*, p. 219.

17. James' account of his nitrous oxide experiment can be found at http:// www.des.emory.edu/mfp/jnitrous.html

INDEX

active imagination
  as alchemical practice, 156, 223
  danger of, 116, 144
  gnosis as, 153
  guardedness concerning, 115–16
  during hypnagogic state, 27
  increase in synchronistic and paranormal
    phenomena, 122–23
  inferior function in, 136, 156
  method and results, 117–19, 143–44,
    243n12
  recordings of, 214, 223
  roots of, 50
  symbols produced, 120
  during time of distress, 120–21
  unconscious remarks, 121
"Adaptation, Individuation, Collectivity"
    (Jung), 133
Adler, Alfred, 71, 98, 161–62, 185
Adler, Gerhard, 170
Africa, 140–42, 148–50
Aion (Jung), 189, 193
alchemy, 116, 143, 155–59, 223
Alchemy (von Franz), 156
Ancient Pagan and Modern Christian Symbolism
    (Inman), 89
Andreas-Salomé, Lou, 101
anima, 40, 94, 121–22, 129
Answer to Job (Jung), 20, 153, 200
"Apocalyptic Landscapes" (Meidner), 109–10
Apparitions (Jaffé), 208
archetypes
  in collective unconscious, 2, 33, 97,
    151, 191
  language of, 123

  in Nazism, 160, 167, 180
  overrunning of conscious decision, 167
  vision of doctor, 187–88
Aschaffenburg, Gustav, 71
Assagioli, Roberto, 236n25
Association for Analytical Psychology, 130
automatic writing, 58, 123, 137

Babette (Jung's patient), 58, 89
Bachofen, Johann, 53, 74
Baeck, Leo, 172
Bailey, Alice, 165
Bailey, Ruth, 150, 197–98, 199
Bair, Deirdre, 173, 232n4
Bancroft, Mary, 176–79
Beckett, Samuel, 182
Bergson, Henri, 141
Bettelheim, Bruno, 67
Binet, Alfred, 61–62
Binswanger, Ludwig, 98
Bion, Wilfred, 182
Bitter, Wilhelm, 173–76
Black Book (Jung), 129, 214
Blake, William, 219, 222
Blavatsky, Helena Petrovna, 44
Bleuler, Eugen, 55–57, 62, 64, 81, 99
Bly, Robert, 209
Boa, Fraser, 209
Boddighaus, Martha, 94
Bollingen Foundation, 186
Book of the Law, The (Crowley), 123
Briner, Mary, 178
Brome, Vincent, 129
Buber, Martin, 132, 166
Buddha, 183

Bulletin of the Analytical Psychology Club of New York, 171
Burckhardt, Jacob, 53, 89
Burckhardt, Titus, 157
Burghölzli Asylum, 53, 55, 56–57, 58, 64, 81–82

C. G. Jung Institute, 184, 207, 209, 210
C. G. Jung (Jaffé), 208, 222
Campbell, Joseph, 166, 209
Canaris, Wilhelm, 177
Care of the Soul (Moore), 211–12
Casa Gabriella lectures, 165–66, 172, 182, 193
Chang Tsu, 23
Charcot, Jean-Martin, 61
Churchill, Winston, 174
Clark University, 83–84, 88
Collected Works (Jung), 139, 186, 200
collective unconscious
    ambiguous definitions of, 3
    archetypes in, 2, 33, 97, 151, 191
    astrological ages as symbols of, 190
    versus Freudian personal unconscious, 160
    in hypnagogic visions, 97
    Jung's experiences of, 25, 86–87, 149
    mystical experience of, 2–3
    in Nazism, 160, 167, 180
    Symbols of Transformation (Jung), 97
Corbett, Sara, 213–14
Creuzer, Friedrich, 89
Crookes, William, 44
Crowley, Aleister, 123, 157, 217

death
    afterlife, 42, 204
    curiosity about, 21, 42
    dreams about, 107–8
    premonition of, 144
    presence of dead, 19, 122
    reawakening of dead, 45, 108
    séances, 47–50
de Crinis, Max, 174
Demian (Hesse), 124
Dorn, Gerhard, 155, 157, 183
dreams. *See also* visions and fantasies
    about reawakened dead, 45, 108, 144
    career decisions and, 37, 38–39
    childhood dreams, 21, 22
    collective unconscious in, 86–87
    Freud's dreams, 86
    mythological significance of, 107–8

phallus dream, 21, 86, 231n13
portent of shift in life, 100, 107, 154
revelatory nature of, 88–89
self-regulation of psyche in, 99
Dulles, Allen W., 176–80, 245n55
du Prel, Carl, 44

Eastern philosophy
    Hinduism, 183, 187
    I Ching, 139, 142–43, 184, 189
    Taoism, 143, 183–84
    Tibetan Buddhism, 22, 184
    yoga, 165, 238n6
Eckhart, Meister, 153
Edison, Thomas, 44
Eisenhower, Dwight D., 179
Eliade, Mircea, 165
Ellenberger, Henri, 28, 110, 127
Encounters With Soul (Hannah), 208
Ensor, James, 217–18
Eranos conferences, 165–66, 172, 182, 193
Essays on Contemporary Events (Jung), 170
Estés, Clarissa Pinkola, 209
Evans, Richard I., 1
Evans-Wentz, W. Y., 183
Evola, Julius, 157

Face to Face interview, 154, 197, 199, 201, 205
fantasies. *See* visions and fantasies
Faust (Goethe), 18, 38
Federal Polytechnic, 181
Feet of Clay (Storr), 6, 127
Ferenczi, Sándor, 71, 84
Flournoy, Theodore, 97
Flying Saucers (Jung), 191
Forel, Auguste, 55
Fragments of a Faith Forgotten (Mead), 123
Freeman, John, 154
Freud, Sigmund
    break with Jung, 78–79, 96–103, 105
    correspondence with Jung, 68–70
    dream analysis of Jung, 86–87
    on dreams, 88, 90
    dreams of, 86
    fainting fits, 85, 101
    as father figure, 69, 78–79, 99
    influence on Jung, 61, 63, 70–71
    interest in mythology, 93
    Jung's death wish against, 85, 87, 101
    Jung's reservations concerning, 65, 68–69, 84

Kreuzlingen gesture, 98
meeting of Jung, 70–71, 83–84, 88
mistrust of Jung, 76, 77–78
obedience of followers, 99, 102
obituary, 185
on paranormal phenomena, 75–78, 235n18
psychoanalysis concept, 65
Psychoanalytical Association, 71
on sex, 69, 73, 84
Fröbe-Kapteyn, Olga, 165

Gabriel, Peter, 242n45
Galton, Francis, 59
Gebser, Jean, 19, 165, 167
Geisteskranker als Künstler, Ein (Morgenthaler),
   218
German Faith Movement, 164
Germany
   dark side (blond beast), 159–60, 167–68
   Hitler, 159, 163, 167–68, 174–75, 179
   Hitler, plots against, 173–76, 177–78
   incursions throughout Europe, 185
   International Society, 163–64, 165, 166–67
   Jews, 161–62, 166, 169–72
   Nazi exploitation of Jung, 168, 171, 173
   Nazism, Jung's stance on, 167–72
   Swiss intelligence on, 176–80
   völkisch groups, 164–65
Gisevius, Hans Bernd, 177–79
Glover, Edward, 3
gnosis and Gnosticism, 5, 7–8, 31, 123–24,
   152–54, 161
Gnostic Jung and the Seven Sermons to the Dead,
   The (Hoeller), 124
"God Complex, The" (Jones), 105–6
Goethe, Johann Wolfgang von, 18, 26, 38,
   45, 154
Göring, Matthias Heinrich, 163, 166, 171
Grail Legend, The (Emma Jung), 198
Green, Martin, 73
Groddeck, Georg, 163
Gross, Hans, 72
Gross, Otto, 72–75, 133
Gurdjieff, G. I.
   body of teachings, 206
   compared to Jung, 131
   on consciousness, 136–37
   female followers, 64, 131
   on fulfilling of obligations, 134
   Gurdjieff work, 232n23
   self-remembering, 28–29

on transformation through interpersonal
   friction, 131
Gurney, Edmund, 137
guru, Jung as, 6–8, 127, 146, 206
guru, Jung's inner, 113–14

Habilitationsschrift (Jung), 66
Haeckel, Ernst, 90
Hall, Manly P., 155
Hannah, Barbara, 146, 175–76, 207, 208, 209
Harding, Esther, 196
Harris, Frieda, 217–18
Harvard University, Tercentenary Conference,
   182
Hauer, J. W., 164–66
Hauffe, Frederika, 44, 49
Hauke, Chris, 211
Hayman, Ronald, 85, 168–69, 232n4, 233n10
He: Understanding Masculine Psychology
   (Johnson), 211
Heaven and Hell (Huxley), 115
Hegel, Georg Wilhelm Friedrich, 32, 232n26
Heidegger, Martin, 3, 206
hell, 215–16
Henderson, Joseph, 202
Hesse, Hermann, 8, 73, 124, 128, 132, 134
Hidden Symbolism of Alchemy and the Occult
   Arts (Silberer), 154
Hillman, James, 209–10, 212
Hillyer, Robert, 171
Hinduism, 183, 187
History of Greek Civilization (Burckhardt), 89
Hitler, Adolf
   incursions throughout Europe, 185
   Jung's assessment of, 167–68, 174–75, 179
   as leader, 159, 163, 168
   plots against, 173–76, 177–78
   on völkisch movement, 164
Hoeller, Stephan, 4, 7, 8, 124
Holy Grail, 100, 113, 198
"Holy Grail of the Unconscious, The"
   (Corbett), 213–14
homosexuality, 39–40, 232n4
Honegger, Johann Jakob, 90–94
Horney, Karen, 163
Humboldt, Alexander von, 17
Huxley, Aldous, 8, 115
hypnagogia, 27, 97–98, 119–20

I Ching, 139, 142–43, 184, 189
India, 182

individuation
  alchemy as, 156–58
  through connection to land, 83
  contribution to society, 133–34
  earlier writers on concept of, 10
  as evolutionary process through eternity,
    145, 203
  fusion of disparate parts of personality,
    49–50
  Gnosticism and, 152–53
  through hypnagogic visions, 27
  incest as symbol of, 96
  Jung's ability to foster in patients, 66
  Jung's experience of, 6–7, 28–29, 38, 41,
    144, 199
  through mandala meditation, 125–26, 192
  need for personal secret, 24
  as ongoing journey, 11
  personal significance of, 5–6
  prophetic revelations on, 123
  psychic maturity beyond norm, 128
  psychosynthesis, 78, 236n25
  Way of Individuation, The (Jacobi), 208
  of Western civilization as whole, 190
Individuation in Fairy Tales (von Franz), 209
Inman, Thomas, 89
International General Medical Society for
    Psychotherapy (International Society),
    163–64, 165, 166–67, 173, 183
International Psychoanalytical Association, 71,
    72, 93, 95, 105
Iron John (Bly), 209

Jacobi, Jolande, 13, 170–71, 202, 207–8,
    232n4
Jaffé, Aniela
  authorship of *Memories, Dreams, Reflections*,
    13, 208, 228n2
  in film, 209
  writings, 202, 207, 208, 222
James, William, 28, 44, 88, 135, 223
Janet, Pierre, 61–63
Jaynes, Julian, 238n17
Jews
  in International Society, 166
  Jung's attitude toward, 161–62, 169–72
  Jung's attraction to Jewish women, 63, 67, 75
  in psychoanalysis field, 69, 162
  in Psychological Club, 185
Johnson, Robert A., 211
Jones, Ernest, 85, 101, 105–6

Joyce, James, 181–82
Jung, Carl Gustav
  archaeology, interest in, 37, 89, 224
  as artist, 121–22, 216–19
  asocial nature, 14, 16
  career choice, 37–38, 51–53, 117
  childhood influences, 16–23
  children, 14, 68, 122, 129, 145
  crisis (creative illness), 110, 124–25,
    127–28, 144, 188, 214
  drinking habit, 40, 43, 56, 82, 85, 182
  final years, 198–204
  guardedness concerning discoveries, 4,
    47–48, 115–16, 123, 139, 189
  marriage, 61
  military service, 54, 83, 116, 124–25
  nature, love of, 20, 32, 83
  neurosis, overcoming of, 27–28
  private practice, 61, 81
  sanity, fear for, 52, 108, 111
  schooling, 22, 25–27, 31–32, 34, 36–37
  scientific persona, 1, 5, 48, 116, 189, 205,
    216
  writing style, 2–4, 97, 193–94, 195, 206,
    223–24
Jung, Carl Gustav, Sr., 17
Jung, Emilie Preiswerk
  death, 144, 145
  mental breakdown and hospitalization, 18,
    26, 70, 122
  as mother, 25–26
  move to home near Jung, 83
  séances, 47
  trance states and No. 2 voice, 18–19,
    29, 42, 45–46, 47
Jung, Emma Rauschenbach
  at Burghölzli, 63, 81
  correspondence with Freud, 95
  death, 197–98
  formality with children, 14
  marriage, 61
  pregnancy, 129
  in Psychological Club, 130, 132
  tolerance of Jung's affairs, 94–95, 130
  wealth, 60, 61, 64, 81
Jung, Franz, 112, 219–20
Jung, Gertrude "Trudi," 25, 83, 204
Jung, His Life and Work (Hannah), 208
Jung, Paul
  doubts about religion, 16, 30–31
  illness and death, 41–42

on Jung's future, 27, 36, 37
poor relationship with Jung, 17, 22
Jung and Film (Hauke), 211
Jung and the Post-Jungians (Samuels), 211
Jung Codex, 152
Jung Cult, The (Noll), 221
Jungian thinkers, 207–12

Kandinsky, Wassily, 218
Kant, Immanuel, 33, 36, 44
Kazantzakis, Nikos, 215
Kerényi, Karl, 165
Kerner, Justinus, 44
Keyserling, Hermann, 142
Keyserling's School of Wisdom, 142, 165, 172
Klint, Hilma af, 217–18
Knickerbocker, H. R., 174
Knight, Richard Payne, 89
Koestler, Arthur, 194–95
Krafft-Ebing, Richard von, 51–52, 66
Kretschmer, Ernst, 163–64
Küsnacht, 75, 77, 83, 122. *See also* Tower

Lang, Josef, 124
Lawrence, D. H., 147
libido, 96
Lindbergh, Charles, 246n9
Little Book on the Human Shadow, A (Bly), 209
Lodge, Oliver, 44

Maeder, Alphonse, 56, 99
Man and His Symbols (Jung), 202–3, 205
mandalas
attunement to inner state, 125–26
flying saucers as, 191–92
in Jung's dreams, 37, 117
metaphysical system as, 50
as products of psyche, 22
in *Red Book* (Jung), 217, 218
in *Secret of the Golden Flower* (Wilhelm, ed.), 222–23
Self and, 143
Systema Mundi Totius, 125
Marcuse, Herbert, 73
Maslow, Abraham, 6, 66, 234n9
Matter of Heart (Whitney), 209
Max, Peter, 218
Mayer, Gerald, 176–77
McCormick, Edith Rockefeller, 106, 130
McCormick, Fowler, 106, 147
McCormick, Joseph Medill, 82, 106

Mead, G. R. S., 92, 123, 152
Meidner, Ludwig, 109–10
Meier, Carl A., 207
Mellon, Paul and Mary, 186
Memories, Dreams, Reflections (Jung)
alternative thinking, 8–9
appeal to broad audience, 205
on development of Jung's psychology, 224
fantasies, 111
India trip, 183
paintings, 222
paranormal phenomena, 77
writing of, 13–15, 208, 228n2
Miller, Frank (pseud.), 97–98
Moltzer, Mary, 94, 121, 125
Mondrian, Piet, 218
Moore, Thomas, 211–12
Morgenthaler, Walter, 218
Morning of the Magicians, The (Pauwels), 201
Müller, Friedrich von, 52–53
Myers, Frederick, 44, 137
Myers-Briggs Personality Test, 135
Mysterium Coniunctionis (Jung), 116, 155, 156, 224
Myth of Meaning, The (Jaffé), 208
mythology, 23, 88–90, 92–93, 96, 97–98, 164–65

Nag Hammadi Library, 152
Nature Word (Schwaller de Lubicz), 215
Neumann, Erich, 166, 170, 207
New Age movement, 7, 8, 189–92, 245n6
Nicoll, Maurice, 131
Nietzsche, Friedrich
on chaotic precondition for rebirth, 168
on dreams, 90
individuation concept, 10
influence on Jung, 26, 45, 215, 248n5
Nazi defamation of, 181
on outsider's contribution to society, 134
posthumous publication of notebook, 222
as thinker and feeler, 137
on underlying meaning of cultural works, 84
No. 2 (Other), 1, 29–30, 32, 34–36, 75, 99
Noll, Richard, 206, 221

objective psyche, 2, 114, 128. *See also* collective unconscious
occult. *See* paranormal phenomena
Ochwiay Biano, 141, 147
Oeri, Albert, 16, 175

On the Aesthetic Education of Man (Schiller), 119
On the Psychology and Pathology of So-called Occult Phenomena (Jung), 47
Origin and History of Consciousness, The (Neumann), 207
Ouspensky, P. D., 134, 231n13

paranormal phenomena. *See also* synchronicity
  active imagination and, 122
  ambivalence concerning, 4, 137–39, 219
  automatic writing, 58, 123, 137
  exteriorised libido, 77
  Freud's bookcase episode, 75–76
  hauntings and apparitions, 4, 19, 22, 45–46, 77, 138
  in Jung's family background, 18–19, 44–45
  popular interest in, 9, 43–44
  premonitions, 60, 110, 144
  presence of dead, 19, 122
  psychosynthesis, 78, 236n25
  reawakening of dead, 45, 108
  séances, 47–50
  transference, 138
Pauli, Wolfgang, 181, 193
personality types, 135–37
Philemon Foundation, 211, 221
Philemon vision, 113–14, 123–24
Pindar, 10
Police (rock band), 242n45
Porter, George, 147
Power of Myth (Campbell), 209
Preiswerk, Helene "Helly," 46–51, 63
Preiswerk, Luise "Luggy," 47, 49
Preiswerk, Samuel, 19, 230n10
Probleme der Mystic und ihrer Symbolik (Silberer), 154
Problems of the Feminine in Fairy Tales (von Franz), 209
Psyche (Rohde), 89
psychiatry
  complexes, 59
  counter transference, 66
  Jung's career choice, 51–53
  "kill or cure" method, 82
  patient-friendly approach, 55–56
  psychological tension, 62
  reality function, 62
  role of past traumas, 61
  word-association tests, 58–59
psychoanalysis

  emphasis on sexual repression, 73, 98
  as Jewish science, 69, 162
  Jung's commitment to, 70–71, 75, 81, 102
  Jung's first practice of, 65–66
Psychological Club, 124, 130–33, 142, 165–66, 177, 185
"Psychological Foundations of Belief in Spirits, The" (Jung), 138–39
Psychological Reflections (Jacobi), 208
Psychological Types (Jung), 62, 135–37
psychology
  alchemy and, 155
  analytical psychology, 7, 95, 97, 130, 135, 155
  experiment in group psychology, 130–31
  Gnosticism and, 153
  history and, 151
  Nazi Germany and, 169, 179
  parapsychic phenomena, 138–39
  self-transformation, 64, 75
Psychology and Alchemy (Jung), 156, 157, 224
Psychology and Religion (Jung), 182
Psychology of the Unconscious, The (Jung), 96–97
psychosynthesis, 78, 236n25
Pueblo Indians, 147–48

Rauschenbach, Berta, 60–61
Red Book, The (Jung)
  artwork, 113, 122, 216–19
  central theme, 216
  fantasies and active imaginations, 214
  Jung family's attitude toward, 219–21
  Jung's psychology, 213, 222, 224
  Nietzsche's influence on, 215, 248n5
  publication of, 213–14, 219, 221–23
Regardie, Israel, 157–58
Reich, Wilhelm, 73, 79, 163, 236n27
"Relations Between the Ego and the Unconscious, The" (Jung), 5, 156
religion, 20, 21, 30–31, 36, 153, 229n2.
  See also Eastern philosophy
Re-Visioning Psychology (Hillman), 210
Rhine, J. B., 194, 195
Ricoeur, Paul, 84
Riklin, Franz, Sr., 121
Roerich, Nicholas, 218
Rohde, Erwin, 89
"Role of the Unconscious, The" (Jung), 159–60
Russell, Bertrand, 136

Samuels, Andrew, 211
Sartre, Jean-Paul, 23
Saviours of God, The (Kazantzakis), 215
Schellenberg, Walter, 174, 177
Schiller, Friedrich, 119
Scholem, Gershom, 165, 172
School of Wisdom, 142, 165, 172
Schopenhauer, Arthur, 32–33
Schwaller de Lubicz, René, 147, 157, 215
Schwyzer, Emile, 91–92
scientific materialism, 1–2, 43
Secret of the Golden Flower, The (Wilhelm, ed.),
    143, 159, 222–23
Self, 22–23, 51, 125–26, 156–58, 183, 190.
    See also individuation
Serrano, Miguel, 200
Seven Sermons to the Dead (Jung), 122, 123–25,
    140, 144, 187, 219
Shadow and Evil in Fairy Tales (von Franz),
    209
Shamdasani, Sonu, 7, 63, 211, 219–20, 221,
    223, 224
She: Understanding Feminine Psychology
    (Johnson), 211
Sigg, Hermann, 140
Silberer, Herbert, 79, 120, 154
Society for Psychical Research (SPR), 137–38
Soul's Code, The (Hillman), 212
Spielrein, Sabina, 65–68, 74, 81, 112, 121
Spiritual Diary (Swedenborg), 215
spiritualism. *See* paranormal phenomena
Spring Publications, 210
Steiner, Rudolf
    body of teachings, 206
    compared to Jung, 230n9
    in counterculture, 73
    female followers, 64
    Geothe as role model for, 18
    on Jews, 162
    on visionary states, 160–61, 224
Stekel, Wilhelm, 71, 99
Steppenwolf (Hesse), 128, 134
stone, 23–25, 108–9, 217
Storr, Anthony, 3, 4, 6, 97, 127, 206
Study of History (Toynbee), 134
supernatural phenomena. *See* paranormal
    phenomena
Swedenborg, Emanuel, 44, 115, 120, 215–16,
    224
Symbolik und Mythologie der alten Volker
    (Creuzer), 89

Symbols of Transformation (Jung), 1, 96–97, 99,
    111, 112, 135
synchronicity
    action of psyche on outside world, 10, 78
    active imagination and, 122
    Jung's experiences of, 113, 143, 223
    Lachman's experiences of, 220, 241n31,
        242n41, 246n13
    meaningful coincidences, 193–97, 246n13
Synchronicity (Jung and Pauli), 193–97

Taoism, 143, 183–84
Tausk, Victor, 79
Tavistock Clinic lectures, 2, 118–19, 167, 182
Temple, William, 175
Theatrum Chemicum (Dorn), 183
Thus Spake Zarathustra (Nietzsche), 45, 134,
    181, 215, 248n5
Tibetan Book of the Dead, The
    (Evans-Wentz, ed.), 183
Tibetan Buddhism, 22, 184
timeless consciousness, 140–41, 148–49
Tower, 144, 145–47, 148, 198, 217
Toynbee, Arnold, 134
transcendent function
    in alchemy, 156, 158
    in career choice, 37–38, 117
    guardedness concerning, 115–16
    outgrowing of problems, 35, 143–44
    symbols produced, 120, 203
    union of conscious and unconscious minds,
        117, 156, 202–3
"Transcendent Function, The" (Jung), 116,
    156
Travel Diary of a Philosopher, The (Keyserling),
    142
Tresemer, David, 220
Two Essays on the Worship of Priapus (Knight),
    89

UFOs, 191–92, 194, 246n9
Undiscovered Self, The (Jung), 135, 202

Valentine, Basil, 158
Ventura, Michael, 210
visions and fantasies
    active imagination and, 117–19
    blood and solar-hero, 111–13
    descent, 111, 113
    destruction, 106–7, 109
    during hypnagogic state, 27, 97–98, 119–20

visions and fantasies (*cont.*)
inner figures in, 113–14
making reality of, 36
near-death experience, 186–89
Philemon, 113–14, 123–24
precognition, 60, 109–10
reawakening dead, 108
recordings of, 214
shitting God, 30, 229n2
von Franz, Marie-Louise, 97, 118, 156, 184, 198, 202, 208–9

Wandlungen und Symbole der Libido (Jung), 96–97
Was Jung a Mystic? (Jaffé), 208
water, 19–20, 21
Way of Individuation, The (Jacobi), 208
Way of the Dream, The (von Franz), 209
We: Understanding the Psychology of Romantic Love (Johnson), 211
Wehr, Gerhard, 47
Weininger, Otto, 170
Weizsäcker, Adolph von, 168–69
Wellcome Trust Center for the History of Medicine at University College London, 211
We've Had a Hundred Years of Psychotherapy... (Hillman and Ventura), 210
White, Victor, 200
Whitehead, Alfred North, 137

Whitney, Mark, 209
Wilhelm, Richard, 142–43, 154
Will to Power, The (Nietzsche), 222
Wilson, Colin, 42, 57, 134, 194, 231n23, 232n4
Wittgenstein, Ludwig, 170
Wolff, Kurt, 13, 228n2
Wolff, Toni, 64, 94–95, 108, 128–30, 132, 184, 197
Wölfli, Adolf, 218
women
attraction to Jewish women, 63, 67, 75
attractiveness to, 63, 64
as companions, 199
conventional views about, 66–67
Jungian thinkers and writers, 207–9
mistrust of, 18
polygamous tendencies, 64, 67–68, 69, 74–75, 87, 94–95
Women Who Run With the Wolves (Estés), 209
word-association tests, 58–59
"Wotan" (Jung), 180
Wundt, Wilhelm, 59

Yale University, Terry Lectures, 182
Yeats, W. B., 137
yoga, 165, 238n6

Zimmer, Heinrich, 165, 183
Zöllner, Johann, 44

ABOUT THE AUTHOR

Gary Lachman is the author of several books on the links between consciousness, culture, and the Western esoteric tradition, including *Rudolf Steiner: An Introduction to His Life and Work; In Search of P. D. Ouspensky; A Secret History of Consciousness;* and *Politics and the Occult.* As a critic and journalist his work has appeared in *The Times Literary Supplement, The Independent on Sunday, Fortean Times, The Guardian* and other journals in the United States and United Kingdom, and he is frequent guest on BBC Radio Three and Four. A founding member of the rock group Blondie, in 2006 he was inducted into the Rock and Roll Hall of Fame, and his *New York Rocker: My Life in the Blank Generation* (written as Gary Valentine) is an account of his years as a musician. Born in New Jersey, he has lived in London since 1996, where he lectures frequently on his work.

If you enjoyed this book, visit

www.tarcherbooks.com

and sign up for Tarcher's e-newsletter to receive special offers, giveaway promotions, and information on hot upcoming releases.

TARCHER
PENGUIN

Great Lives Begin with Great Ideas

New at **www.tarcherbooks.com**
and **www.penguin.com/tarchertalks**:

Tarcher Talks, an online video series featuring interviews with bestselling authors on everything from creativity and pros~~~~ and Freemasonry

If you would like to place a
of this book, call 1-800-8